CONSUMER GUIDE TO

MORTGAGE MODIFICATION

HOW TO LOWER YOUR MORTGAGE PAYMENTS WITH THE HOME AFFORDABLE MODIFICATION PROGRAM

DEAN ALLEN KACKLEY

ANKERWYCKE

Cover by Tony Nuccio.

Printed in the United States of America

18 17 16 15 14 5 4 3 2 1

Library of Congress Cataloging-in-Publication Data

Kackley, Dean Allen, author.
The consumer guide to mortgage modification : how to lower your mortgage payments with the Home Affordable Modification Program / Dean Allen Kackley.
pages cm
Includes bibliographical references and index.
ISBN 978-1-62722-763-6 (alk. paper)
1. Home Affordable Modification Program (U.S.) 2. Mortgage loans—Law and legislation—United States. 3. Loan workouts—United States. 4. Mortgage loan servicing—United States. 5. Foreclosure—United States—Prevention. I. Title.
KF697.M63K33 2014
332.7'220973—dc23

2014040734

Discounts are available for books ordered in bulk. Special consideration is given to state bars, CLE programs, and other bar-related organizations. Inquire at Book Publishing, ABA Publishing, American Bar Association, 321 N. Clark, Chicago, Illinois 60654-7598.

www.ShopABA.org

For Susan Carrington

Ultimately, my desire is to help resolve the residential mortgage debacle and restore peace of mind to millions of American families—one borrower at a time.

—*Dean Kackley*

Contents

Preface

Mortgage problems? This book will help. It's the consumer's version of federal rules for modifying home loans.

If you don't know what to do. If you've applied for a modification, but it's taking too long. If you've received a modification but still can't make your payments. Even if you've been turned down. Rely on this valuable resource during a long, unfamiliar, and discouraging process. It can shift the balance of power and help you get control.

Cut through technical jargon and specialized knowledge. Homeowners, landlords, and their trusted advisors now have a simple and complete reference when working with lenders. Step by step, it explains what you need to know and do to get a loan modification.

Making Home Affordable® (MHA) was launched in February 2009 as part of the Obama Administration's comprehensive approach to help homeowners avoid foreclosure, according to the U.S. Department of Treasury, which runs the program. Its Home Affordable Modification Program (HAMP) sets rules for more than 85 percent of all home loans. You ask: What are the rules? Can I lower my payments? Is my lender required to modify my loan? Do I qualify? Does my lender play by the rules? Here are the answers to your questions, plus 12 questions to ask your lender.

Now you can understand the guidelines that the big lenders like Bank of America, Chase, Citi, Ocwen, and Wells Fargo use to modify home loans. They claim they want to help. It doesn't matter—they are overwhelmed, and they work for somebody else. Borrowers must take responsibility for themselves. This book makes that possible.

The ABA Consumer Guide to Mortgage Modification includes helpful suggestions and practical tools. Use the forms, grids, and worksheets to calculate your new payment, complete financial information, and qualify for a modification. Look up unfamiliar but crucial terms in the glossary.

This is the user's manual for homeowners, landlords, and their professional advisors to get the most out of HAMP. Knowledge *is* power. Get the results you want and deserve.

Introduction

If you can't afford your mortgage payment or your loan balance is more than the value of your property, help is available.

The federal Making Home Affordable (MHA) program started in April 2009 with a simple, some might say naive, premise: modify problem loans so payments are affordable and sustainable for financially distressed homeowners. Five years later, though, less than a third of those thought to need help actually received it, as slightly more than a million modifications have barely scratched the surface.

In June 2012, the program expanded exponentially to include landlords and rental properties and guidelines so complex as to leave the average property owner dazed and confused. Later, program expiration was extended to the end of 2015, but the problem will be around for at least another decade.

The program works through lenders to help homeowners and owners of residential rental properties avoid foreclosure. The centerpiece of MHA mortgage relief is the Home Affordable Modification Program (HAMP). Written for lenders, loan servicers, and mortgage investors, the guidelines would overwhelm most borrowers with technical jargon, specialized knowledge, and sheer density. This book is the consumer's version for borrowers and their trusted advisors, a simplified but complete resource to use when working with lenders.

HAMP consolidates best practices and institutional thinking to establish an industry-wide standard for loan modification, which is the priority and starting point for other MHA foreclosure alternatives. Guidelines instruct lenders how to identify "at risk" homeowners and how to modify their home mortgages so monthly payments will be "affordable and sustainable." Recent revisions now include owners of rental properties and homeowners previously declined for HAMP modifications.

The purpose of this book is to level the playing field, to identify eligible borrowers, and to help them modify their loans. It explains technical terms, concepts, and procedures in useful and usable ways. It is current—crucial because the state of mortgage modifications changed entirely with HAMP, and then changed again in June 2012, with periodic refinements. Earlier information is out of date.

An essential ingredient of this book is my actual current work with HAMP, supplemented by personal knowledge and experience. I am an attorney and real estate broker. I counsel clients regarding distressed mortgages and loan workouts with lenders and loan servicers, saving tens of thousands of dollars in payments and hundreds of thousands of dollars in principal reductions.

Facing the Problem

Relying on the generosity of banks to solve the problem hasn't worked. Just to get their attention has taken new state consumer protection laws, federal Wall Street reform legislation, formation of the Consumer Financial Protection Board, and the U.S. Department of Justice supported by 49 states attorneys general. It's the same mistake we made when we relied on banks to lend responsibly in the first place. Homeowners in distress need to get educated. Then, instead of leaning on banks, they can stand up or push back when needed.

While the situation according to the U.S. Department of Treasury and my own observation has improved, here's the magnitude of the problem:

- Value of equity lost by homeowners—$171 billion. This is not lost property value. It's only the portion (equity) lost by the homeowner, which amounts to everything before the loan goes underwater.
- Underwater home mortgages—11 million. That's 11 million homeowners with no equity hoping desperately for their homes to float on rising fair market values. On the contrary, in the foreseeable future, these are short sales or foreclosures waiting to happen.
- Foreclosure sales—about 60,000 per month. That's three-quarters of a million homes lost in a year, vastly more of which go to lenders than to private buyers.
- Sales by lenders of properties received in foreclosure—about 50,000 per month. This number was higher a year ago but now has fallen below the number of foreclosure sales. The result increases the institutional (shadow) inventory of unsold properties.
- Short sales—about 25,000 per month. At this rate, it would take 36 years to sell the 11 million homes with underwater mortgages.
- Modifications—of the 2.18 million trial modifications started through early 2014, only 1.35 million (62 percent) became permanent and fewer than a million (43 percent) are still active.

According to government estimates, three million to four million American families can benefit from loan modifications. In fact, the number probably approaches twice that many, and now countless owners of residential rental properties have been added. Whatever the total, many millions of Americans suffer daily from fear, confusion, discouragement, and shame. A large fraction lives under the dark cloud of foreclosure and loss of home—more than 10 million foreclosure filings during 2009 through 2013. Further aggravating the problem, accumulated stress jeopardizes health, family, productivity, and self-esteem. The human cost is staggering.

My practice is built on a thorough understanding of HAMP guidelines and related resources, which have been incorporated into a system of analysis and calculations that is used in my work and explained in this book. I suggest reading through the book and appendices rather quickly to form a foundation. Then, return to each chapter, reference, and exercise to build a sturdy and effective loan modification, step by step.

How It Works: Program Basics

Learning Points:

- How this book can help save your home.
- How to use the Home Affordable Modification Program (HAMP).
- The origins and purpose of HAMP.

An anxious homeowner worried about making or missing mortgage payments needs to know about HAMP. It might mean the difference between keeping and losing a home. Help is also available for owners of one- to four-unit residential rental properties. Here is a brief overview.

What to Expect

Why does it take so long and seem so complicated? This personal experience might help borrowers to understand the systemic resistance—and endless delays—commonly encountered.

Picture yourself sitting on a three-legged stool. Now imagine trying to sit on a stool with only two legs, then one, and finally with none at all. When I learned lending from Wells Fargo Bank two and a half decades ago, it took deposits out of the vault and loaned them to qualified homeowners. We were accountable to our customers and shareholders. Careful with the money entrusted to it, the bank taught me about the three-legged stool.

Three essential ingredients of good lending, when in balance, characterize a qualified borrower: (1) ability to repay the loan from predictable income, (2) willingness to repay the loan exhibited by a credit record of timely payments, and (3) commitment to repay the loan by pledging a cash down payment or equivalent equity. Balance the stool, and then make the loan.

During the past decade or so, first, one leg was pulled out from under the stool as FICO scores replaced human judgment in making loans despite questionable credit histories. Another leg went as private mortgage insurance (PMI) and higher interest rates allowed borrowers to risk 10 percent, then 5 percent, and finally none of their own money as a down payment. The third leg came loose with stated-income, no-income, and no-documentation loans made on wishful thinking or no thinking at all. Finally, when all three compromises combined in no-qualification loans, the stool collapsed.

Despite irresponsible lending—and borrowing—taken to catastrophic extremes, many responsible lenders and borrowers still think in terms of the three-legged stool. Rare in the past, but commonplace today, loan modifications and foreclosure alternatives represent a new and unfamiliar lender-borrower relationship. Typically, lenders look for, and borrowers try to show, financial and credit strength and stability. Until recently, rising real estate prices supported everybody, reduced risk, and concealed poor decision making.

Most borrowers whom I counsel have encountered a hardship that makes paying their mortgage difficult or impossible. They are traumatized, first by the hardship itself, next by the devastation wrought on their family's lives and lifestyle, and finally by their inability to meet obligations. It runs contrary to lifelong values.

For a lender to look for, and a borrower to show, reasons to modify a loan contradicts the ordinary lender-borrower relationship and would probably disqualify a conventional loan application straight away. It is even more confusing to explain and analyze these contradictions logically. From start to finish, keep in mind that this requires some uncomfortable upside-down thinking by both lender and borrower. At the same time, by addressing the problem honestly and responsibly, borrowers and lenders alike might begin to recover needed confidence and rebuild mutual trust.

What Is HAMP?

For homeowners with a legitimate financial hardship, HAMP provides temporary relief while resetting the loan interest at today's rate. It is like refinancing with five to seven years of lower payments while getting past the hardship.

Wide-ranging changes on June 1, 2012, expanded and extended the program. It now expires on December 31, 2015, and consists of two "tiers." Tier 1 is the original program introduced in 2009, with changes consolidated in the servicers' handbook released from time to time and most recently March 3, 2014. Tier 2 broadens the program's reach to homeowners who were declined for a modification, who failed to complete a Trial Period Plan, who defaulted on a final modification, or whose financial hardships have changed. Tier 2 also includes non-occupant owners of rental properties consisting of one to four residential units, which now falls within a broadened definition of "home."

HAMP consolidates best practices and institutional thinking to establish an industry-wide standard for modifying home loans. Crafted by the U.S. Department of Treasury, FDIC (Federal Deposit Insurance Corporation), and some pretty astute industry gurus, the guidelines instruct lenders how to identify "at risk" homeowners and how to modify their mortgages so monthly payments will be "affordable and sustainable."

The guidelines, first and foremost, are intended to help homeowners stay in their homes. Once eligibility—including hardship—is established, a borrower must be either already delinquent in payments or not yet delinquent but at "imminent risk" of default.

Based on information furnished by the borrower, and on computer modeling from a huge set of data, a lender compares the cost of modifying a loan with the cost of foreclosure. If modification yields higher present value to the lender, then a specific sequence of steps must be taken to reduce the borrower's monthly mortgage payment. If not, the lender must offer other foreclosure alternatives.

A three-month trial period follows when affordability of modified payments, documentation, and commitment of borrower can be confirmed. Then, according to the final modification agreement signed by both borrower and lender, the loan terms are permanently changed.

Lenders servicing nearly 85 percent of all home loans signed on to the program, obliging them to comply. However, the final decision must be approved by the actual owner of the loan, the "investor," and some investors are contractually restricted from modifying loans.

How to Use HAMP

Despite its clear intention to set standards and procedures for lenders, HAMP can be used by borrowers and their advisors either to initiate a modification or to respond to a lender's initiative. Especially for borrowers who are experiencing a financial hardship, but whose payments are current and whose profile does not fit at-risk modeling, waiting for a lender's initiative may aggravate an already difficult situation.

As outlined below, and throughout this book, the guidelines proceed in a logical progression: eligibility, feasibility, affordability, verification, and modification. Except for the net present value test, in which the lender evaluates the relative benefit of modification versus foreclosure, most elements are transparent and accessible to a borrower for independent analysis.

Make the effort to thoroughly complete a financial statement and to calculate the various formulas that determine qualifications. This enables you to give accurate yet scrubbed information to your lender and to verify the responses you receive. Confirm everything according to HAMP guidelines. Do not assume that your lender's offer or non-approval complies or that customer service and analytical

TIP

While most lenders participate in HAMP, many have not sufficiently trained their staff on the program. Learning as much about the program as possible prior to approaching your lender substantially increases the chances that you'll succeed in modifying your home loan.

personnel understand everything. This is unfamiliar and shifting terrain for borrowers, their advisors, and lenders alike. In each person's own unique way, everybody involved is overwhelmed.

For details about documentation, submission, asking for what you want, and responding if you do not get it, refer to chapter 14, "Working with Your Lender," page 115. Because the need for modifications significantly exceeds lenders' current resources, I strongly encourage you to take the initiative. Act now.

Background

In February 2009, President Obama put into motion the Making Home Affordable plan. It consists of four components. The most ambitious, and the one addressed in this book, is HAMP, which concentrates on loan modifications intended to help millions of struggling homeowners make their mortgage payments and stay in their homes. First announced in March by the U.S. Treasury, its detailed guidelines were released in April.

After three years, the U.S. Treasury reported that nearly 4.7 million requests had been received, 3.3 million (70 percent) processed, and 1.4 million (30 percent) pending or displaced; 2.0 million (43 percent) had been approved and 1.3 million (27 percent) denied. Private and anecdotal numbers might vary, but the question remains: Of those approved, how many actually resulted in "affordable and sustainable" permanently modified mortgages? Estimates are about a million.

HAMP is primarily for financial institutions regulated by the federal government, including the government-sponsored enterprises (GSEs) Fannie Mae and Freddie Mac. Generally, the guidelines for modifying loans are intended to become standard procedure for the entire mortgage industry. Specifically, they are for homeowners who are experiencing a hardship that affects their ability to make mortgage payments. Significantly, the program has been expanded to include one- to four-unit rental properties. The program also offers financial incentives both to lenders and to borrowers.

Briefly, the second component includes other programs beginning with applicable HAMP eligibility criteria, such as the Home Affordable Foreclosure Alternatives (HAFA) program for those not qualified for a modification. See chapter 16, "Short Sale," page 129. Others are described in chapter 17, "Other Home Affordable Programs," page 135, which includes the Second Lien Modification Program.

The Home Affordable Refinance Program allows homeowners to refinance into today's historically low interest rates despite declines in property values. Limits on loan amounts exceeding current property values—loan-to-value (LTV) ratios exceeding 100 percent—have been removed. Conventional credit and income qualification standards apply.

The third component strongly encourages alternatives to end-game foreclosure for borrowers who are ineligible or unqualified for the Making Home Affordable programs. The fourth component aims to keep interest rates low by strengthening Fannie Mae (founded in 1938) and Freddie Mac (founded in 1970). These GSEs pumped trillions of government-backed dollars into home loans for 70 years, but the real estate and mortgage markets had deteriorated so badly by September 2008 that the U.S. Treasury placed these pillars of the American Dream into conservatorship under the Federal Housing Finance Agency created for that purpose.

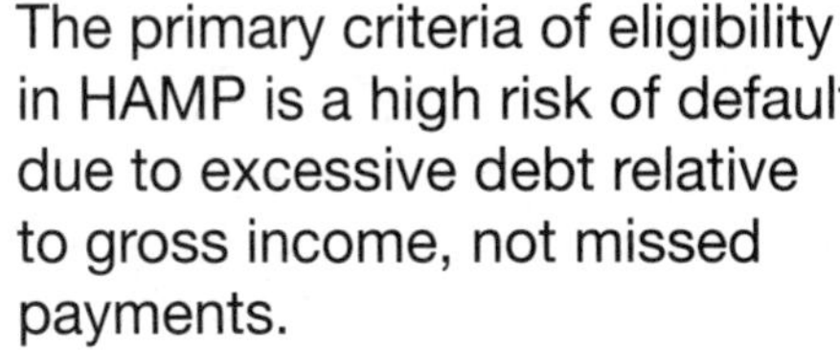

NOTE

The primary criteria of eligibility in HAMP is a high risk of default due to excessive debt relative to gross income, not missed payments.

As with any guidelines that try to balance conflicting interests, HAMP is neither simple to understand nor easy to put into practice. I have developed a system to gather borrowers' information and to present it in compliance with the HAMP guidelines. Participating lenders may interpret the guidelines differently, but they must comply. Nearly 85 percent of all home loans are subject to the program, but many lenders still struggle to actually implement it.

Overview

These programs are, first and foremost, intended to help homeowners stay in their homes. Once eligibility—including hardship—is established, a borrower must be either already delinquent in payments or not yet delinquent but at imminent risk of default. Based on information furnished by the borrower, and on computer modeling from a huge set of data, the lender compares the cost of modifying a loan with the cost of foreclosure. If modification yields higher present value to the lender, then a specific sequence of steps must be taken to reduce the borrower's monthly mortgage payment.

According to the guidelines, the series of required modification steps must be followed "in the stated order of succession until the borrower's monthly mortgage payment ratio is reduced as close as possible to 31%, without going below 31%." The ratio equals principal, interest, property tax, and insurance divided by borrower's gross income. At its most fundamental, the purpose of the guidelines is how to accomplish this objective of reducing the loan payment.

In addition to housing expenses, the borrower's other expenses and obligations are compared against income. If all debt obligations exceed 55 percent of income, that borrower must submit to credit counseling. Though the guidelines set no limit, excessive debt may disqualify an eligible borrower. Once through the foregoing gauntlet, a three-month trial period follows when affordability of modified payments, documentation, and borrower's commitment can be confirmed. Then, according to the final modification agreement signed by both borrower and lender, the loan terms are permanently changed.

If your current mortgage payment is less than 31 percent of your gross income, you will not be eligible for loan modification under Tier 1 of HAMP.

Program Criteria

Eligibility. Borrower, mortgage, property, and lender—all four—must be eligible before modification may be considered under HAMP. With a few exceptions, the borrower(s) of the original loan must be the same for the modified loan. The mortgage must have closed before the end of 2008, must be senior to any other loans, and must be within liberal but specific loan amount limits. The property may be one to four units and must be occupied as the borrower's principal residence for Tier 1 eligibility. The lender must have signed a Servicer Participation Agreement before the end of 2009.

Hardship. In addition to several other general eligibility criteria, a borrower must be experiencing a hardship that impairs the ability to make timely mortgage payments. Several events are listed in a hardship statement, called an affidavit, together with representations that the borrower attests are true. The hardship must be supported with financial and other suitable documentation.

Target monthly mortgage payment. The HAMP objective for modifying a mortgage is to reduce a borrower's monthly housing expense to (as close as possible to, but not less than) 31 percent of borrower's income. This is called the target monthly mortgage payment ratio. Therefore, to be eligible for modification, a borrower's current ratio must exceed 31 percent of gross income.

Risk of default. Late payments are *not* a condition to begin the modification process. A borrower may be current but likely to miss a payment soon due to financial hardship. The guidelines call this "imminent risk of default." Lenders may use their own criteria to determine the risk. For example, Fannie Mae screens borrowers based on debt coverage and cash reserve ratios. If a borrower's income is less than 1.2 times debt obligations, and liquid assets are less than 3 times monthly housing expenses, then the borrower is judged to be at imminent risk of default. In that case, delinquent payments are not necessary for that borrower to be considered for loan modification.

Feasibility: modification versus foreclosure. With eligibility decided, and the mortgage either delinquent or determined to be at risk of default, then the lender uses a computer model to calculate the "net present value" of modification versus foreclosure. If the benefit from modification exceeds that from foreclosure—that is to say, if modification would cost the lender less than foreclosure—then HAMP requires modification. Otherwise, modification is optional, although alternatives should be considered before proceeding with a foreclosure.

Affordability: reducing the payment. By applying a sequence of specific steps, called the Standard Modification Waterfall, a lender arrives at the target monthly mortgage payment, which equals no less than 31 percent of the borrower's monthly gross income. After calculating the target payment, the following steps are applied in order to reduce the payment until the target is reached.

- Step 1 confirms the amount owed, which includes the unpaid principal balance plus amounts advanced by a lender to cover unpaid property tax and insurance but must not include late fees or administrative costs.
- Step 2 reduces the interest rate but no lower than 2 percent.
- Step 3 extends the term but no longer than 40 years.
- Step 4 allocates the rate and term to an interest-bearing portion that is less than the total unpaid principal balance. The remaining portion, though due when the loan is paid off, accrues no interest or payment in the meantime.
- Reduction of the loan amount ("principal forgiveness") is optional for lenders.

Confirmation: trial period. After estimating the owed amount, interest rate, amortization term, and interest-bearing principal amount, the lender offers the borrower a modified payment for a three-month trial period. This period gives the lender time to verify and update the borrower's information and to prepare the final modification agreement. The borrower must accept the Trial Period Plan, supply requested information, and make all payments before the period ends.

Modification. If the borrower meets all requirements, the modification takes effect on the first day of the month following the trial period. The lender may adjust monthly payments

Reference and Key Definitions

The rules are called the "Handbook for Servicers of Non-GSE Mortgages."[1] If necessary, refer to them by their title and insist that your lender play by them.

"Lender" You chose your lender when you took its money, or your lender chose you when it bought your loan or the right to service it. Let me explain how I use certain terms:

"Servicer" means the mortgage company that receives your payments, bundles them together with thousands of others, retains its fee, and passes the remainder along to the investor according to the terms and conditions of their servicing contract. If you miss a payment, its collections department jumps into action. If you want or need mortgage relief, the servicer's loss mitigation department joins the team.

"Loss mitigation" means the servicer's effort to control and reduce its loss on a defaulting loan. It solicits delinquent borrowers, or responds to their initiative, with offers to consider modification of the loan or sale of the property. This department administers the Making Home Affordable programs for participating servicers. Your application for a modification or short sale runs the loss mitigation gauntlet.

"Investor" means the owner of your mortgage and tens of thousands like it. A loan consists of the borrower's obligation to pay and, by extension, the recipient's right to receive payment. The recipient "invested" the loan principal with the expectation of receiving a return on its investment (interest).

Investors are passive, having contracted routine tasks to the servicer. Some might have the same name as the servicer, but they have very different functions. They manage huge amounts of other

continued

continued

people's money, subject to securities regulations, according to representations and warranties of their investment prospectuses.

Except very rarely, investors were not organized to deal with individual mortgages and borrowers. They are more concerned with credit swaps, derivatives, insurance, and other hedges against loss and litigation. Further complicating decision making, some mortgages have more than one investor.

"Insurer" means either the PMI company that insured a high LTV loan for an individual borrower or a financial behemoth like AGI that insured a pool of thousands of high LTV loans for an investor. Either, or both, adds another, more distant layer to the decision making process.

"GSE" means government-sponsored enterprise, also known as Fannie Mae and Freddie Mac. After suffering substantial losses, they were placed into conservatorship under the FHFA in September 2008. At that time, together they owned or guaranteed about half of the $12 trillion residential mortgage market, easily the biggest investors. If one owns or guarantees your loan, expect its own variation on the Making Home Affordable program.

"Delegated authority" means that the investor has given broad discretion to the servicer for making loss mitigation decisions. Usually, this is good for implementing Making Home Affordable programs.

"Lender" means, when I use it, one or more of the above, depending on context. It refers generically to the collective entity (adversary) on the other side of your loan. Most often, it means the servicer and those represented by the servicer.

consistent with information received during the trial period. The modification agreement permanently changes the terms of the original loan. Once modified under HAMP, a loan may not be modified again under Tier 1 of the program, though it might be eligible for Tier 2 consideration.

Escalation. A procedure gives borrowers and their trusted advisors a way to question results, dispute errors, and bring abuse of guidelines to the attentions of HAMP administrators.

Summary

HAMP has become an effective way for homeowners to save their homes during financial hardship. Participating lenders and mortgage investors follow a logical sequence of steps. The objective is to avoid foreclosure, while arriving at affordable and sustainable payments for homeowners and owners of rental properties. For eligible borrowers, payments are reduced primarily by lowering the interest rate and extending the term, though principal reduction is an option.

Where to Start: Eligibility

Learning Points:

- The requirements to start the HAMP application.
- The two "tiers" and their similarities and differences.

Start with eligibility. Borrower, mortgage, property, and lender must conform to a dozen criteria to be considered for a HAMP modification. Most homeowners experiencing a financial hardship will be eligible.

Compare your situation with the following criteria. First is a quick list, then a more detailed explanation, followed by clarification about many common factors affecting HAMP eligibility. Keep in mind the two tiers of eligibility. Tier 1 is generally synonymous with HAMP prior to June 1, 2012. Its criteria are stricter, but modification terms are better than Tier 2.

Criteria: Summary

1. Loan origination.
   Tier 1: Senior mortgage that originated on or before January 1, 2009.
   Tier 2: Same.
2. Loan previously modified.
   Tier 1: The mortgage was not modified previously under the program.
   Tier 2: The mortgage may have been modified under Tier 1 but was not modified under Tier 2.

3. Delinquency.
   Tier 1: Payments are delinquent or default is reasonably foreseeable.
   Tier 2: Payments are at least two months delinquent, or, for owner-occupied properties only, default is reasonably foreseeable.
4. Property.
   Tier 1: The property is a single-family (one- to four-unit residential) property.
   Tier 2: Same.
5. Occupancy.
   Tier 1: The property is borrower's principal residence.
   Tier 2: The property may be either borrower's principal residence or a rental property.
6. Condition.
   Tier 1: The property is not condemned and is habitable.
   Tier 2: Same.
7. Hardship.
   Tier 1: Borrower must document a financial hardship and state that available liquid assets are insufficient to make the monthly mortgage payments.
   Tier 2: Same.
8. Payments.
   Tier 1: The pre-modification monthly mortgage payment must be greater than 31 percent of borrower's gross monthly income.
   Tier 2: Post-modification monthly mortgage payments range from 25 to 42 percent of gross income depending on lender.
9. Escrow account.
   Tier 1: An escrow account for property taxes and insurance must be established before beginning the trial period if one does not already exist.
   Tier 2: Same.
10. Loan limits.
    Tier 1: Limits apply to the maximum unpaid principal balance (UPB).
    Tier 2: Same.
11. Program expiration.
    Tier 1: The modification request must be submitted on or before December 31, 2015, and the modification must be permanent on or before September 30, 2016.
    Tier 2: Same.
12. Servicer participation.
    Tier 1: Lender/servicer entered a Servicer Participation Agreement.
    Tier 2: Same.

Tier 1 and Tier 2 Compared

Far-reaching changes effective June 1, 2012, expanded the program to two tiers. Tier 1 is the original program introduced in 2009, as amended. HAMP Tier 1 refers to HAMP modifications and trial periods before the effective date and to Tier 1 activities after the effective date.

Tier 2 broadens HAMP eligibility to include homeowners declined for a modification who failed to complete a Trial Period Plan or who defaulted on a final modification. It also includes non-occupant owners of rental properties consisting of one- to four-residential units. The loan may not have been modified previously under Tier 2.

To begin, the loan must satisfy basic HAMP eligibility criteria, which are the same for Tier 1 and Tier 2:

- Loan origination on or before January 1, 2009.
- Financial hardship with limited liquid assets.
- One- to four-unit residential property.
- Property is not condemned.
- Escrow account.
- Loan principal balance limitations.
- Submission and modification effective dates.
- Lender/servicer participation.

The borrower and loan are then evaluated on remaining Tier 1 eligibility criteria:

- Loan not previously modified under HAMP Tier 1.
- Borrower's principal residence.
- Delinquent or at "imminent risk" of default.
- Pre-modification payment greater than 31 percent of gross income.

If borrower or loan fails any of these criteria, or is not approved for Tier 1 modification, the servicer must consider Tier 2. First, the remaining Tier 2 eligibility criteria must be satisfied:

- Loan not previously modified under HAMP Tier 2.
- Rental property or borrower's principal residence.
- Default or risk of default (owner-occupied properties only).

Narrower eligibility criteria for Tier 1 than for Tier 2 align with the relative benefits of modifications under each Tier. If granted a modification under the stricter Tier 1 criteria, a borrower can receive an initially lower interest rate for five or more years. Moreover, modification under Tier 2 carries a "risk adjustment" that adds 0.5 percent to the permanent interest rate.

Tiers 1 and 2 are nevertheless components of the same program. Borrower, loan, and property must satisfy common basic eligibility criteria, the lender must participate in HAMP, and deadlines must be met.

NOTE

If you don't qualify under Tier 1, which has superior modification terms for the borrower, your lender must consider you for a Tier 2 modification.

Common Criteria Explained

Let's start with the eight basic HAMP eligibility criteria common to both Tier 1 and Tier 2, as well as for other programs under Making Home Affordable.

First Lien Mortgage Loan Originated on or before January 1, 2009

The loan to be modified must be the only loan secured by the property, or it must have priority over any other loan secured by the property. Almost always, it is the larger loan. It might have been used to purchase the property or to refinance an earlier loan. It must have been originally funded and closed before January 1, 2009. This date applies to purchase and refinance loans; it is not the date of a modification or forbearance.

Second loans (junior, subordinate, equity lines) are not eligible for HAMP but might be eligible for another MHA program. A lender is not required to use the guidelines to modify an ineligible loan, nor is a lender or borrower eligible for the HAMP incentive payments. Still, the logic and principles are the same for any loan, so make your case as you would if the loan were eligible. If the senior mortgage is modified under HAMP, when the modification becomes final, the second mortgage is eligible for the Second Lien Modification Program (2MP). See chapter 17, "Other Home Affordable Programs," page 135.

Documented Financial Hardship (A) with Limited Liquid Assets (B)

(A) Documented financial hardship. This is the heart and guts of HAMP, which intends to bring relief by reducing a borrower's mortgage burden, while justifying such relief to lenders who must rationalize the reductions. The Request for Mortgage Assistance (RMA) form defines several standard conditions involving reduced income or increased expenses that contributed to the hardship. A separate statement usually accompanies and elaborates the standard form.

Whether referred to by the lender as the hardship affidavit, letter, statement, or explanation, it should include a description of the events leading to the hardship, its financial impact, its severity, and when or if it is expected to end. Because hardship is pivotal, and the narrative is so important, the subject will be dealt with in detail in chapter 4, "Hardship: Statement and Affidavit," page 33.

(B) Limited liquid assets. Available liquid assets are insufficient to make the monthly mortgage payments. This is another of those frustrating "requirements," like the perplexing need to be late on payments before lenders will talk seriously to borrowers about modifying their loans. By the way, for homeowners, delinquency is *not* necessary for HAMP loan modifications.

However, no matter how frugal and conscientious, no matter how tight borrowers have cinched their financial belts, they can expect to go through most of their savings before being eligible for a loan modification. Borrowers are allowed to have emergency funds equal to three times the monthly debt payments. Fannie Mae limits the reserve to three times monthly housing expenses, which is a lower amount and contradicts HAMP, but prevails for Fannie Mae loans and several other lenders nevertheless. Definitions and calculation are covered later.

Despite this limitation, if possible, borrowers should get started while they still have money in the bank. The modification process can easily take three months, so savings will have plenty of time to dwindle down to emergency status or less. If borrowers have a significant stash in a liquid account, but their condition will change soon—repaying a loan, replacing a worn-out vehicle, advancing college tuition, covering medical expenses, etc.—they should prepare to supply an explanation and proof.

Most lenders want two months of bank statements. They notice large transfers or expenditures and frown on anything resembling a "shell game"—whether a borrower tries to show more money to get a loan or less money to modify one. On the other hand, if borrowers expect an unusual windfall (bonus, commission, gift, personal loan, inheritance), they may want to get started quickly before they receive it and have to declare it.

> **TIP** The modification process may take three or more months, so it's prudent to start the process early if you know your financial situation will worsen in the weeks ahead.

The operative word is "liquid," also referred to as "cash reserves." When preparing an income and expense statement (aka financial statement, statement of financial condition, or whatever terminology the lender uses), be sure to separate liquid from other money assets. "Liquid" means the money can be withdrawn within a short period of time. Obvious examples are checking and savings accounts. Others are sellable stocks, bonds, mutual funds, money market funds, and certificates of deposit of any maturity.

Excluded are retirement accounts, whether self-administered (IRA, 401(k), Keogh, etc.) or otherwise administered (employer, pension), and deferred compensation or stock options. Make sure these are clearly separated on the financial statement. Not specified are funds designated for a special or tax-preferred use (college or health saving accounts), and other age- or time-restricted funds (unavailable until maturity or until reaching a specified age), which arguably should also be excluded as being not readily accessible. Refer to the format in appendix G, "Financial Statement," page 161.

> **TIP** Initiate a loan modification process prior to accessing retirement accounts, stock options, or other illiquid assets. These illiquid assets will not impact your HAMP eligibility. By reducing payments first, you can preserve more of these assets.

The Property Is a One- to Four-Unit Property

It may be a conventional single-family dwelling, condominium, planned unit development (PUD), townhouse, cooperative share, and even a pre-built or manufactured home so long as state law classifies it as real property. It can include more than one unit but not more than four units. The expanded guidelines aspire to keep occupants in their homes, whether they are homeowners or tenants. Therefore, vacation homes not rented full time are ineligible. Whether property use must be strictly residential is unclear though highly probable; that is, whether a portion of the property may be used for commercial or business purposes is not expressly covered by the guidelines.

The Property Is Not Condemned

This does not require much discussion. If condemned, a loan modification alone probably will not solve whatever problems afflict the property. Even HAMP has no interest in sustaining a property that's not habitable. A lender's representative will probably lay eyes on the structure before the modification becomes final, which will frustrate any attempt to sidestep this criterion. Consider a short sale (see chapter 16, "Short Sale: Modification Alternative," page 129). A former requirement regarding vacancy has been eliminated, and the property may be vacant.

Escrow Account Must Be Established

If one does not already exist, an escrow account for property taxes and insurance must be established prior to the beginning of the trial period. An escrow account, oftentimes called an "impound" account, is an amount paid monthly in addition to principal and interest payment and held separately by the lender.

The amount is the annual property tax plus hazard and, if applicable, flood insurance premiums, divided by 12. It's paid in monthly increments with the loan payment. The lender then pays the property tax and insurance premiums on the borrower's behalf. An escrow account ensures that those amounts will be available to be paid when due. This is a common requirement for many loans, and you already may be paying into an escrow account.

This criterion mentions the trial period. It is a three-month period during which payments are modified, but the permanent modification will not take effect until all three payments, including escrow amounts, have been paid as agreed. This is an essential ingredient of the final loan modification and must be carefully considered. Find more on this in chapter 9, "Pre-Modification: Trial Period," page 77.

The UPB Does Not Exceed Maximum Limits

The loan balance excludes capitalized amounts, including delinquent interest, escrow advances, prior forbearance amounts, property preservation costs, and foreclosure expenses. Such amounts, however, might be added to determine the modified loan amount.

The maximum loan balance is determined by number of units in the property and may not exceed the following amounts at the time of modification:

- 1 unit (single-family dwelling): $729,750
- 2 units (duplex): $934,200
- 3 units (triplex): $1,129,250
- 4 units (quad- or four-plex): $1,403,400

Program Expires on December 31, 2015

Two important dates to keep in mind: The initial package, or modification request, must be submitted on or before December 31, 2015, and the modification effective date when the loan becomes permanently modified must be on or before

September 30, 2016. The initial package includes the lender's required forms and evidence of income.[1]

Using the last day of September might have an unexpected consequence for anyone waiting until the last minute. The modification effective date, by definition, occurs on the first day of the month following completion of the Trial Period Plan. Therefore, to occur on or before September 30, the last actual date would be September 1, reducing by a month the time allotted to complete the modification from start to finish.

Whether a full nine months (submit by December 31, 2015, and finish by September 30, 2016), or the abbreviated eight months (submit by December 31, 2015, and finish before September 1, 2016), the three-month trial period would need to begin by June 1 or July 1 at the latest. From the last submission date, approval of the initial package and related qualifications must be completed in five or six months. Do not delay, because usually it takes longer and servicer motivation might wane.

Servicer Entered a Participation Agreement by October 3, 2010

The recipient of mortgage payments (the servicer) must implement and use HAMP guidelines if it enters a Servicer Participant Agreement, which entitles it to receive monetary incentives. Every recipient of federal economic stimulus funds after HAMP began, and most FDIC-insured depositories, must participate.

Servicers of roughly 85 percent of eligible loans have committed, and all the big players like Bank of America, Wells Fargo, Chase, CitiMortgage, GMAC (dissolved), and Ocwen signed on. Refer to MakingHomeAffordable.gov to know whether a lender participates and whether a loan is owned by Fannie Mae or Freddie Mac. Also refer to the Servicers and Investors section below in this chapter.

Tier 1 Criteria Explained

If all of the preceding common criteria are met, the lender then evaluates borrower and loan on the four remaining Tier 1 eligibility criteria:

To find out if your lender participates in HAMP and more about the program, visit MakingHome Affordable.gov.

The Mortgage Has Not Previously Been Modified under HAMP

The important message: When doing a modification, make sure to get it right the first time. If you have been declined and your circumstances change, you may again apply for a modification. Loans modified under HAMP Tier 1 might be eligible for HAMP Tier 2. Loans modified, but not under HAMP, may still be eligible for HAMP modification.

The Property Is Borrower's Principal Residence

The guidelines are, first and foremost, intended to help homeowners stay in their homes. "Principal residence" means the dwelling where the borrower lives most of the time. It may be any eligible property. If more than one unit (but not more than four), one must be occupied as the principal residence.

Payments Are Delinquent or Default Is Reasonably Foreseeable

Borrowers do not have to be behind in their payments to be eligible for a HAMP Tier 1 modification. A formula determines "risk of imminent default," the likelihood that a borrower will miss a payment in the near future, which will be covered in detail later. Otherwise, payments usually are considered delinquent when 60 days (two payments) late.

Pre-modification Monthly Mortgage Payment Ratio Is Greater Than 31 Percent

This ratio compares monthly mortgage payment to monthly gross income. The "monthly mortgage payment" includes loan payment *plus* property tax, hazard insurance, flood insurance, and homeowner association (HOA) fees, as applicable.

The ratio applies only to the first mortgage, which is the eligible mortgage, and does not include private mortgage insurance or special bonds and assessments. Its components and calculations are covered in chapter 7, "Reduce Your Payments: The Modification Waterfalls," page 53. Ultimately, through a series of predefined adjustments, the purpose of the guidelines is to reduce the ratio to 31 percent; thus, it must start above that level.

Tier 2 Criteria Explained

Failure at any Tier 1 evaluation stage—eligibility, qualification (underwriting), or feasibility (net present value, or NPV, test)—results in consideration of borrower and loan for Tier 2. Notably absent is the Tier 1 mortgage payment ratio criterion, which means that the monthly mortgage payment may be higher *or lower* than 31 percent of gross monthly income.

The Mortgage Has Not Previously Been Modified under HAMP Tier 2

This is much broader than it appears. With so little time between the start and expiration of HAMP Tier 2, it would be too late to apply again anyway after a Trial Period Plan or final modification failure. So what's the point?

Not excluded are failures under HAMP Tier 1, which, prior to June 1, 2012, encompassed all HAMP activity. Therefore, the following are eligible for reconsideration under HAMP Tier 2:

- Default on HAMP Tier 1 permanent modification if (1) the Tier 1 modification effective date was more than 12 months before Tier 2 *evaluation*, which is later than submission of the Tier 2 Initial Package, or (2) the borrower experiences a change in circumstances (see the Change in Circumstance section below).
- Default on HAMP Tier 1 Trial Period Plan, without any apparent limitations on time or circumstances.
- Non-approval of HAMP application prior to June 1, 2012, or HAMP Tier 1 afterward (for reasons other than fraud, money laundering, or tax evasion).

The Property Is a Rental Property or Borrower's Principal Residence

A "rental property" is owned by borrower exclusively for rental purposes. It must be (a) occupied as a tenant's principal residence; (b) if rent is not charged or collected, then occupied by a dependent, parent, or grandparent of borrower as the family member's principal residence; or (c) vacant and available for rent.

The property may be the borrower's principal residence, which is the same as Tier 1 criteria. It excludes a second or vacation home not occupied full time. A property offered for rent on a seasonal basis is not eligible, being neither a principal residence nor strictly a rental property.

Payments Are Delinquent or Default Is Reasonably Foreseeable

Loans secured by rental properties must be delinquent, meaning that two or more payments are due and unpaid. A loan secured by borrower's principal residence must be either delinquent or at "imminent risk" of default, which is the same criteria as for Tier 1.

You may qualify for a Tier 2 modification even if your current monthly payment is less than the 31 percent of gross income minimum required under Tier 1.

Change in Circumstances

A mortgage previously evaluated for HAMP, but not approved, may again be considered if the borrower's circumstances change. Typically, reasons for non-approval involve ineligibility, negative NPV test results, or unaffordable payments even after modification. Therefore, reconsideration implies a change affecting those criteria and presumes that the borrower has already exhausted all disputes, appeals, and escalations of the non-approval.

If the non-approval occurred before June 1, 2012, then a borrower is entitled to one reconsideration simply by requesting it. If the non-approval occurred after June 1, 2012, then the borrower's circumstances must have changed, and such changes must meet lender's predetermined definitions. At its discretion, a lender may reconsider borrowers multiple times whenever circumstances vary.

Factors Affecting HAMP Eligibility

Questions arise about specific details affecting individual borrowers, properties, and loans. Here are the answers to several common situations about (1) borrowers and their financial and legal circumstances, (2) properties securing the mortgage to be modified, and (3) loans secured by the same property. Others not covered here should be addressed with your lender, a housing counselor, or the Making Home Affordable administration.

Borrowers and Their Financial and Legal Circumstances

Borrower is not a "person." The borrower must be a natural person. For example, a corporation, partnership, limited liability company, or nonprofit organization is not eligible for HAMP.

continued

continued

Living trust. A property owned by an *inter vivos* (life) revocable trust does not render the borrower ineligible for HAMP, if the borrower is a trustee of the trust, is a primary beneficiary of the trust, and signs HAMP documents as both an individual and trustee. Occupancy of the trustee-borrower determines Tier 1 or Tier 2 eligibility.

Co-borrower is not an occupant. This is especially relevant when a divorce or separation has occurred. If one borrower occupies the property, but another does not, the occupying borrower may be considered alone for HAMP. The non-occupying co-borrower must satisfy two conditions: (1) record a quitclaim deed relinquishing all rights to the property and (2) comply with investor requirement for signing HAMP documents.

Excessive credit obligations. Credit obligations include mortgages, credit cards, automobile loans or leases, and student or other installment loans. If all credit payments, including the *modified* mortgage payment, exceed 55 percent of the borrower's gross income, then the borrower must agree to credit counseling. Previous, even recent, counseling doesn't count.

Default after modification. A borrower loses eligibility for HAMP Tier 1 by defaulting on a final modification or a Trial Period Plan, whether an original HAMP, Tier 1, or Tier 2. A borrower loses eligibility for HAMP Tier 2 by defaulting on a final modification or a Trial Period Plan under HAMP Tier 2.

Active litigation. Active litigation regarding the mortgage to be modified does not render the borrower ineligible for HAMP.

Borrower in bankruptcy. At its discretion, a servicer may consider borrowers in open Chapter

continued

The general rule prevents a borrower from eligibility after rejecting a HAMP modification offer. Even in such a case, a relevant change in the borrower's circumstances might permit reconsideration. Default on a Tier 2 trial or permanent modification renders a borrower ineligible for a HAMP Tier 1 modification no matter what the circumstances.

Nothing in this area limits a borrower's ability to dispute NPV input values and request reevaluation. Likewise, non-approved for HAMP Tier 1 automatically triggers evaluation for Tier 2 without any need for change in circumstances. Ultimately, regardless of circumstance, any mortgage loan not approved for modification must be considered for other available loss mitigation options, including Home Affordable Foreclosure Alternatives (HAFA).

Limits on Multiple Modifications

Generally, a loan may be modified only once under each HAMP Tier. Failure to complete any HAMP trial or permanent modification prohibits HAMP Tier 1 consideration on the same property. Failure to complete a HAMP Tier 2 trial or permanent modification prohibits any HAMP consideration on the same loan.

Whether the primary borrower or a co-borrower, any individual may receive only one HAMP Tier 1 modification. After defaulting on a Tier 1 trial or permanent modification, a borrower loses eligibility for any other Tier 1 modification.

An individual may receive up to three HAMP Tier 2 permanent

modifications of three different mortgage loans. After defaulting on a Tier 2 trial or permanent modification, a borrower loses eligibility for any other HAMP modification on the same loan.

For example, Borrower A received a HAMP modification for her home loan. She also cosigned Borrower B's home purchase loan. Borrower B is limited to a HAMP Tier 2 modification because Co-borrower A may receive only one HAMP Tier 1 modification.

Later, Borrower B defaults on his Tier 2 modified loan; both he and Borrower A lose eligibility for any further HAMP modification *of that loan*. However, if Borrower A defaults on her Tier 1 modified home loan, she subsequently may be eligible for a HAMP Tier 2 modification. In this example, either borrower still may be eligible for a HAFA short sale or deed-in-lieu of foreclosure alternative on either property or loan.

Servicers and Investors

The recipient of mortgage payments "services" the loan on behalf of an "investor" or investment entity that actually owns the loan and the right to be repaid. This "servicer" collects payments from hundreds or thousands of loans, keeps its fee, and pays the balance to the investor. The servicer also conducts loss mitigation activities like collections, settlements, modifications, and approval of short sales. Ultimately, however, the investor must approve changes to loan terms (modifications) and repayment amounts (principal reductions and short sales).

continued

7 or Chapter 13 bankruptcy proceedings for HAMP. However, servicers *must* consider such borrowers if their bankruptcy counsel or trustee submits a request.

Borrower discharged in bankruptcy. A borrower remains eligible for HAMP despite a Chapter 7 discharge if the mortgage to be modified was not reaffirmed.

Failure to file a tax return. If a borrower failed to file a tax return, the borrower is not eligible for HAMP without a documented reason approved by the servicer.

Waiver of legal rights. Lender may *not* require the borrower to waive legal rights as a condition of HAMP.

Monetary contribution. Lender may *not* require the borrower to make any "good faith" or other advance payment to be considered for HAMP.

Properties Securing the Mortgage to Be Modified

Loan-to-value (LTV) ratio. The LTV ratio does not affect a borrower's eligibility. There is no minimum or maximum LTV ratio for HAMP.

Federal Declared Disaster (FDD) relief. Servicers should grant three months of forbearance during HAMP evaluation of a borrower whose home or business is located in a Federal Emergency Management Agency–declared disaster area.

Loans Secured by the Same Property

Balloon loans. A loan with a past due balloon payment, or balloon payment due during the trial period, does not render the borrower ineligible for HAMP.

continued

continued

Secondary loans. A HAMP modification affects only the senior loan and does not affect other loans secured by the same property. Such secondary mortgages (e.g., equity loan or homeowner line of credit), however, must remain subordinate to the senior modified loan. Standard modification paperwork accomplishes this. Nothing suggests that a secondary lender needs to approve modification of a senior loan. Modifying subordinate loans using the 2MP is discussed in chapter 17, "Other Home Affordable Programs," page 135.

Equity loans and lines of credit. Though usually subordinate to another loan, if an equity loan or home equity line of credit is the only loan or is senior to other loans secured by the same property, then it is eligible for HAMP.

Charged-off loans. A mortgage to be modified that has been charged off by the lender does not render the borrower ineligible for HAMP, unless the lender also released the borrower in writing from liability under the loan.

To receive financial incentives, a servicer must enter a Servicer Participant Agreement, which in turn requires compliance with HAMP guidelines. Servicers of roughly 85 percent of eligible loans signed on. Many smaller lenders refused, but, even more challenging, several large loan servicers have been inconsistent or incomplete in their implementation. Aside from such internal shortcomings, and despite committing to the Servicer Participant Agreement, implementation of HAMP guidelines is also subject to potential restrictions of pooling and servicing agreements.

Typically, lenders pool scores of similar loans into a package, and sell the package for tens of millions of dollars to an investor, like a Wall Street brokerage or a financial institution. With the proceeds, lenders can make more loans, then package and sell those loans, and relend that money. Investors raise the money to buy the package by issuing mortgage-backed securities. The securities earn a yield based on the collective interest payments from loans in the pool and are secured by the mortgages that secure those loans.[2]

CAUTION

Your mortgage may not be owned by the institution that you send your payments to but rather by an investment entity. Ask your lender up front if the owner of your loan participates in HAMP modifications.

Most servicers collect payments and enforce mortgages as the investor's agent according to the terms and conditions of the pooling and servicing agreement. That agreement, in turn, reflects the promises made by the investment organizer to those actually putting up the money. These agreements preexisted HAMP and supersede HAMP's requirements. A servicer that agreed with HAMP might be prohibited by the pooling and servicing agreement from implementing one or more inconsistent HAMP guidelines.

Where such a conflict occurs, HAMP obliges a servicer to seek resolution with the investor. The investment entity is rarely empowered to alter its agreements, so the investor ultimately prevails, effectively disqualifying an otherwise HAMP-eligible borrower, most often at the end of the evaluation process, not at the beginning. This is HAMP's Achilles' heel, and the source of borrower mistrust and lender lethargy.

Ask your servicer at the front end whether the investor plays by HAMP rules. If not, ask whether the investor approves an alternative proprietary (non-HAMP) loss mitigation program for modifications and short sales. Remember, if the investor is Fannie Mae, Freddie Mac, the U.S. Federal Housing Administration, the U.S. Department of Veterans Affairs, or one of a few other federal agencies, your loan must be evaluated under that agency's variation of HAMP and other Making Home Affordable relief programs.

Summary

Before consideration for HAMP, a borrower and lender must meet several requirements. The original program was intended to help homeowners in financial distress but was extended in 2012 to include help for landlords. To expand HAMP so significantly, a second level or "tier" was added.

Tier 1 continues the original program limited to homeowners. Tier 2 expands the program to include homeowners who failed to qualify or to successfully complete Tier 1, together with owners of one- to four-unit residential properties. In effect, Tier 2 helps home renters by helping their landlords.

Once a lender determines eligibility, the method for qualifying the modification and for calculating the payment differs between the two tiers.

CHAPTER

3

Getting Started: Initial Package

Learning Points:

- How to apply for a modification.
- How to complete the RMA.
- Other documentation needed.

The initial package begins the HAMP evaluation process. It consists of the Request for Mortgage Assistance (RMA) form, IRS form 4506-T or 4506T-EZ, and evidence of income. This chapter discusses completion of the RMA and then explains evidence of income and the IRS forms. Chapter 13, "Paper Trail: Documentation," page 105, covers details about other documentation that will be required. Chapter 4 discusses mandatory financial hardship and the accompanying explanation.

Request for Mortgage Assistance

From its humble beginnings as a simple three-page form with a more complicated name (Request for Modification and Affidavit), the RMA has morphed into seven complicated and disjointed pages with a more simplified name.

Large lenders may adapt the standard form to create their own unique form. For example, Wells Fargo sometimes requires a ten-page version. Ask your servicer or check its website before starting.

Adding the second tier greatly expanded the information needed, especially about rental properties and multiple HAMP modifications. The RMA consists of nine sections:

1. Borrower Information
2. Hardship Affidavit
3. Principal Residence Information
4. Combined Income and Expense of Borrower and Co-borrower
5. Other Properties Owned
6. Other Property for Which Assistance Is Requested
7. Dodd-Frank Certification
8. Information for Government Monitoring Purposes
9. Borrower and Co-borrower Acknowledgment and Agreement

For reference, the standard Making Home Affordable RMA is included as appendix H, "Request for Mortgage Assistance," page 165. The lender may brand the form with its own logo, but it must gather the same information and must accept the standard form if the borrower submits it. I recommend using it.

The guidelines allow use of an alternative "Hardship Affidavit." Identical in what it covers with the full RMA, it excludes income, expense, asset, and real estate information. Lenders may use the form, or a proprietary version. I suspect that its primary use is for non-HAMP Making Home Affordable (MHA) programs like Home Affordable Foreclosure Alternatives (HAFA). What follows regarding the RMA also applies to relevant portions of the Hardship Affidavit.[1]

The introductory paragraph at the top of page 1 of the RMA states the obvious: If you are experiencing difficulty paying your mortgage, and you want help under the Making Home Affordable program, you need to complete the form accurately and provide correct information.

Here's a breakdown of the sections with clarification and suggestions.

Borrower Information

Enter borrower information. If more than one person is a borrower, then enter the co-borrower's information (1) on the same form if sharing income and assets and own any other real estate together (e.g., most spouses) or (2) on a separate form so income, asset, and property information will be allocated appropriately, though a third combined version might be necessary.

If borrowers have filed for bankruptcy, they should check the appropriate box and provide requested details. Likewise, complete information if any borrower is a military service member. Give details in the hardship explanation for section 2.

The next portion about properties owned and modification activity needs clarification. "Single-family property" means residential real estate with one to four units. On this line, do not include the home even if it contains more than one unit. The other questions relate only to MHA modifications, not to proprietary lender programs or forbearance plans. The next line is about the home, then about other properties, and finally about either the home or other properties.

NOTE

In MHA language, "single-family property" means residential real estate with one to four units. It is not limited to a single-dwelling structure.

Hardship Affidavit

An affidavit is a written statement that affirms that its contents are true and accurate. Check all applicable boxes. Typically, income, expenses, and cash reserve items will apply. If unemployed, clarify option (a) or (b) in the "Explanation" space and refer to chapter 17, "Other Home Affordable Programs," page 135. If the check boxes don't describe a specific situation, use the "Other" space. In the "Explanation" space, refer to an attached statement described in chapter 4, "Hardship: Statement and Affidavit," page 33.

Principal Residence

Complete this section and check the appropriate boxes at the top with information about the property you live in, whether or not it secures the loan to be modified. The first line refers to the home address and the loan number for the senior (first) home mortgage. The second line refers only to a junior (second) mortgage, if any. The third and fourth lines refer to a homeowner association, if any. The remainder regarding an escrow or impound account and sale of the property are self-explanatory. The annual homeowner insurance amount should correspond to the monthly amount entered in the next section's expenses.

Income and Expense

Anticipate the results before giving the data to the lender. So, before completing this section, draw upon three resources in the appendices to determine gross monthly income, credit and household expenses, and monthly mortgage payment ratio: appendix G, "Financial Statement," page 161; appendix E, "Income & Expense," page 155; and appendix C, "Modification Worksheet Tier 1," page 149; or appendix D, "Modification Worksheet Tier 2," page 153.

Income suggestions. Monthly gross wages are employment income before tax and other withholdings from a periodic pay voucher (stub). Use line 2 for overtime; use line 9 for tips, bonuses, and commissions not included in business income. Self-employment (business) income is net income typically reported on IRS Schedule C and 1099 forms, determined monthly from a current profit and loss statement. If you receive unemployment income, refer to chapter 17, "Other Home Affordable Programs," page 135. Use child support and alimony only if needed to increase income sufficiently to qualify for the modified payment and refer to chapter 13, "Paper Trail: Documentation," page 105. Read the asterisks; the single asterisk is on the next page (page 3) of the RMA.

Expense suggestions. The itemized property expenses are for the home, regardless of the loan to be modified. Use the minimum monthly payment for credit cards and revolving debt and the regular monthly payment for installment debt. In the "Other" space, I usually add the "Household Expenses" total from the lender's form or use appendix E, "Income & Expenses," page 155. Whether to minimize or maximize expenses depends on the overall debt-to-income ratio. After subtracting all expenses from *net* income, there should be a comfortable, but modest, net surplus after modifying (reducing) the mortgage payment.

Asset suggestions. Enter account balances consistent with account statements that will be submitted. Averages are okay. Keep in mind that eligibility requires insufficient liquid assets to make the monthly mortgage payments. Therefore, those assets should not exceed three times the monthly housing expense and (if not a government-sponsored enterprise loan) other debt obligations. Exclude retirement and pension accounts. If an account appears on the bank statement, but not here, explain the reason in the hardship statement. If so inclined, put vehicle information in the blank spaces; some lenders will ask. For "Value of Real Estate," enter equity (current market value minus mortgage), even if negative, for properties other than the home. You may leave the "Other" space blank (it's not time to brag about jewelry, coin collections, or power boats).

A bifurcated list of required income documentation begins on page 3, completes section 4, and ignores any instructions. The right column relates directly to the left column. If you answer yes to any of the questions in the left column, then check the box. If you check a box in the left column, then provide the items listed in the corresponding areas in the right column. For example, the first line applies to "All Borrowers" and refers to the IRS 4506-T or 4506T-EZ forms, discussed later in this chapter, which you therefore must include in the initial package.

Other Properties Owned

"Other properties" means other than the home, which was listed in section 3. If this RMA requests the modification of a rental property loan, list that property in section 6, not in this section.

Instructions do not differentiate types of properties, so list all other real estate here, including land, commercial, and multifamily residential. Use a separate schedule of real estate owned if needed. Apparently, as space permits, you need to provide information only about the primary loan.

The point of this list: lenders must inform applicants who own single-family (one to four units) rental properties about limits on the number of Tier 2 modifications permitted. Also, eligibility excludes borrowers who own more than four single-family rental properties.

(The single asterisk footnote at the bottom of page 3 relates to the Income and Expense portion of section 4 *on page 2*, as well as "Monthly mortgage payment" on page 3.)

Assistance Requested

Complete this section only if you want to modify a loan secured by a rental property, not your home.

The top portion of section 6 is identical to information provided in section 3 for the principal residence, which is discussed above. It then asks for details about the rental property, all relating to Tier 2 eligibility. You must check one of the boxes and then explain on the appropriate following line. Refer to chapter 2, "Where to Start: Eligibility," Tier 2 Criteria Explained, item 2, page 17.

NOTE

Section 6 asks if the property is a rental or seasonal/second home. A rental property is eligible, so answer yes. A second or seasonal home is not eligible, so answer no.

Use the Rental Property Certification only if you completed the rental property information in section 6, directly above. You must check the box. By checking the box, you promise that the property will be rented for at least five years, with very limited exceptions, and that you do not own more than four other rental properties. READ THIS CERTIFICATION CAREFULLY. Only then should you initial at the bottom.

Dodd-Frank Certification

By signing on page 6, borrowers certify under this section that they have not been convicted of certain financial crimes during the past ten years. Those crimes are felony larceny, theft, forgery, money laundering, or tax evasion. Don't waste time here; you would know. If you're curious, read it for details. It's a requirement of the Dodd-Frank Wall Street Reform and Consumer Protection Act (July 21, 2010).

Government Monitoring

Providing or not providing this information about ethnicity, race, and gender will not affect any decision related to the loan or its modification. Completion of the monitoring form is voluntary, although it will be done by someone sometime, from assumptions drawn from surname, observation, the form previously completed as part of the loan application, etc.

Acknowledgment and Agreement

A list of facts, representations, and agreements precedes actual signing of the RMA. Here is a summary by paragraph:

1. All of the information in the form is true.
2. The information may be verified. Intentionally submitting false information is illegal.
3. A current credit report will be obtained for all borrowers.
4. Intentional default on the mortgage, or giving false or incomplete information, may disqualify any modification and return the mortgage to its pre-modification status.
5. The property is habitable.
6. The borrower will provide all requested documents and answer all questions when asked.

7. The lender (servicer) is not obligated to modify a loan or provide other relief.
8. Credit counseling might be required.
9. These acknowledgments and agreements will become part of any modification or relief agreement.
10. The lender may disclose to the government, and to other specified parties related to MHA mortgage relief programs, any information provided.
11. Borrower consents to be contacted by e-mail and cell phone.

Other representations in the original 2009 Hardship Affidavit might be assumed or included in other documentation. Be aware:

Refer to page 7, "Notice to Borrowers," which includes warnings about criminal prosecution for providing false or misleading information. By signing on the preceding page 6, you agree: "Under penalty of perjury, all documents and information I have provided to my Servicer in connection with the Making Home Affordable Program, including the documents and information regarding my eligibility for the program, are true and correct."

- Modification is subject to the terms of the Trial Period Plan, which must be completed successfully before obligating the lender to permanently modify.
- Failure to complete the trial period returns the loan to its prior status.
- An escrow account must be established, if one does not already exist.

Time is of the essence, especially when responding to lender communications and requests for documents, which must be provided promptly.

Each borrower then signs the RMA, affirming that its contents are true and accurate, adds Social Security number and date of birth, and dates it.

Additional Provisions

Page 7 includes the "Homeowner's Hotline," which gives free counseling about the RMA and Making Home Affordable programs in English and Spanish (and possibly other languages). The phone number is 888-995-HOPE (4673). It also includes the "Notice to Borrowers" described in the *Caution* above.

IRS Forms

The IRS form required as part of the initial package is the Request for Transcript of Tax Return. The standard version is IRS Form 4506-T.[2] Its somewhat simplified and appropriately named alternative is IRS Form 4506T-EZ.[3] For reference, copies are in appendices I and J, pages 173 and 177. Some of my clients resist anything associated with the taxman, but this is harmless if you filed honest returns.

Signing the form gives the IRS permission to release the tax return, or transcript summary, to a lender for the years indicated on the form. The purpose is either to verify the tax return provided to the lender or to obtain the information in the tax return if not provided. Late filing of a tax return can delay a modification request. Failure to file can terminate a request. Of course, fraudulent filing can make a modification meaningless.

Most of the information is self-explanatory and instructions are usually included. Here are a few suggestions: Use the September 2013 version of Form 4506-T and the January 2012 version of Form 4506T-EZ. For item 5, "third party" information, enter the lender's name and leave the rest blank unless you know it. On the "T" form, line 6 "Transcript Requested," enter "1040" and check box "a" for "Return Transcript." On both forms, for the "Years Requested," enter the last day of the tax year for three years (e.g., 12/31/2011, 12/31/2012, and 12/31/2013—not simply 2011, 2012, 2013). Really, don't underestimate the importance of minutia. Sign, date, and include a telephone number.

Evidence of Income

Refer to the RMA, section 4, Combined Income and Expense of Borrower and Co-borrower, the second portion, on page 3, entitled Required Income Documentation. What follows here explains the bifurcated (two-part) list. If you check the left column, then supply the information listed in the corresponding right column as explained here:

☑ **IRS Form 4506-T or 4506T-EZ.** Refer to the preceding section in this chapter.

☑ **Pay stub(s) for employment income.** Typically, pay stubs or vouchers show the employer's name and location, as well as gross pay, deductions and withholdings, and net pay for the pay period and for totals year to date. Supply two or three, enough to cover a full calendar month, and then continue to submit them monthly to maintain a current file. Refer to chapter 13, "Paper Trail: Documentation," Income Categories, page 110. If you do not receive a formal pay voucher, check with your lender for instructions; alternatives are available.

☑ **Profit and loss statement for self-employment income.** The profit and loss is an income and expense statement for a business. If you report income on IRS form 1040, Schedule C, then prepare and submit one for the current year to date and for the preceding year if you have not yet filed that tax return. A simple monthly summary might suffice, though more detail may be needed depending on the size and complexity of the business. QuickBooks or other business accounting software works. An audited or third-party prepared statement is rarely needed. Refer to chapter 13, "Paper Trail: Documentation," Income Categories, page 110. Place the name of business and date range at top of the profit and loss statement. For months, specify first through last dates. For all dates, use mm/dd/yyyy format. Sign and date at the bottom.

☑ **Description of variable income.** If you receive employment income that varies from time to time (e.g., overtime or bonus), then explain it and provide supporting evidence. Often, such amounts will appear as separate entries on a pay voucher and IRS Form W-2. The lender wants to establish a reliable monthly average. Especially if you need the additional income to qualify for the modified mortgage payment, ask for instructions and cooperate. It might involve a letter from an employer, which should be written for the employer's signature. Refer to chapter 13, "Paper Trail: Documentation," Income Categories, page 110.

- ✓ **Proof of entitlement income.** Such proof might be an entitlement letter (e.g., from Social Security), a benefits statement (e.g., from a pension fund), a coverage declaration (e.g., from a disability insurer), or other documentation acceptable to the lender. It must state the amount, frequency, and duration of the benefit. It also must indicate that the income will continue for at least three more years. The same applies to public assistance programs, including unemployment, but the minimum remaining duration is only nine months. Refer to chapter 13, "Paper Trail: Documentation," Income Categories, page 110.
- ✓ **Proof of alimony or child support.** If you voluntarily disclose alimony and child support received, then provide copies of the settlement and custody agreements that state the award amount and remaining duration, which must be at least three years. Furthermore, full, regular, and timely payments must be shown with reasonably reliable evidence, such as bank statements (circle amounts), deposit slips, or *signed* federal income tax returns.
- ✓ **Proof of real estate rental income.** Usually, include personal federal income tax returns—*signed*—with Schedule E, Supplemental Income and Loss. However, if (1) you prefer not to disclose other information in your tax return or (2) properties or rents have changed since filing, then substitute copies of actual signed leases. Also, include a schedule of real estate owned, especially if you own several rental properties. Segregate rent from a property securing the loan to be modified. Refer to chapter 13, "Paper Trail: Documentation," Income Categories, page 110.

CAUTION

Do not disclose the amount of alimony or child support you pay, unless such income helps you qualify to make the modified payment or to reduce an excessive overall debt-to-income ratio. Refer to chapter 13, "Paper Trail: Documentation," Income Categories, page 110.

- ✓ **Tax returns.** Sign and date page 2. This is the most overlooked detail that I encounter. Repeat: sign and date page 2. Include federal personal returns only, not state taxes, for the most recent year filed. Include all schedules and pages. For late filing, also include the extension. A second year might be required, but let the lender ask.
- ✓ **Bank statements.** If you show an account balance among your asset on the RMA page 2, then provide the two most recent consecutive monthly statements, bank, investment, brokerage, or otherwise. Circle and label wages, entitlements, and rent by property. For accounts that report quarterly, include one statement. Every month, submit the current statement,

whether or not the lender asks. It will avoid delays later. Explain the reason if an account appears on a statement but is not listed on the RMA.

- □ **Other income (not mentioned in the RMA).**

  Investment income. If equaling less than 20 percent of total income, it does not require documentation. For investment income exceeding 20 percent of total income, use the approach for real estate rent. Interest and dividends, deferred compensation, royalties, retirement distributions, and other returns on investments may be shown with periodic statements covering at least three months (quarterly or annual should suffice) substantiated by a second year of tax returns with Schedule E. Point out changes in income, which contribute to hardship and qualification. Changes in investment asset value are secondary but relevant.

  Non-borrower cohabitant contributions. The guidelines do not require borrowers to disclose income earned by a spouse or partner who cohabitates but who is not a borrower and is not obligated on the promissory note. Nor do the guidelines require disclosure of amounts received from non-borrower occupants, such as children or a renter living in the principal residence. As a general rule, do not disclose these amounts, unless such income helps you qualify to make the modified payment or to reduce an excessive overall debt-to-income ratio.

  To use a spouse or domestic partner's income, supply the same documentation as for the borrower. Room and board income needs a written agreement, probably supported by bank statements showing regular deposits, and may be used only in connection with modifying a mortgage secured by a principal residence, not by a rental property.

  Refer to chapter 13, "Paper Trail: Documentation," Income Categories, page 110.

- □ **Excluded income (not mentioned in RMA).** A lender may not consider income tax refunds; non-borrower non-occupant income offered, for example, by friends or family living separately; grants, including mortgage assistance payments; severance payments; unemployment benefits; or payments from non-MHA unemployment assistance programs.

NOTE

You are not required to include or prohibited from including non-borrower cohabitant income. The decision whether to include or exclude should be based on how it impacts your qualification for HAMP modification.

Summary

The minimum needed to get started with a modification application is the initial package, which consists of the Request for Mortgage Assistance, IRS forms requesting information about tax returns or the most recent returns themselves, and evidence of income. Use the lender's versions of the forms or find them at the Making Home Affordable and IRS websites.

Follow the line-by-line instructions in this chapter. When giving income and expenses, review appropriate sections in this book to ensure presenting the best possible information.

Most online forms cannot be saved, so print them blank, complete them by hand, and then submit the handwritten version or go back online and complete the electronic version in one sitting. Keep copies of everything submitted to the lender.

Hardship: Statement and Affidavit

Learning Points:

- The need for financial hardship.
- Definitions of financial hardship.
- How to effectively explain your situation.

Financial hardship justifies modification. It is the key to establishing eligibility.

Affidavit

An affidavit is a written statement that affirms its contents are true and accurate. The Request for Mortgage Assistance (RMA) includes a list of events or conditions that have contributed to the difficulty in making mortgage payments and serves as an affidavit. A stand-alone Hardship Affidavit can be used in special cases. Both include an area to write a narrative explanation, but most lenders expect a separate statement or letter.

Hardship

Be prepared to write a factual explanation that is concise and to the point. Yours does not have to be a special or unique situation; however, it must be supported by documented evidence. The RMA provides inadequate space to explain in detail any of the hardship events that it lists. Instead, in the space provided, refer to a separate statement covered in this chapter and attach it with the comprehensive explanation.

Be brief and direct. Try to remember that those reading the explanation have read hundreds, have heard every possible reason in many variations, and have many more to read before the end of their day.

That said, some lenders use the hardship explanation as the central document for understanding what borrowers want. Lenders will stick primarily to guideline formulas and internal policies but may be influenced when applying them. If borrowers have anything to say about a unique solution or form of relief that they prefer, they should state it in the hardship explanation.

> **TIP**
> Write a separate letter explaining your financial difficulties and attach it to the RMA form.

The Making Home Affordable guidelines state that "HAMP does not distinguish between short-term and long-term hardships for eligibility purposes." Nevertheless, when asked, I usually describe duration as "indefinite," especially considering the length of time to complete some modifications. However, borrowers are obliged to inform their lender of a material change in circumstances, either good or bad, that might affect the final modification decision.

The following addresses acceptable reasons for hardship.

Hardship "Events"

The RMA form lists five types of hardship:

- Reduced household income.
- Increased expenses.
- Unemployment.
- Excessive monthly debt payments.
- Insufficient cash reserves.

It then adds a space for "Other" and the area for "Explanation." Check all that apply, add other circumstances if not listed, and refer to the separate hardship statement in the explanation area.

Explanation

To construct the hardship statement, consider this expanded list of seven events that might cause financial hardship. Both current HAMP guidelines and the original HAMP Hardship Affidavit mention all of the following:

- Reduction in or loss of income that was supporting the mortgage.
- Change in household financial circumstances.
- Recent or upcoming increase in the monthly mortgage payment.
- Increase in other expenses.
- Lack of sufficient cash reserves to maintain payments on the mortgage.
- Excessive monthly debt payments and overextension with creditors.
- Other reasons for hardship detailed by the borrower.

Most are self-explanatory, but the following comments and examples might help frame the hardship reasoning and the written explanation. It's not intended to cover every possible situation. If you have a strong commitment to stay in the house, state that fact and your reasons.

TIP

HAMP does *not* consider retirement accounts or a college fund as liquid assets and does not require borrowers to use these assets as a condition for mortgage modification.

Hardship Events Explained

1. Reduction in or loss of income that was supporting the mortgage. Reduced hours and furloughing days are common examples of reduced income. Other obvious examples are loss of job, unemployment, reduced number of days per week or month, temporary layoff, etc. For those who are self-employed, a decline in business, especially due to economic conditions, is equivalent.

If two or more people are obligated on the loan, then an event happening to one is sufficient. For example, the wife continues working as usual, but the husband loses his job. The wife gets a raise, but not enough to compensate for husband's lost income. Also, an adult child or partner living permanently in the household, who is not obligated on the loan but who has contributed regularly to monthly expenses including mortgage costs, experiences a reduction or loss of income or relocates; both the regular contributions and the cause of their reduction would need to be documented.

2. Change in household financial circumstances. If number 1 applies, then this also applies. However, it more specifically asks for—and should focus on—such changes as birth of a child or adoption, caring for an aging family member, a debilitating injury or illness either temporary or permanent; divorce or separation (but be prepared to show a property settlement agreement, even if just preliminary—some lenders will require final dissolution); if borrowers have been the victim of theft, fraud, scam, or other loss that affects their ability to make mortgage payments; and losses to retirement or investment accounts, if retired or depend on interest or dividends to pay the mortgage.

3. Recent or upcoming increase in the monthly mortgage payment. The loan itself can be the source of hardship that justifies its modification. The increase already may have occurred or is expected to occur soon, say within three to six months, though this is not specifically defined.

Here's a quick summary of loans that are especially vulnerable to such changes:

- Subprime and "Alt-A"—alternatives to A-rated (prime) credit—loans often have interest rates that are fixed for an initial period, typically two years, then adjust periodically. Because of the higher perceived risk, such loans carry higher interest rates. Despite general declines in interest rates, the rates on many of these loans have actually increased along with payments.
- Others have fixed payments for an initial period, typically one year, based on an artificially (very) low introductory interest rate. The rate changes periodically, sometimes every month, which means the fixed payment does not cover the interest charge, and the shortfall is added to the loan balance. Amortization is when the loan balance decreases. Instead, the loan balance increases, resulting in "negative amortization." As the balance swells, the interest applies to a larger amount, which further increases the interest cost.
- Option ARM (adjustable rate mortgage) loans allow a choice of payments: (1) at the artificially low introductory rate that covers less than the current interest due (negative amortization), (2) at the actual current adjusted rate that covers the current interest due (interest only), (3) at the current adjusted rate plus principal that eventually will pay off the loan over 30 years, or (4) over 15 years (amortization). It's your choice. Many borrowers qualified at and paid the lowest amount, which has resulted in negative amortization and a steadily increasing loan balance. They have no realistic possibility of paying off the loan without refinancing, which depends on increasing property values. The opposite has happened. As values plummeted, the owner's equity—if there ever was any—has vanished, and the carrying cost of the mortgage has continued to rise.

4. Increase in other expenses. This may be closely related to number 2, but I recommend concentrating on expenses other than the mortgage that are significant: either a large one-time expense that needs to be paid over time or an expense that is likely to continue for six to 12 months. Nothing in the guidelines prohibits increasing expenses by purchasing discretionary or luxury items, but a brand-new luxury car, sailboat, or a new home loan may be difficult to explain.

Examples of suitable expenses: a health condition that requires more, or more costly, treatment; vocational training, especially in connection with changing or improving a career due to job loss; uninsured losses from fire, flood, or other natural disasters; unexpected repairs to a home or automobile; an increase in property tax, assessments, or homeowner association (HOA) fees.

5. Lack of sufficient cash reserves to maintain payment on the mortgage and cover basic living expenses at the same time. The guidelines include in cash reserves such assets as cash, savings, money market funds, marketable stocks, or bonds. These are often called liquid assets. Note that certificates of deposit of any maturity are included in cash reserves, without regard to penalties. Cash reserves do not include retirement accounts and assets that serve as an emergency fund.

The emergency fund is an amount intended to sustain a borrower (and family) for three months. However, the items to be included when determining the amount vary among three apparent possibilities. First, this hardship event refers to the mortgage payment and basic living expenses. Second, the guidelines then limit the emergency fund to mortgage, property tax and insurance, and other debt payments. Third, Fannie Mae further limits the amount to just the mortgage payment, property tax, and insurance. This becomes more important if borrowers have not missed a payment.[1]

Ask the lender what items it includes. Try to use (1) all debt, including credit cards, other revolving accounts, credit lines, the senior mortgage, and any junior mortgage; (2) property tax, insurance, and HOA fees; and (3) household, medical, and other recurring expenses.

The less included by a lender, the less likely a borrower is to survive the modification gauntlet without missing a payment, usually the mortgage payment. So, here is my advice.

Expect to provide bank statements, probably from two or three recent consecutive months. Some consolidate several accounts, so the statement will disclose all accounts. If any is not cash or liquid, be sure to explain in the hardship statement or separate letter of explanation.

Be conscious of accounts (1) designated for special purposes, like college funds and health savings accounts; (2) that are time or age qualified, like annuities or funds that mature at a date well into the future or at age 65, for example; or (3) held jointly with, or for the benefit of, a non-borrower. HAMP does not state whether such accounts are considered cash reserves. I think not, but lenders may think otherwise.

Many of my clients have gone through substantial savings, stock options, deferred compensation, and retirement accounts in an effort to stay current on their mortgage payments. Try to avoid this mistake despite emotional attachments to the home. Consider the following:

First, if you are using, or expect to use, savings to pay your mortgage or other expenses, then get started on a loan modification immediately. Second, determine for yourself what kind of emergency reserve you need. Third, before tapping your reserve, make an objective inventory of obligations and payments and decide now which to pay and not pay as resources dwindle. Fourth, do not dip into your retirement funds, deferred compensation, stock options, children's college fund, or non-borrower accounts before initiating a loan modification. Fifth, unless you are offered a favorable loan modification, resist when lenders suggest that you spend your (or your family's) future by touching such funds.

6. Excessive monthly debt payments and overextension with creditors. This extends number 5 to resources beyond cash reserves to borrowing power. The guidelines do not specifically require—but do imply—that the debt incurred, the resulting payments, and overextension with creditors was in order to make mortgage payments. The larger consideration—and the one that you should focus on—is whether you have used credit cards, a home equity loan, or other credit to pay normal living expenses due to an increase in those expenses or a decline in income.

7. **Other reasons for hardship detailed by the borrower.** A cause of hardship that is not already listed, or unusual or extreme circumstances, may be described here. Examples of such circumstances include incarceration of a spouse, military reassignment, and disability from medical or psychological causes. Though not required, explain reasons for defaulting on a prior modification, if applicable. Borrowers must provide evidence that supports their claim, which may be different from or in addition to the documentation typically required by lenders. This will need to be tailored to borrowers' special situations.

Be certain to identify the explanation as the "hardship statement," or similar term. Include the loan number, borrower's(s') name(s), and the property address. Then all borrowers sign and date it near the bottom.

Summary

The central theme of the Making Home Affordable program is to help homeowners, and now landlords, to withstand financial hardship imposed by the Great Recession and onerous mortgage loans. Therefore, HAMP eligibility depends on the borrower's financial hardship, which falls into one or more of several standard categories, and must be explained in a written statement.

The statement receives much attention by the lender. It should describe briefly and objectively the borrower's circumstances and intentions. It needs to stay within the boundaries of other eligibility and qualification requirements. If your financial situation has stabilized, say so. Express your desire to keep the property and, if appropriate, any special reasons for wanting to do so.

Delinquency Is Not Required: Risk of Default

Learning Points:

- For homeowners only.
- How to stay current in your payments and still get a modification.

The next step depends on whether a loan is more or less than 60 days late, and whether it is secured by your home. This concession is for homeowners trying to remain current despite their financial hardship.

If payments are 60 or more days delinquent, or will be when the initial package is submitted, then skip this step. If the property securing the loan to be modified is not the principal residence, then skip this step. Eligibility requires loans secured by rental properties to be 60 days late.

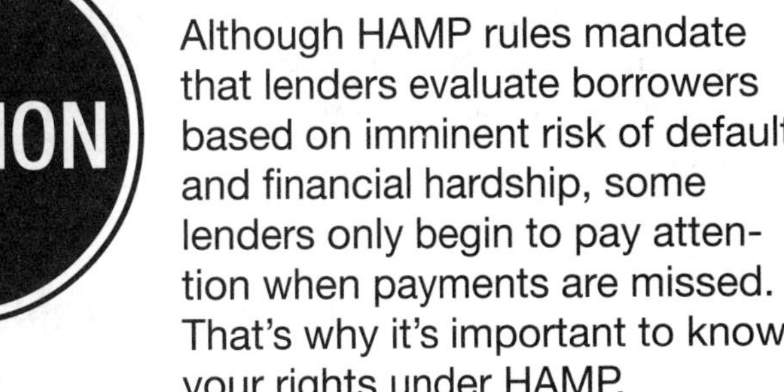

Although HAMP rules mandate that lenders evaluate borrowers based on imminent risk of default and financial hardship, some lenders only begin to pay attention when payments are missed. That's why it's important to know your rights under HAMP.

Many people I talk with have been frustrated that lenders would not consider mortgage relief until a borrower had missed at least one or two payments. Many people struggling with their payments, but who were current, faced almost certain delinquency. They confronted a serious dilemma: either they could try to be responsible, make impossible payments on time, and maintain a good credit rating until they were simply wiped out, or they could miss payments and damage their credit—but finally get their lender's attention.

Fortunately, HAMP would remedy this perplexing problem for homeowners, when lenders and investors comply. Despite the mandate, many lenders still seem to notice more quickly those loans in default than those paid current.

Difficulty persists in breaking the old mold. Some lenders still fail to perceive a problem until the pain reaches them, regardless of the difficulties borrowers are suffering. Gradually, the light may dawn and, when it does, this is how things should look.

If default is "reasonably foreseeable," then the guidelines require a lender to consider the borrower and loan for modification, the same as when a borrower and loan are already in default. This status is also referred to as an "imminent risk" of default, meaning that default is likely to occur very soon. How does a lender determine whether default is reasonably foreseeable? From the guidelines: "A borrower who is an owner-occupant [and] is current or . . . is less than 60 days delinquent and who contacts the servicer to request HAMP consideration must be evaluated to determine if he or she is at risk of imminent default."[1]

A lender's determination must evaluate the borrower's financial condition in light of the described hardship, liquid assets, liabilities, income, monthly obligations, and a reasonable allowance for living expenses. The process of making this determination is called an "imminent default screen." The borrower must document hardship and financial condition for verification by the lender.

HAMP allows lenders to develop their own screening criteria. On the other hand, Fannie Mae has developed an imminent default screen that servicers must use for its loans. I have tried to combine Fannie Mae's imminent default screen with HAMP guidelines, and to generalize standards that might satisfy a broad range of lenders and servicers. However, they might interpret this differently, and many may have simply adopted the Fannie Mae model. Pay attention to the lender's possible variation.

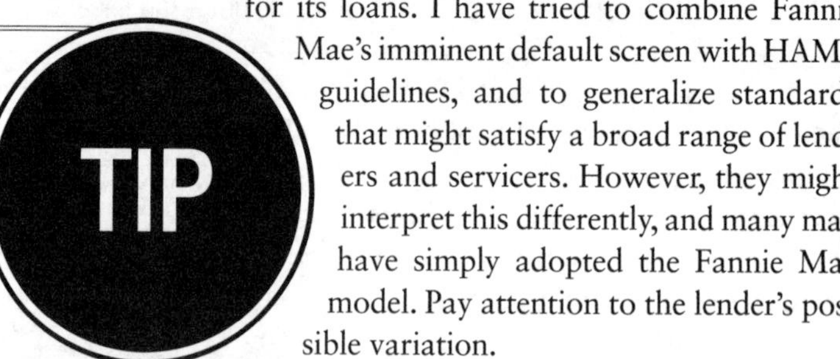

Ask your lender if it uses HAMP or Fannie Mae criteria to determine if a loan is at imminent risk of default and then apply the criteria in this chapter to your own situation.

Overview: Imminent Risk of Default

To summarize:

- Borrower and loan meet HAMP eligibility criteria. Refer to chapter 2, "Where to Start: Eligibility," page 9.
- Specifically, the property securing the loan to be modified is borrower's principal residence, not a rental property.

- The subject mortgage is presently current or is delinquent less than 60 days.
- However, circumstances suggest that default is "reasonably foreseeable."
- Whether default is reasonably foreseeable is determined by using an imminent default screen.
- The imminent default screen evaluates the borrower's documented financial circumstances, hardship, and subject property.
- If the nondelinquent loan is found to be at imminent risk of default, then it must be considered for modification or other foreclosure relief.

The following quickly reviews the formulas used to assess whether a loan is at imminent risk of default. First, note the importance of furnishing complete documentation so a lender can fully evaluate your situation without delay while you look for more—or more current—information. For help in presenting information and estimating qualification, refer to appendix G, "Financial Statement," page 161, and appendix K, "Documentation List," page 181. Ultimately, however, the servicer's criteria determine imminent risk of default for a loan.

Determining Imminent Risk of Default[2]

In a typical imminent default screen, all three factors must be true:

1. **Debt coverage ratio** is less than 1.20.

   (a) monthly disposable net income
   (b) current principal and interest (monthly)
   (c) ratio equals (a) divided by (b)

Debt coverage ratio refers to the relationship of net income to loan payments and reveals the income "cushion" that remains after making those payments. In this usage, income is monthly disposable net income, which means whatever income is left after payroll deductions and all credit obligations, including housing and living expenses, but excluding the mortgage payment to be modified. Debt is current principal and interest, which means the monthly payment for the loan to be modified.

In effect, borrowers have cash remaining for personal and discretionary spending equal to one-fifth (20 percent) *or less* of their loan payment. For example, if the monthly net (take-home) income is $4,500 and the allowable expenses are $1,500, then the disposable net income is $3,000. If the loan payment is $2,500 or more, then this imminent default screen is satisfied ($3,000 divided by $2,500 equals 1.20). The remainder ($3,000 disposable net income minus $2,500 loan payment) is $500 cash in hand after paying all expenses, including the mortgage.

2. **Cash reserves** are less than three times PITIA.[3]

   (a) cash reserves
   (b) current monthly mortgage payment
   (c) ratio equals (a) divided by (b)

The topic of cash reserves was discussed extensively in chapter 2, "Where to Start: Eligibility," page 9, and in chapter 4, "Hardship: Statement and Affidavit," page 33. "Current monthly mortgage payment" means principal and interest paid to the lender plus property tax and insurance paid directly or into an escrow account held by the lender plus HOA fees and other assessments, if any. It does not include any second mortgage, equity line of credit, or mortgage insurance premium.

For this criterion, Fannie Mae is more restrictive than what HAMP criteria suggest. Though not in context of imminent default, HAMP hardship guidelines refer to an emergency fund that equals *all* debt payments for three months. All debts include payments for all mortgages, other installment loans, revolving credit, and credit lines and might even extend to common living expenses.

For example, assume the monthly mortgage payment of principal, interest, tax, and insurance is $2,500 and other monthly debt payments for an equity loan, an automobile lease, and credit cards is $1,500. Fannie Mae would allow a cash reserve of $2,500 times three months equals $7,500. HAMP would allow a cash reserve of $2,500 plus $1,500, which equals $4,000, times three months equals $12,000.

The HAMP allowance can be significantly larger than Fannie Mae's limit, resulting in a larger allowable cash reserve. To state the obvious, the larger the cash reserve, the higher the comfort level. Now that you know the difference between Fannie Mae's restrictive approach and the HAMP alternative, ask your lender which one it uses: three times the monthly mortgage payment or three times the mortgage payment plus all other debt payments, with or without living expenses. You may need to ask more than once to get a clear answer.

3. **Monthly mortgage payment ratio** is greater than 31 percent.

   (a) current monthly mortgage payment
   (b) monthly gross income
   (c) ratio equals (a) divided by (b)

Current monthly mortgage payment was discussed in number 2 above; it includes mortgage principal and interest, property tax and insurance, and homeowner association fees, if any (PITIA). Monthly gross income is top-line income before withholdings, deductions, taxes, retirement contributions, etc. For self-employed income, use taxable net income or earnings actually received.

This also is an eligibility requirement.[4] It expresses the relationship of the housing expense (not including a second mortgage, if any) to borrowers' total income. For example, if the monthly mortgage payment is $2,500 and monthly gross income is $6,000, then this imminent default screen is satisfied ($2,500 divided by $6,000 equals 41.67 percent). However, if the monthly mortgage payment is $1,860 and monthly gross income is $6,000, then this imminent default screen is not satisfied because the ratio is not *more than* 31 percent ($1,860 divided by $6,000 equals 31 percent).

In the lending world, 31 percent is very conservative (low)—bad for getting a loan but good for getting a modification. In the past, loans commonly have been made with ratios ranging from 38 to 45 percent or higher, or without declaring income or calculating any ratio at all. Of course, this lending practice is a principal culprit of our current predicament.

Summary

A borrower does not need to miss a mortgage payment to be eligible for a loan modification. On the other hand, despite financial incentives, lenders show little initiative in finding and helping such borrowers. The message: As soon as you foresee difficulty, start the modification process for yourself.

Modify or Foreclose? Net Present Value

Learning Points:

- Meaning of net present value (NPV).
- How lenders decide between modification and foreclosure.
- Servicers are primarily responsible to investors, not borrowers.
- How to improve your NPV.

Will your lender make more money—or lose less—by modifying your mortgage or by foreclosing on it? Well, that depends. And it determines whether your lender will modify your loan.

It depends on variables that predict the benefits and costs associated with modifications and foreclosures from the beginning to the end of each process. The predicted benefits and costs vary with each loan and borrower, occur over different periods of time, and may be influenced by region, locale, or neighborhood.

Net Present Value

A participating servicer uses a Making Home Affordable (MHA) computer program, first, to forecast future benefits and costs if it holds and modifies the loan. Next, the program forecasts future benefits and costs if it takes back the property in foreclosure. Then, to make a fair and accurate comparison, it reduces the forecasted benefits and costs that will occur in the future to their "present value."

Reducing future income or expense to present value draws on predictions about expected inflation, market growth, overall employment and cost-of-living prospects, alternative investments for money now in the loan, and other economic variables, plus the reliability of such predictions. Visualize an avalanche of data.

NOTE

Under HAMP, your lender must calculate based on standardized criteria whether modifying your mortgage would serve their financial interest better than foreclosure.

The resulting present value of all benefits and of all costs forecasted by the program is compared. Subtracting the present value of costs from the present value of benefits results in a net present value for modification and an NPV for foreclosure.

I prefer the "benefits and costs" terminology, rather than "income and expense," because we are talking about value, which reaches beyond dollars and cents. Simply stated, value equals benefits minus costs, whether applied to a home, possessions, business, job, friendships, or life. In this instance, of course, it applies to your mortgage and profile as a borrower and whether your lender will modify or foreclose on your loan.

Evaluation Process

Any loan that meets HAMP eligibility criteria,[1] and is either in imminent risk of default[2] or is more than 60 days delinquent, must be evaluated using a standardized computer program called the Base NPV Model, which is available to all lenders through MHA.

The program tries to predict the likelihood that a loan, once modified, will then perform as agreed or whether the borrower will "re-default." The prediction is based on characteristics of a very large number of borrowers and loans reported to a central database by Fannie Mae, Freddie Mac, and participating servicers. Lenders that service more than $40 billion in loans may adapt, or "re-code," the Base NPV Model to their own systems and experience but must utilize standard MHA components.

Calculations draw from such characteristics as current loan balance, property value, loan-to-value (LTV) ratio, monthly mortgage payment, credit score, delinquency status, and other loan and borrower attributes, as well as economic, geographic, and demographic influences. The program then calculates the value to a lender/investor if (1) the loan is modified and (2) the loan is not modified and goes to foreclosure. The lender then compares these two results.

If the NPV is greater by modifying the loan, then the NPV outcome is referred to as "positive." If the net present value is greater by *not* modifying the loan, then the outcome is referred to as "negative."

With few exceptions according to the guidelines, if the outcome is "positive," then the lender must offer the modification. Therefore, *if a loan qualifies, the lender must modify it.*

If the determination is "negative," then the modification is optional at the lender's discretion and subject to permission of third-party investors. If a lender chooses not to modify, then it must consider other foreclosure prevention options, including custom or proprietary non-HAMP modification programs, a deed in lieu of foreclosure, and a pre-foreclosure short sale.[3]

To dispute a negative outcome, refer to chapter 11, "Non-Approval: Required Disclosures and Remedies," page 91. To help predict the NPV test outcome, refer to the section below about using a free online tool developed by the U.S. Department of Treasury and U.S. Department of Housing and Urban Development (HUD).

Running the NPV Test

The NPV computer program, sometimes referred to as a "test," runs once for both HAMP Tier 1 and Tier 2.[4] The day when a servicer first runs a loan through the NPV test is the NPV date for the loan. This date remains constant for all subsequent NPV runs. The only exception is a loan originally evaluated before June 1, 2012, when reevaluated for HAMP Tier 2.

The NPV date holds significance because it determines the version of the NPV model and assumptions that will be used initially and subsequently for appeals or escalations. It also determines the baseline for extensive borrower, loan, and property information, called "input values." Relatively few input values can be disputed, and even fewer actually change after the original NPV test.

Because the variables differ between Tier 1 and Tier 2 modifications, the same NPV test can deliver different results for each tier. The NPV test results apply first to Tier 1 evaluation, if applicable, and then to Tier 2 evaluation.

For example, consider these scenarios:

1. Assume that a homeowner is eligible for a Tier 1 modification, and the NPV Tier 1 result is positive. The servicer must offer the homeowner a HAMP Tier 1 trial modification.
2. Assume that a homeowner is eligible for a Tier 1 modification, and the NPV Tier 1 result is negative, but the NPV Tier 2 result is positive. The servicer must offer the homeowner a HAMP Tier 2 trial modification.
3. Assume that a borrower is not eligible for a Tier 1 modification, and the NPV Tier 2 result is positive. The servicer must offer the borrower a HAMP Tier 2 trial modification.
4. Assume that a borrower is not eligible for a Tier 1 modification, and the NPV Tier 2 result is negative. The servicer may, but is not required to, offer the borrower a HAMP Tier 2 trial modification.

Predicting NPV Results

The website CheckMyNPV.com, developed by the U.S. Treasury and HUD, allows borrowers and their advisors to conduct their own NPV evaluation. The tool requires the same extensive borrower, loan, and property input values as the Base NPV Model. Likewise, it uses the same formula used by mortgage servicers.

However, differences in borrowers' input data from the lender's input values might result in different outcomes.

Use the tool before submitting the initial package to anticipate results, and then adjust the data if necessary and possible. Once submitted, the initial package triggers the NPV test, which in turn sets the NPV date and establishes the NPV input values and assumptions.

If borrowers were denied a HAMP modification because of a negative NPV test result, the non-approval notice will list the NPV input fields and values used by the lender. Review the input values. Borrowers can use the same values to verify the lender's results. Or, if borrowers disagree with any, they can substitute their values and use CheckMyNPV.com to run an alternative scenario. In either case, if the result is positive, then dispute those input values and request a reevaluation.[5]

CAUTION

CheckMyNPV.com allows you to make the same calculations as your lender must under HAMP, although the website cautions that results are "only an estimate of a mortgage servicer's NPV evaluation."

CheckMyNPV.com offers good information and ample help. Use the supporting materials to prepare before beginning the actual evaluation. Assemble all the input values in advance. Save a copy of the evaluation and share it with the mortgage servicer to discuss options available.

Principal Factors Influencing NPV Test Results

Knowing about some of the factors incorporated in the Base NPV Model might help borrowers better understand the NPV test, which is the least transparent element of HAMP. It might suggest how to improve borrowers' chances for a positive result.

Though data will come from sources built into the model, and immune from external influence, consider how to emphasize or "weight" your variable input values to your advantage. Also, consider how you might enhance your hardship statement by integrating these attributes.

For example, future increases or decreases in home prices affect a borrower's willingness to stay in a house and, likewise, impact a lender's potential loss from foreclosure. Tell your lender if you are willing to stay with an "underwater" property and why.

The NPV test compares the present value of projected future cash flows if a mortgage is modified and if it is not modified. The following factors can significantly influence such future cash flows.

Value of Property Compared with Size of Mortgage

A loan balance far exceeding the value of a property diminishes the prospects for accumulating equity, discourages the owner, and raises the risk of re-default. In fact, many owners simply abandon such underwater loans. On the other hand, value approaching or exceeding the loan balance encourages the owner but also improves probable return to the lender from foreclosure. It's difficult to predict the effect on the NPV test.

The presence of a second mortgage often aggravates these cases and the risk for re-default. The added debt further buries the possibility of ever regaining equity. For some, the mortgages far exceed the property value, and a modification that does not forgive principal—does not actually reduce the loan amount—will inevitably result in a short sale and a loss to the lender. Foreclosure aside, the property simply will not appreciate in value fast enough to catch up to the mortgage before the owners must sell.

Principal forgiveness is optional under the guidelines, so don't be surprised when lenders resist or ignore this alternative. Because principal forgiveness has been so rare, contributing in part to the woeful record of pre-HAMP modifications, statistics are not yet available to support its effectiveness. Recent litigation over lender abuses, however, jarred the door open slightly.

NOTE

A reduction by the lender in your loan amount is called "forgiveness." Don't be confused by the term "forbearance," which temporarily suspends payments or permanently suspends partial payments while leaving the entire principal balance intact and due sometime in the future.

Eventually, I believe, the NVP test will demonstrate that to give up principal now is less expensive for a lender than to give it up later *and* incur the costs of foreclosure. Slowly in that direction, the NPV calculation now incorporates the Principal Reduction Alternative[6], which still remains optional for lenders even with a positive NPV result.

Determining Value

Current market value is an essential component of the NPV test calculation. It can be determined by using an automated valuation model (AVM) or a broker's price opinion (BPO). An AVM is yet another computer model, which draws on data contributed by appraisers and other sources, then narrows the data by location, square footage, room count, and similar value determinants to estimate an individual property's value. It does not take into consideration the unique qualities of an individual property and therefore is the most disputed element of the NPV calculation.[7] A BPO is a professional statement of value by a licensed real estate agent or broker. Different from a market valuation for listing or selling, the BPO addresses specific criteria contained in a form acceptable to the lender.

A full appraisal, like the one completed for several hundreds of dollars when the borrowers got the loan, is very rare for a modification, unless done by the lender's staff or in connection with a dispute. The value of the collateral is now less important than whether the borrower can afford and sustain payments.[8] Borrowers might obtain an AVM from a friendly title or escrow company, but the BPO carries a price tag.

Instead, make your own estimate from recent sales in your neighborhood of properties similar to yours, or from a recent property tax reassessment. At some point, someone representing the lender will lay eyes on the property, with or without notification. An interior inspection requires the borrower's consent.

Trends in Prices

Whether the values of similar properties in a marketplace have tanked, bottomed out, or turned the corner will affect an owner's optimism and attitude and may influence a lender's receptivity and flexibility.

Has the property declined in value more than, less than, or about the same as others in the marketplace? Different market segments have behaved differently. For example, in some areas, condominium or super-custom segments have been pounded harder than starter and family homes. Underdeveloped and overbuilt subdivisions and declining neighborhoods may take longer to recover. Statistics paint with broad strokes. If a situation warrants a closer look, give a brief specific description of the property's unusual circumstances.

Other conditions, even if already factored into the Base NPV Model, may affect value trends and deserve specific mention. Examples include geographic influences (positive or negative), economic conditions such as factory closings or relocation of major employers, and natural disasters.

Likelihood of Foreclosure

How seriously delinquent are loan payments? Is the property value significantly below the loan balance? How badly have a borrower's financial prospects deteriorated? Has the file been referred to an attorney or trustee? Has a foreclosure sale been scheduled? The further along in this process, the more likely the NPV result will turn negative. These circumstances should already have been clearly described in the hardship explanation, along with how they will be relieved by modifying the loan.

Likelihood of Default after Loan Modification

Lenders and third-party investors may be skeptical that a loan modification might only delay the inevitable and might cost them more in the long run. Part of the skepticism comes from the miserable track record of past modifications. Many past modifications served to reorganize the loan problem, not correct it. They even increased payments after a temporary reduction by adding late payments and fees onto a loan that was already delinquent and impossible for the borrower to pay. This irony likely distorts the statistical data used in the Base NPV Model and, in so doing, exaggerates the problem.

Relevant variables affecting the likelihood of default after the loan modification include the following:

- **Payment record.** Does the borrower exhibit a pattern of late payments: since purchasing the property, since obtaining the loan, since the hardship began, since first missing mortgage payments? The later borrowers began missing payments, if any, the better; it suggests that they have more to lose by re-defaulting. Remember, borrowers do not have to be delinquent to modify the loan. If the payment history was responsible until—and especially after—the hardship began, one can assume that the borrower will make timely payments when the hardship ends, *if* the loan is modified and payments are reduced. If the borrower paid when payments were affordable, then they will pay again when payments become affordable again.

- **Credit quality.** Refer above to payment record. Few other credit accounts and delinquencies bode well for a helpful modification. The lender will pull a credit report, but don't assume that anyone will have time to interpret patterns. If the pattern is good, then mention it in the hardship statement.
- **Borrower's debt burden.** This also will be revealed in the credit report. It is one of the identified hardship events, so a manageable amount of debt after modification is acceptable. However, a borrower still upside-down after modification needs other solutions. A lender may differentiate debt accumulated before the hardship event, which should exhibit a responsible pattern, from what accumulated since (and because of) the hardship event. To stop making mortgage payments, however, shortly after obtaining a new car loan may raise questions. To stop making mortgage payments shortly after obtaining a new home loan can disqualify a modification.
- **LTV ratio.** Refer above to value of the property compared with the size of the mortgage. The mortgage amount divided by the property value is the LTV ratio. A second mortgage combines to a larger amount and the combined loan-to-value ratio, or CLTV. Any result greater than 100 percent is commonly referred to as negative equity, or "underwater." For example, a property with a $550,000 mortgage and now valued at $500,000 has an LTV of 110 percent ($550,000 divided by $500,000). Add a $100,000 equity loan and the CLTV is 130 percent ($650,000 divided by $500,000).
- **Duration of delinquency**. Prospects improve for a loan modified earlier in the delinquency cycle rather than later. It also suggests that a nondelinquent loan in imminent risk of default has a better chance for success, despite lenders' persistence in giving priority treatment to delinquent loans.

Summary

It all comes down to whether the mortgage investor, for which your servicer collects your payments and enforces your agreement to pay, will benefit more (or lose less) by modifying your loan or foreclosing. A key determinant is the NPV test. It estimates the value today of possible modified payments in the future, together with the value recovered by foreclosing, and compares them.

A complex computer model calculates the comparison from information about your income, loan, and payment history and from data collected about the economy, property values, and modified loans. A borrower's best chance to influence the outcome relates to personal income and expenses. If declined for a negative NPV outcome, or to get an idea of the outcome in advance, use a website designed for that purpose, CheckMyNPV.com.

Reduce Your Payments: The Modification Waterfalls

Learning Points:

- How your payment gets reduced.
- How to figure your modified payment.
- How to prepare *before* talking to your lender.

Yes, that's correct. HAMP uses the term "waterfall" to describe the sequence of steps that a lender must follow to modify a loan. Even "cascade" might be better. "Waterfall" feels like approaching a cliff, flowing inescapably over the edge, careening off rock ledges, and tumbling inexorably to the bottom. In fact, the "sequence" of mandatory steps dictated by the guidelines can cause a significant drop in your payments, with a soft landing.

Familiarity with the sequence may prove very important. Here is a recent illustration: During a six-hour period, I talked for nearly three hours with three different HAMP customer service representatives at one of the very largest lenders, which services a gigantic portfolio of loans eligible for modification. It clearly has systems in place and an operational computer model.

After I furnished income and expense numbers, the representative concluded that my client didn't qualify for a modification. Actually, he explained, the computer told him that my client didn't qualify and told him to supply me with the telephone number of a free nonprofit mortgage counseling agency. I thanked him, rechecked the numbers and my calculations, and called back later.

To avoid making a long story out of a short one, suffice it to say that my second conversation was nearly identical to the first. On my third call, I reached a representative who showed greater initiative. After a long but productive discussion, we agreed that the computer conclusion was incomplete and to proceed with the modification. The scenario involved principal reduction of $60,000, interest rate reduction of nearly 5 percent, and monthly payment reduction of $1,600. Pay attention—this might be important.

Introduction to Modifying Loans

The process of modifying a loan consists of four steps called a "modification waterfall." The steps vary, first, between Tier 1 and Tier 2 and, second, between the *Standard* Modification Waterfall, which uses the full amount owed to the lender, and the *Alternative* Modification Waterfall, which uses a reduced loan amount.

Tier 1 and Tier 2 Waterfall Steps Summarized

Tier 1. Servicers must evaluate homeowners and loans that are eligible for HAMP Tier 1 according to the following Standard Modification Waterfall steps in the stated order, **until reaching** the *target payment ratio* of 31 percent of gross income.

1. **Capitalize:** Determine the remaining amount of the loan and other amounts owed to the lender.
2. **Reduce the interest rate:** Lower the monthly payment by reducing the interest rate to as low as 2 percent.
3. **Extend the term and re-amortize:** To further reduce the monthly payment, stretch payments over a longer period up to 40 years.
4. **Principal forbearance:** Reduce the portion of principal on which interest is charged to further reduce the monthly payment as needed.

Tier 2. Owners of rental properties and others who are not eligible for Tier 1 must be evaluated similarly but according to steps tailored to Tier 2 criteria. *Only after applying all waterfall steps* does a lender calculate the target payment ratio and determine whether it falls within the *acceptable debt-to-income (DTI) range* of 25 to 42 percent of income.

1. **Capitalize:** Determine the remaining amount of the loan and other amounts owed to the lender, as for Tier 1.
2. **Adjust the interest rate:** Change the interest rate to a predetermined fixed rate.
3. **Extend the term and re-amortize:** Change the remaining loan term to 40 years.
4. **Principal forbearance:** Convert the portion of the loan that exceeds 115 percent of the property value to non-interest-bearing principal.

Differences between Tier 1 and Tier 2 Waterfall Steps

Tier 1 methodology focuses on a fixed target using flexibility in applying the waterfall steps. The target payment, explained in detail below, is precisely 31 percent of income. The methodology applies each step in order as necessary until reaching the target but no further. The values determined when applying the steps become the terms of the modification.

Contrast Tier 2 methodology, which focuses on a flexible target while applying the waterfall steps without variation. The target payment can range from 25 to 42 percent of income, provided the modified payment achieves at least a 10 percent reduction. However, the methodology applies the fixed criteria of each step until completing all steps.

Tier 1 results reflect a modified interest rate, amortization term, and monthly payment tailored to the individual homeowner's qualifications. On the other hand, Tier 2 results reflect a rate, term, and payment (relative to loan amount) that are identical for every owner of a rental property and others who are not eligible for Tier 1.

Standard and Alternative Modification Waterfalls

Servicers must evaluate every eligible loan using the Standard Modification Waterfall, which consists of the four steps enumerated above for Tier 1 and Tier 2. If third-party investor limitations restrict a servicer's application of one or more steps, the servicer must attempt to complete the waterfall procedure within such limits and seek a waiver of the restrictions from the investor.

If the eligible loan principal balance exceeds 115 percent of the current property value, then servicers also must evaluate it using the Alternative Modification Waterfall, which adds a step after Step 1.

The step reduces the principal balance to 115 percent of the current property value before applying the remaining Standard Modification Waterfall steps. The effect for such loans is to evaluate them twice: once for the full loan amount and once for the reduced hypothetical loan amount. Evaluation runs through the Base NPV Model with the purpose of ensuring that lenders consider whether principal reduction produces a "positive" NPV result, though principal reduction still would be optional.

Called the Principal Reduction Alternative (PRA), details about this added step are discussed in the Principal Reduction Alternative section of this chapter starting on page 68. Such principal reduction, generically referred to as "debt forgiveness" and staged over three years, permanently reduces the loan amount.

Monthly Mortgage Payment Ratio[1]

The monthly mortgage payment ratio calculates the relationship between housing expenses and income. It relates to the senior mortgage on the principal residence and applies to both Tier 1 and Tier 2 but in different ways, explained in the pertinent section below.

Tier 1 eligibility requires, among other things, that the pre-modification ratio exceeds 31 percent; Tier 2 has no pre-modification ratio requirement. The post-modification objective for Tier 1 is the "target" ratio; for Tier 2 is the "range."

The monthly mortgage payment is for your primary residence, regardless of the loan to be modified.

Commonly referred to as the "housing-to-income" or "front-end" ratio, it's the target of the payment reduction steps. Unfortunately, the guidelines also refer to it as the DTI ratio, which suggests that it would include junior mortgages, loans secured by other real estate, credit cards, and other "debt," but it does not. It includes only the specified obligations associated with the home, whether or not it is the subject of the desired modification.

Monthly Mortgage Payment

- principal and interest (P&I) payment
- property taxes
- homeowner's insurance
- flood insurance
- HOA fees

Monthly Mortgage Payment Ratio

- (a) monthly mortgage payment
- (b) monthly gross income
- (c) ratio equals (a) divided by (b)

The "monthly mortgage payment" means the principal and interest paid to the lender for the primary home loan, *plus* monthly allotments for property taxes and insurance, homeowner association (HOA) fees, and certain other assessments. It does not include the payment for any second mortgage or for mortgage insurance.

To arrive at the monthly mortgage payment ratio, divide the monthly mortgage payment by monthly gross income. "Monthly gross income" means salary, wages and other employment income, or self-employment compensation actually received, before taxes and other withholdings. Gross income also includes non-employment income from investments, entitlements (like pensions or social security), net real estate rental income, and alimony and child support (*if* you choose to disclose it), but it does not include unemployment compensation.

Lenders use several ratios. Confusion may arise from terminology. According to the guidelines, monthly mortgage payment *not only* includes the principal and interest (P&I) payment *but also* includes taxes, insurance, and other fees. Principal and interest are components of the target payment but total less than the target payment amount.

The resulting ratio, expressed as a percentage, represents the portion of income used to pay basic housing expenses. For details regarding the components of gross income, refer to appendix G, "Financial Statement," page 161.

Common Waterfall Steps

The New Loan Amount

The first waterfall step for both Tier 1 and Tier 2 determines the remaining amount of the loan and other amounts owed to the lender. The process of arriving at the total is called "capitalization."

Step 1. Capitalize the Loan Amount

Find the loan balance in the current monthly mortgage statement, log into the online account, or call the lender's customer service number. When calling a lender, have the loan number, last four digits of the borrower's Social Security number, property address, and plenty of patience.

A close look at the loan balance will reveal the following:

- The loan balance will be lower than the original loan amount, if payments have included both principal and interest (amortizing loan).
- The loan balance will be the same as the original loan amount, if payments have included interest but not principal (interest only).
- The loan balance will be more than the original loan amount, if payments have been less than the interest amount (option ARM, or adjustable rate mortgage). The difference between the interest due and the lower payment has been added to the loan balance (negative amortization).

Clarify whether the loan balance includes late fees and interest. If so, subtract late fees; if not, add late interest (the interest portion of missed payments) but not the principal portion, which remains part of the unpaid loan balance.

If the lender advanced payments for such expenses as unpaid property tax or insurance, add those amounts too. In addition, lenders may add fees paid to others for loans referred to foreclosure, as well as prior forbearance amounts granted to a borrower. In the rare event that a second lender must subordinate to a modification, the HAMP lender must pay the fee, if any.

The guidelines refer to the loan amount throughout this process generally as the "unpaid principal balance" (UPB).

Lenders must waive late fees when modification becomes final and may not add them to the UPB. They may not charge, or add to the loan balance, any of the costs incurred to modify a loan—including credit report, appraisal or valuation, escrow and settlement fees, and lender administrative and business overhead expenses.

Here's a summary for both Tier 1 and Tier 2:

- Start: current loan amount (principal balance)
- Plus: past due interest, but not past due principal
- Plus: escrow advances for property tax and insurance
- Plus: escrow advances for HOA or other assessments
- Plus: third-party expenses for
  - property preservation,
  - property title, valuation, and related expenses, and
  - foreclosure services
- Plus: Forbearance amounts previously granted to borrower
  - Exclude: late fees
  - Exclude: lender's expenses related to modification
- Result: Estimated capitalized principal balance

The resulting total is the estimated capitalized principal balance. It's "estimated" because it will change by the amount of more missed interest payments and lender-paid escrow amounts that accrue before final modification.

If borrowers are current with their payments, it equals the loan balance. If borrowers are late with their payments, it is calculated like this:

- actual principal balance × annual interest rate = annual interest
- annual interest ÷ 12 (months) = monthly interest
- monthly interest × number of missed payments = interest past due
- interest past due + loan balance = new balance
- new balance + allowed lender costs = capitalized loan amount

For example:

- loan balance × interest rate = interest/year

  Example: $200,000 × 6.00% = $12,000 annual interest

- annual interest ÷ 12 (months) = interest/month

  Example: $12,000 ÷ 12 = $1,000/month

- monthly interest × missed payments = interest past due

  Example: $1,000 × 3 = $3,000

- interest past due + loan balance = new balance

  Example: $3,000 + $200,000 = $203,000

- new balance + allowed lender costs = capitalized loan amount

  Example: $203,000 + $1,000 (unpaid property taxes) = $204,000

Though not mandatory, the lender may voluntarily reduce the estimated capitalized principal balance at any point in the waterfall process. Or the PRA might result in a reduction for certain loans. In either case, the remaining waterfall steps apply to both amounts. Likewise, subsequent waterfall steps are different for Tier 1 and Tier 2 modifications. Tier 1 is for homeowners whose home loan was not previously modified, and Tier 2 is for rental property owners and homeowners ineligible for Tier 1.[2]

Step 4: Principal Forbearance

Loan then consists of:

(a) Capitalized Principal Balance (the entire amount owed)
(b) Interest-Bearing Principal
(fully amortizing)
(c) Non-Interest Bearing Principal
(forbearance amount resulting in a balloon payment)

Divide the Loan Amount

In Step 1, the loan amount probably increased by late interest payments and other expenses. After changing the interest rate in Step 2 and lengthening the term in Step 3, dividing the loan into interest-bearing and non-interest-bearing portions can further reduce the monthly payment. The process is called forbearance. Thus, the other waterfall step common to Tier 1 and Tier 2:

Step 4. Principal Forbearance

Forbearance means that a lender refrains, or forbears, from receiving payments for a portion of the loan. In this instance, the lender actually *forgives* interest (does not charge or collect it during or at the end of the loan term) on that portion of the loan. Because no payments are received, that portion of the loan is not amortized (is not paid over time), so the lender *forbears* from collecting a portion of the principal during the loan term. However, unlike the interest, the lender eventually collects the principal in a lump-sum balloon payment at the end of the loan term, or earlier if the borrower sells the property or refinances the loan.

Step 4 reduces the monthly payment by separating the loan into two parts. On one part, interest is charged: the interest-bearing principal. On the other part, interest is not charged: the non-interest-bearing principal. For example, applying interest to 80 percent of the principal balance (interest-bearing principal) reduces the payment by about 20 percent. The borrower still owes the remaining 20 percent of the principal balance (non-interest-bearing principal) but makes no payments on that portion.

The loan now has three components: (1) the new principal balance, which is either the total amount owed from Step 1 or the PRA amount; (2) the interest-bearing principal balance calculated in this step, which is the amount subject to regular principal and interest payments; and (3) the deferred principal balance, or forbearance amount, which is the non-interest-bearing difference between (1) and (2).

Tier 1 Waterfall

Tier 1 methodology focuses on a fixed target: a monthly mortgage payment that equals 31 percent of gross income. It applies the following waterfall steps in order until the target is reached, but no further.

Homeowners who have *not* been offered a HAMP Trial Period Plan (TPP) trial modification should continue to the next section. Others should skip to Tier 2 Waterfall on page 65.

1. **Capitalize:** Determine the remaining amount of the loan and other amounts owed to the lender.
2. **Reduce the interest rate:** Lower the monthly payment by reducing the interest rate to as low as 2 percent.
3. **Extend the term and re-amortize:** To further reduce the monthly payment, stretch payments over a longer period up to 40 years.
4. **Principal forbearance:** Reduce the portion of principal on which interest is charged to further reduce the monthly payment as needed.

The results reflect a modified interest rate, amortization term, and monthly payment tailored to the individual homeowner's qualifications.

Target Monthly Mortgage Payment[3]

Tier 1 uses the monthly mortgage payment ratio in determining both eligibility and the modified payment. The ratio before modification must be greater than

Monthly Mortgage Payment

principal and interest (P&I) payment
property taxes
homeowner's insurance
flood insurance
HOA fees and other assessments

Monthly Mortgage Payment Ratio

(a) monthly mortgage payment
(b) monthly gross income
(c) ratio equals (a) divided by (b)

Tier 1 *Target* Principal & Interest

Target: gross income × 31%
Minus: escrow (tax, insurance, etc.)
Equals: new principal and interest

31 percent; the ratio after modification must be as close as possible to 31 percent but not less.

Two elements compose the ratio: the monthly mortgage payment and the gross monthly income of all borrowers. The ratio equals payment divided by income. Keep in mind that payment includes not only the principal and interest loan payment but also monthly property tax, homeowner insurance, and HOA fees or other assessments if applicable. It does not include a second mortgage or line of credit, or mortgage insurance.

Monthly gross income includes salary and wages before taxes and withholdings, self-employment profit, income from investments, entitlements like pensions or social security, net real estate rental income, and alimony and child support *if* the borrower chooses to disclose it. It does not include unemployment compensation. The resulting ratio, expressed as a percentage, represents the portion of income used to pay qualified housing expenses.

The target monthly mortgage payment ratio is 31 percent, meaning the payment equals 31 percent of gross income. Lenders must reduce monthly mortgage payments until reaching the target ratio by using the following sequence (waterfall) of reduction steps.

As a practical matter, the reduction affects only the monthly principal and interest payments because lenders don't influence property taxes, insurance, fees, and assessments. The reduced principal and interest payment, plus the other listed expenses, equal a new lower amount called the "target monthly mortgage payment."

Step 1. Capitalize the Loan Amount[4]

Adding together the total sum owed to the lender, including the current principal balance and other allowable amounts, is called capitalization, and the result is called the "estimated capitalized principal balance." Often referred to as the UPB, it's the starting point for applying the waterfall steps that actually reduce the payment.

Step 2. Reduce the Interest Rate

This is the first step to actually modify the payment—and an advantageous starting point. First, lower the monthly payment by lowering the interest rate, maybe significantly, but not below 2 percent.

When calculating interest, use the UPB found in Step 1. For amortizing, use the remaining term of the loan, ignoring any balloon payment. All monthly payments must include principal amortization. Some might involve a balloon payment. Interest-only payments and negative amortization are prohibited.

For example, a loan originated eight years (96 months) ago that is fully payable over 30 years (360 months) with a balloon payment due after 15 years has a "remaining term" of 264 months (360 minus 96 months), regardless of the scheduled balloon or interest-only payments.

Financial calculators, spreadsheet software, and online utilities can help to determine the four common variables: principal, interest, amortization, and payment. If borrowers know three variables, they can calculate the fourth.

Use a payment calculator or appendix Q, "Payment Constant," page 201, a chart of payments for different interest rates and amortization periods and how to use it for the loan amount with simple multiplication and division using an elementary calculator.

When finding the modified interest rate, remember that the *principal and interest* payment is less than the *monthly mortgage payment.* It is 31 percent of gross income, *minus* the monthly escrow amount of tax, insurance, and assessments.

Here's a way to keep track:

Monthly Gross Income		Target Monthly Payment
$________________	× 31% =	$ (A) ________________
Monthly Property Tax	____________	
+ Homeowner Insurance	____________	
+ Flood Insurance	____________	
+ HOA Fees	____________	
+ Escrow Shortage	____________	
Total	=	Monthly Expense Amount $ (B) ________________
(A) minus (B)	=	Target Principal & Interest $ ________________

Find the target payment interest rate. In Step 1, you found the principal balance, and in this section (Step 2), you identified your remaining term and your principal and interest payment. To keep track, record them here:

Capitalized Principal Balance	$ ________________
Remaining Term	________________
Target Principal & Interest	$ ________________
Solve for:	
Interest Rate	________________%

Step 2: Reduce the Interest Rate

Current Monthly Mortgage Payment
Less: P&I Payment
Equals: Fixed Portion (e.g., escrow)
Target Monthly Mortgage Payment
Gross Monthly Income × 31%
Less: Fixed Portion
Equals: Modified P&I Payment
Calculate: Modified P&I Interest Rate
For: Capitalized UPB
If less than 2%, then use 2%
And: Go to Step 3.

Use a payment calculator or appendix Q, "Payment Constant," example 2, page 202, to find the interest rate. This is the modified target payment interest rate. If the rate is less than 2 percent, then use 2 percent and continue to Step 3.

The modified rate is fixed for five years, then increases 1 percent per year until it reaches the market rate for 30-year fixed-rate mortgages at the time of the modification. For clarification, after five years, the interest rate steps up annually to the rate *now*, *not* the rate then. The rate is then fixed for the remaining term. It's like refinancing now, but with some breathing room to get back on track.

Step 3. Extend the Term and Re-amortize

Stretch payments over a longer period, up to 40 years (480 months), to further reduce the monthly payment. As the term lengthens, the repayment is spread over more but smaller payments.

Amortization is the process of paying off a loan over time. As an increment of principal is paid each month, together with the interest charged against the outstanding balance, the principal declines. Each month, as the principal balance decreases, the interest charge also decreases, and a larger portion of the payment goes to reducing the principal balance. The process, and the pay-down of the loan, accelerates over time.

Step 3: Extend the Term

IF monthly mortgage payment @ 2.000% is greater than "target monthly mortgage payment,"
THEN extend amortization.
IF more than 480 months,
THEN go to Step 4.

If Step 2 does not yield a 31 percent target payment ratio, then the payment will be further reduced by extending the term. Extend the term until reaching the target payment, but not longer than 480 months from the modification effective date.

Find the amortization term. In order to apply this Step 3, you must have found in Step 2 that your target interest rate is 2 percent. Here is a variation of the chart used:

Capitalized Principal Balance	$ ______________
Target Principal & Interest	$ ______________
Interest Rate	2.000%
Solve for:	
Amortization Term	______________

Use a payment calculator or appendix Q, "Payment Constant," example 3, page 202, to find the amortization term. If the term is less than 480 months, then it is the modified amortization term. Otherwise, use 480 months and continue to Step 4.

When servicing agreements or state regulations prohibit extending the loan due date, the amortization term for such loans might be lengthened to reduce monthly payments, but a principal balance will remain unpaid at maturity (the original due date). That remainder must be paid in a lump-sum balloon payment. HAMP does not permit interest-only or negative amortization loans.

Step 4. Principal Forbearance[5]

Getting to Step 4 means that the interest rate has been reduced to 2 percent and the amortization term has been increased to 480 months, but the resulting monthly mortgage payment still exceeds 31 percent of gross monthly income. The objective of Step 4 is to find a smaller loan amount that produces the target result.

Find the interest-bearing principal amount. To utilize this Step 4, you must have found in Step 2 that your target interest rate is 2 percent and in Step 3 that your amortization term is 40 years (480 months). Here is another variation of the charts used:

Capitalized Principal Balance	$ ______________	(A)
Target Principal & Interest	$ ______________	
Interest Rate	2.000%	
Amortization Term	480 months	
Solve for:		
Interest Bearing Principal	$ ______________	(B)
(A) minus (B) equals	______________	
Deferred Principal	$ ______________	

To find the interest-bearing principal amount using a payment calculator, enter 2 percent annual rate (divided by 12 months), 40-year (480 months) term, and the target monthly principal and interest payment. Then solve for the loan amount.

Or, use a 302.83 payment constant[6] for 2 percent and 480 months: Divide the target principal and interest payment by the payment constant to find a new "multiplier," and then multiply it by 100,000 to find the interest-bearing unpaid principal amount.

In either case, the *non*-interest-bearing "principal forbearance" amount is the difference between the interest bearing principal and the Step 1 capitalized principal.

Example using the payment constant:

Assume $1,000 target principal and interest payment ÷ 302.83 constant = 3.302 multiplier × 100,000 = $330,200 (B)

Capitalized UPB	$427,000 ______________	(A)
Target Principal & Interest	$ 1,000______________	
Interest Rate	2.000%	
Amortization Term	480 months	

Solve for:	
Interest-Bearing UPB	____________ $330,200 (B)
(A) minus (B) equals	____________
Deferred Principal	$ 97,800

From $427,000 principal balance, subtract $330,200 interest-bearing principal to find $97,800 *non*-interest-bearing deferred (forbearance) principal.

Setting the Interest Rate

For purposes of estimating the modified interest rate, a financial calculator or amortization table will arrive within 0.125 percent of the rate set according to the guidelines. Refer to Step 2. It's probably close enough.

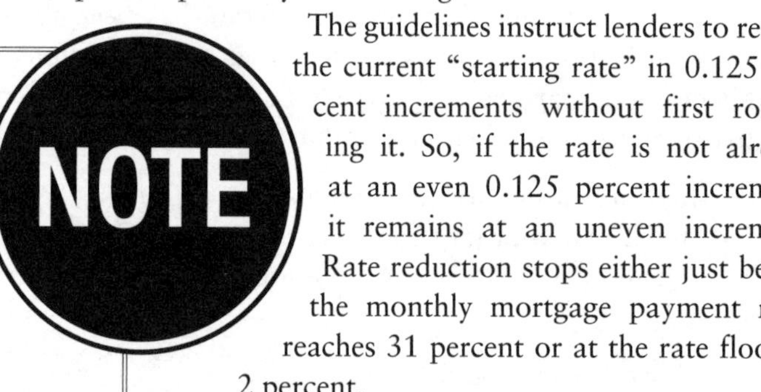

Adjustable Rate Mortgages (ARMs) use the current rate unless the rate is scheduled to adjust[7] within 120 days. The new rate, referred to as the "reset rate," is the Step 2 "starting rate" and the beginning point for setting the modified interest rate.

The guidelines instruct lenders to reduce the current "starting rate" in 0.125 percent increments without first rounding it. So, if the rate is not already at an even 0.125 percent increment, it remains at an uneven increment. Rate reduction stops either just before the monthly mortgage payment ratio reaches 31 percent or at the rate floor of 2 percent.

With a few exceptions noted below, the resulting interest rate is then

- fixed for the first five years,
- followed by 1 percent annual increases,
- until the rate reaches the "interest rate cap," and
- where the rate is fixed for the remaining loan term.

Simply stated, the interest rate cap is the 30-year fixed rate at the time of the modification, not later when the cap rate becomes effective. Referenced in Step 2, it means the Freddie Mac Weekly Primary Mortgage Market Survey (PMMS) Rate, which can be found at FreddieMac.com:

- for 30-year fixed-rate conforming loans
- as of the date when the modification agreement is prepared
- rounded—up *or* down—to the nearest 0.125 percent

For example:

Starting Rate	5.950%
Rate Reduction Increments (0.125% × 29)	−3.625%
Target Payment Rate	2.325%
Years 1–5	2.325%
Year 6	3.325%
Year 7	4.325%
Assume: PMMS 30-Year Fixed Rate	4.520%
Rounded Up *or* Down	4.500%

Year 8	4.500%
Fixed for Remaining Loan Term	4.500%

Exceptions to this procedure:

- If debt forgiveness, either voluntary or PRA, reaches the 31 percent target ratio without the necessity of fully reducing the interest rate, then the resulting interest rate is fixed for the remaining loan term and not subject to annual increases or the interest rate cap.
- If PRA reduces the capitalized principal balance by 5 percent or more, then Steps 2 and 3 become interchangeable. The lender may reduce the interest rate or increase the amortization term, or both, in any combination to arrive at the 31 percent mortgage payment ratio.
- Lenders may deviate from waterfall steps if the outcome results in a more favorable modification for the borrower. Examples include fixing the starting rate for the remaining loan term, perhaps at 2 percent without any subsequent increases, and increasing forbearance or forgiveness rather than increasing the amortization term.

Tier 2 Waterfall

Tier 2 applies to owners of rental properties, homeowners evaluated but not qualified for Tier 1, and others who have lost their Tier 1 eligibility. Servicers must evaluate them for Tier 2 according to the same Standard Modification Waterfall steps but without the same flexibility as Tier 1. *Only after applying all waterfall steps* does a lender calculate the target payment ratio and determine whether it falls within the acceptable DTI range of 25 to 42 percent of gross income.

1. **Capitalize:** Determine the remaining amount of the loan and other amounts owed to the lender, as for Tier 1.
2. **Adjust the interest rate:** Change the interest rate to a predetermined fixed rate.
3. **Extend the term and re-amortize:** Change the remaining loan term to 40 years.
4. **Principal forbearance:** Convert the portion of principal that exceeds 115 percent of the property value to non-interest-bearing principal.

The Tier 2 waterfall focuses on a flexible target payment range from 25 to 42 percent of income but applies predetermined values in the waterfall steps. The modified payment must achieve at least a 10 percent reduction in the pre-modification principal and interest payment.

Acceptable DTI Range

For Tier 2 homeowners and rental property owners, the pre-modification monthly mortgage payment ratio doesn't matter. The objective of the modification waterfall is to reduce the P&I payment *for the modified mortgage* by at least 10 percent.

The resulting post-modification monthly mortgage payment (the PITIA) ratio *for your home loan* must not be less than 25 percent or more than 42 percent. This range is acceptable DTI range.

To repeat, the 10 percent reduction relates to the *modified mortgage*, and the acceptable DTI range relates to the *home loan*. In Tier 2, those loans may or may not be the same.

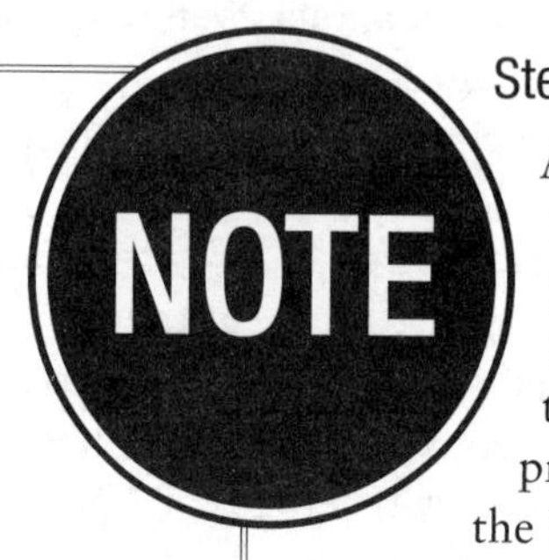

If a rental property secures the mortgage to be modified under Tier 2, then add net rental *income* from the property to *gross monthly income* or add net rental *loss* from the property to the *monthly mortgage payment.*

Step 1. Capitalize the Loan Amount[8]

Adding together the total sum owed to the lender, including the current principal balance and other allowable amounts, is capitalization, and the result is the estimated capitalized principal balance. Often referred to as the UPB, it's the starting point for applying the waterfall steps that actually reduce the payment.

Step 2: Adjust the Interest Rate

Start:	PMMS rate
Round:	up to nearest 0.125%
Add:	risk adjustment of 0.00%
Equals:	Tier 2 rate

Step 2. Adjust the Interest Rate

Homeowners not eligible for Tier 1 and rental property owners adjust their interest to a fixed rate determined when the NPV evaluation occurs. The interest rate, referred to as the Tier 2 rate, is fixed for the remainder of the loan term when the modification becomes final.

The Tier 2 rate equals the PMMS Rate rounded up to the nearest 0.125 percent plus a "risk factor." The PMMS Rate is the conforming 30-year fixed Freddie Mac Primary Mortgage Market Survey Rate[9] published during the week when the NPV evaluation occurs. It reflects the average interest rate for home mortgages nationwide for the week preceding the NPV test.

The Base NPV Model rounds the PMMS Rate up to the nearest 0.125 percent and then adds a risk factor. Tier 2 is more lenient than Tier 1 and, therefore, is perceived as riskier for lenders. Lending practice rewards lenders for the higher risk with a higher interest rate, expressed here as a "risk adjustment." Department of the Treasury determines and publishes the risk adjustment factor. Originally, it decided to add 0.5 percent to the PMMS Rate, but reduced it to 0 percent on April 22, 2014. The Base NPV Model applies the computed rate uniformly to all loans analyzed during the same week.

Find the Tier 2 rate. Go to FreddieMac.com. Find the PMMS Rate near the bottom left of the home page. Round the rate up to the nearest 0.125 percent, and then add the risk factor, currently 0.000 percent. The result would be the fixed rate if the actual NPV test had been run this week.

For example:

Assume: PMMS 30-Year Fixed Rate	4.520%
Rounded Up	4.625%
Add Risk Adjustment	0.000%
Fixed for Remaining Loan Term	4.625%

Different from Tier 1 in another way, after finding the predetermined rate, Tier 2 proceeds to Steps 3 and 4 without regard for the adjusted interest rate, which actually might have increased. In other words, the Tier 2 modified monthly mortgage payment ratio, and whether it falls within the acceptable DTI range, is not determined until all waterfall steps have been completed.

Step 3. Extend the Term and Re-amortize

Tier 2 simply extends the term to 480 months. Ultimately, the term will be measured from the effective date of the modification.

Step 4. Principal Forbearance[10]

Find your Tier 2 non-interest-bearing forbearance principal amount. If the loan-to-value (LTV) ratio is 115 percent or less, then there is no forbearance. If the LTV is greater than 115 percent, then the forbearance amount is the lesser of (1) the difference between the capitalized UPB and the property value multiplied by 115 percent or (2) the capitalized UPB multiplied by 30 percent.

Capitalized UPB	$ ____________	(A)
Estimated Property Value	$ ____________	(B)
LTV: (A) divided by (B)	____________	%
If LTV greater than 115%, *then*		
(1) Multiply (B) by 115%	$ ____________	(C)
(1) Subtract (C) from (A)	$ ____________	(D)
(1) Multiply (A) by 30%	$ ____________	(E)
Lesser of (D) and (E) equals		
Deferred (forbearance) Principal	$ ____________	
If LTV is 115% or less, *then*		
Deferred (forbearance) Principal	$ ____________	None

Calculate the Payment and Ratio

Step 1: Capitalized Loan Amount	____________	(A)
Step 4: Principal Forbearance	____________	(B)
Interest-Bearing Principal: (A) minus (B)	____________	(C)
Step 2: Interest Rate	____________	%
Step 3: Amortization		480 months

Use a payment calculator or Appendix Q, *Payment Constant*, page 202, to find the payment for (C) interest-bearing principal.

Calculated Monthly Principal & Interest	______________________	(D)
Current Minimum Monthly Loan Payment*	______________________	(E)
Divide (D) by (E)	______________________	%

If greater than 90 percent, then STOP. You do not qualify for Tier 2.
If less than or equal to 90 percent, then

Monthly Mortgage Payment (PITIA) *	______________________	(F)
Net Rental Loss if any **	______________________	(G)
Add (G) plus (F)	______________________	(H)
Monthly Gross Income all borrowers	______________________	(I)
Net Rental Income if any **	______________________	(J)
Add (I) plus (J)	______________________	(K)
Divide (H) by (K)	______________________	%

If 25 percent to 42 percent, then you are eligible for Tier 2.

* For your primary residence loan.

** For the subject property securing the loan to be modified under Tier 2, if rent is received.

Principal Reduction Alternative

Alternative Modification Waterfall

Servicers must evaluate every eligible loan using the *Standard Modification Waterfall*, which consists of four steps applied for Tier 1 and Tier 2 depending on eligibility.

LTV Greater Than 115%

(a) capitalized principal balance
(b) current property value
(c) LTV equals (a) divided by (b)

If the eligible loan principal balance exceeds 115 percent of the current property value, then servicers also must evaluate it using the Alternative Modification Waterfall, which adds a step after Step 1. In other words, if the LTV ratio of the current loan balance to the current property value is greater than 115 percent, then a second evaluation must start with this lower amount.[11]

The step reduces the capitalized principal balance to 115 percent of the current property value before applying the remaining Standard Modification Waterfall steps. The effect for such loans is to evaluate them twice: once for the full capitalized principal balance and once for the reduced principal balance. This is the Principal Reduction Alternative, which might be called waterfall step 1A.

Owners of properties significantly underwater should follow Steps 2 through 4, *first*, using the estimated capitalized principal balance determined in Step 1 and, *second*, using the lower PRA reduced principal amount equal to 1.15 times the current property value.

Lenders evaluate the alternative waterfall through the Base NPV Model. The purpose is to ensure that lenders consider whether principal reduction produces a positive NPV result. Ultimately, the interest rate, loan term, and forbearance values produced by this or any principal reduction must prove more beneficial to the lender than foreclosure.

For Tier 1, if PRA reduces the loan by 5 percent or more, then Steps 2 and 3 become interchangeable. The lender may reduce the interest rate or increase the amortization term, or both, in any combination to arrive at the 31 percent target mortgage payment ratio. If principal reduction alone, PRA or voluntary, produces the target ratio, then the current interest rate is fixed, the loan term remains unchanged, and subsequent waterfall steps are skipped.

Reduction of the loan principal amount is called debt forgiveness. PRA principal forgiveness is staged over three years, and permanently reduces the loan amount. However, principal reduction is optional for lenders even with NPV positive results. A lender may voluntarily forgive principal at any point in the Standard Modification Waterfall.

Nothing is more unfamiliar to a lender than voluntarily reducing the amount owed. It runs contrary to the most fundamental principal of good banking: preservation of capital. However, some seem more inclined to reduce loan balances since the $40 billion settlement with the U.S. and most states' attorneys general. Some lenders refer to the settlement as the Department of Justice program.

CAUTION

The IRS and many states tax debt forgiveness as ordinary income. The extraordinary benefit of principal reduction has a shadow. Consult your professional tax advisor. Find some details available in the "Debt Forgiveness Tax" section below.

Equity Share Arrangements

Mortgage investors that agree to reduce principal may recapture some or all of it by sharing future increases in property value. For clarity, the loan servicer arranges principal reductions, but the mortgage investor actually takes the hit. So, when loan amounts are reduced through the PRA, an investor may enter an equity sharing arrangement with the borrower. HAMP awards incentives if the arrangement includes the following borrower protections:

The value used by the servicer to find the PRA LTV ratio determines the beginning property value from which any increase is measured. The modification agreement defines an independent method of finding the new value when the borrower satisfies the modified loan—sells the property, refinances the loan, or fully pays it. The difference is value appreciation. Thus, the arrangement might be called a Shared Appreciation Modification (SAM). Each servicer must include its equity sharing arrangement in its PRA policy statement.[12]

On satisfaction by the borrower of the modified loan, the servicer obtains the new value, calculates the change minus cost of capital improvements, and shares the balance. The borrower may receive no less than 50 percent, and the investor may receive no more than the PRA amount less HAMP incentives.

The arrangement credits the property owner with capital improvements made to enhance or preserve value after the modification. Guidelines are unclear whether adjustments are made for the cost of sale or refinance, or for any difference between the purchase price paid by the buyer and the value obtained by the servicer. Agreements that I've reviewed use the gross sale price before deducting costs of sale, like commission, title insurance, or concessions. The arrangement only applies if the property increases in value. If the net difference is zero or less, as in a short sale, there is no equity to share, so the arrangement would not take effect.

An example that I recently reviewed forgave 60 percent of the capitalized principal balance over three years, an amount exceeding $250,000. The investor only required 25 percent of the appreciation, despite authority to receive up to 50 percent. If sold, the property value would be the gross sales price before costs of sale.

Debt Forgiveness

Lenders may voluntarily forgive loan principal at any point in the standard modification waterfall. Lenders also may reduce the principal amount using the PRA and receive HAMP monetary incentives. Here are a few details about HAMP PRA.

PRA policy. Because servicers operate within many different investor limitations, servicing agreements, and state laws, outcomes can be different for similar loans. To ensure fair treatment for all loans, HAMP insists that lenders clarify such limitations and treatment in a written policy. It does not insist, however, that lenders share their policies with borrowers or their advisors. If you question a PRA outcome, ask for clarification within the context of the lender's PRA policy.

PRA forgiveness. Any PRA amount begins as the non-interest-bearing forbearance amount or a portion of it.[13] Actual principal reduction occurs in three equal installments on the first, second, and third anniversaries of the trial period effective date. That date usually is three months earlier than the permanent modification effective date. Therefore, typically, the first installment happens nine months after the modification effective date, and then over the next two years.

That said, if the borrower sells the property or refinances the loan more than 30 days after the modification effective date, the entire PRA amount is forgiven. When the property appreciates in value by more than 15 percent and sells anytime after 30 days, the borrower might actually realize a profit.

PRA variance. As mentioned above for Tier 1, if PRA reduces the capitalized principal balance by 5 percent or more, then Steps 2 and 3 become interchangeable. The lender may reduce the interest rate, increase the amortization term, or both in any combination to arrive at the 31 percent mortgage payment ratio.

Debt forgiveness tax. The IRS taxes debt forgiveness, as do many states. The lender declares a loss and reports it as income to the borrower during the year the debt was forgiven. Two federal exemptions are available. One is for insolvency. The other is for a loan secured by the borrower's principal residence and used to purchase or improve the home or to refinance the purchase loan. The homeowner exemption does not apply to any portion of a loan used to cash out the owner's equity. The exemption originally expired on December 31, 2012. It was extended through 2013; further extension is pending congressional approval. Consult your professional tax advisor. Refer to chapter 15, "Circumstances and Consequences," page 121.

Property Value

Servicers use three methods to establish the current market value of the property, which must occur less than 90 days before the NPV evaluation. The value and the capitalized or PRA principal balance comprise the elements of the LTV ratio. Guidelines refer to this as the "mark-to-market" LTV, which means the value was brought current with market conditions when conducting the NPV evaluation.

The three methods are an AVM, a BPO, or a conventional appraisal. An AVM uses recently gathered data collected from appraisers and other sources, adjusted to specific property characteristics, and then tests the result for reliability. Failure of an AVM to meet reliability standards leads to validation by a BPO prepared by a real estate professional from personal observation and market analysis. An appraisal is required only when other results are questionable or when value is in dispute.

Summary

A sequence of four steps determines the modified payment and whether it meets HAMP guidelines. Steps differ somewhat between Tier 1 and Tier 2, especially in determining the interest rate and loan term. With a mortgage calculator or spreadsheet, and with realistic and accurate income numbers, a close estimate of the modified payment is possible.

Called the Standard Modification Waterfall, the sequence includes determining the loan amount including delinquent interest, the new interest rate, an extended term if necessary, and forbearance of interest payments on a portion of the loan. Another step, actual reduction of the loan amount, must be considered, but is not required.

The Other Burden: Monthly Debt Expenses

Learning Points:

- Definition of "debt-to-income ratio."
- What lenders include in "income" and "expense" categories.
- Implication of excessive debt ratio.

Many homeowners experiencing a hardship and seeking mortgage relief feel pressure from other obligations too. Most have extended other credit in an effort to make mortgage payments and meet daily living expenses. It can be a very lonely place, despite the reality that many millions of others are in the same predicament and are feeling equally isolated and helpless.

A majority of people I talk with have a second mortgage. It makes sense. To maximize purchase financing, and avoid private mortgage insurance (PMI), many buyers at the peak of the market used an 80 percent loan-to-value (LTV) first mortgage and added a second mortgage. Combined, their mortgage debt stretched to 90 percent, 100 percent, even 105 percent of the property's purchase price.

Others with equity in their homes, either from a down payment or from value appreciation, added a home equity line of credit (HELOC). Thought to be a smart strategy, it covered home improvements, a child's college education, emergencies, even a new car or vacation. Recently, however, many homeowners have used their equity to meet rising expenses or dwindling income.

Monthly Debt Ratio

We have already looked at the relationship between the monthly mortgage payment (housing expense) and income from all sources (gross income), called the monthly mortgage payment ratio. In this section, the guidelines ask for a more comprehensive calculation: income from all sources is compared with gross expenses. It is called the "gross expense-to-income ratio."

For simplicity, I refer to it as the monthly debt ratio. It calculates the relationship between all credit expenses and all income, both before and after modification. Some lenders include an allowance for typical living costs; others ask for specific detailed expenditures. It is commonly referred to as the "debt-to-income" or "back-end" ratio. It measures relative debt burden, overall ability to meet obligations, viability of the loan modification beyond its impact on monthly mortgage payments, and responsible use of borrowed money.

Total Monthly Debt Ratio

(a) monthly gross expenses
(b) monthly gross income
(c) ratio (a) divided by (b)

Lenders use specific accounts, balances, and payments that appear in credit reports, Requests for Mortgage Assistance (RMAs), tax returns, and other modification materials submitted. Gross debt payments include the following:

- Monthly mortgage payment and interest for the principal residence, including property tax, insurance, and assessments such as homeowner association fees (PITIA).
- Monthly payment for other loans secured by the principal residence, either home equity closed-end (lump-sum) or HELOC.
- Mortgage insurance premium.
- Negative net rental income from investment properties owned, if supplied by the borrower (must disclose if property secures the loan to be modified).
- Vehicle lease payments.
- Payment on all other installment loans, repaid in regular periodic payments, with more than ten months of payments remaining (even if in forbearance or deferred status).
- Monthly payment on revolving, credit card, and other open-end accounts.
- Alimony, child support, and separate maintenance payment with more than ten months of payments remaining (disclosure is not required).
- Monthly mortgage payment for a second or seasonal home, including property tax, insurance, homeowner association (HOA) and other assessments (or PITIA).

If payments don't appear on a credit report, lenders will use 3 percent of revolving-account balances, 1.5 percent of installment account balances, and 1 percent of HELOC balances.

Now divide the total of these monthly gross expenses (debt) by monthly gross income to arrive at the gross expense-to-income ratio (debt ratio). Monthly gross income was also a component in the monthly mortgage payment ratio. To repeat, it means all employment and entitlement income and self-employment profit—before taxes, benefits, retirement, and other withholdings. For details regarding the components of gross income, refer to appendix G, "Financial Statement," page 161.

TIP

As a general rule, disclose alimony and child support expense only if it contributes to your financial hardship.

Excessive Debt Ratio

If the monthly debt ratio exceeds 55 percent after the loan modification, a borrower must be willing to work with a HUD-approved housing counselor on a plan to reduce total indebtedness below 55 percent. The guidelines do not suggest a maximum debt ratio, but, as a practical matter, there comes a point when the debt burden simply overwhelms income.

NOTE

For approved housing counseling agencies:

Go to: http://www.hud.gov/offices/hsg/sfh/hcc/fc/
Or call: 1-800-569-4287
There is no charge for this counseling.

Therefore, not every eligible borrower and mortgage will qualify for modification. The guidelines place no limit on the reduction of the principal and interest payment, except the monthly mortgage payment ratio targets. However, the net present value (NPV) test and a lender's good judgment also evaluate the likelihood of re-default (delinquency after modification). A debt ratio at some level above 55 percent—what level is unclear—will disqualify the modification.

Furthermore, the debt ratio does not include other household, medical, insurance, and living expenses or employment withholdings. At some point, sooner than later, borrowers need to list all of their expenses. It's all right if expenses exceed income before the modification, but not afterward. The objective is an affordable *and* sustainable mortgage payment. If expenses exceed income *after* modification, though improved, the situation is not sustainable.

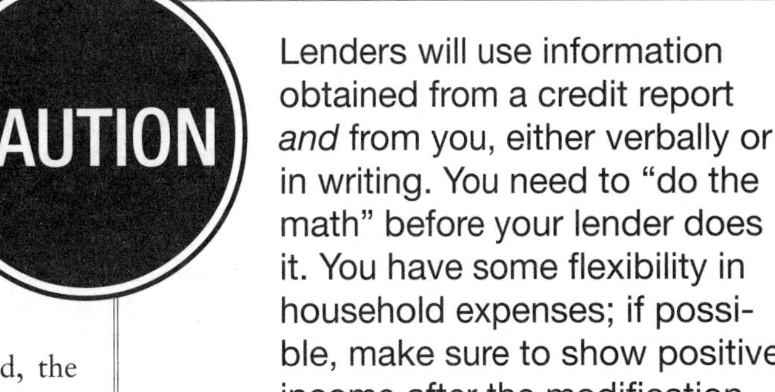

Lenders will use information obtained from a credit report *and* from you, either verbally or in writing. You need to "do the math" before your lender does it. You have some flexibility in household expenses; if possible, make sure to show positive income after the modification.

If any monthly obligations do not appear on a credit report (e.g., personal or family loans), borrowers may need to furnish evidence in the form of a promissory note or other written agreement with detailed terms, conditions, dates, amounts, and signatures.

If you have not already, now is a good time to obtain your one free credit report per year. Go to https://www.annualcreditreport.com/cra/index.jsp.

List all monthly debt payments. Use appendix G, "Financial Statement," page 161, and appendix E, "Income and Expense," page 155, to prepare. But do consider the effect on the debt ratio of disclosing such obligations.

Summary

Many homeowners who encounter problems paying their mortgages also face the burden of other debt. Borrower and lender share the goal of affordability and sustainability after modification, taking into consideration all the borrower's obligations. Though not the primary qualification, lenders consider the borrower's ability to pay all credit payments including the modified mortgage. It indicates overall affordability and whether a modification will succeed.

Pre-modification: Trial Period

Learning Points:

- Definition of "Trial Period Plan" (TPP) and its purpose and requirements.
- How the lender initiates the TPP.
- Factors occurring during the TPP that can influence permanent modification.

A trial period precedes the actual loan modification. Typically lasting three months, the trial period serves two primary purposes: to confirm feasibility of the modification and to formally modify the existing loan. The guidelines require this two-step process, which involves a plan for the trial period and an agreement for the final modification.

First, to confirm feasibility, the TPP requires three monthly payments. The payment amount was calculated in the modification waterfall sequence for reducing payments. In addition to the principal and interest payment, it will include escrow items prorated to monthly amounts. Sometimes referred to as an impound account, escrow items are property tax and insurance premiums. Related items, though not required to be impounded, include homeowner association (HOA) and other fees that can become a lien against the property if not paid.

The second purpose of the trial period is to formalize the modification. The lender has time to verify and update information provided by the borrower, to review any changes in hardship circumstances, and to incorporate any new information into the payment calculations. The lender then prepares the final written Modification Agreement, which is covered in chapter 10.

Trial Period Plan Notice

After approving a TPP, the lender will instruct the borrower on how to make the first trial period payment in the TPP notice, which also specifies the effective date when the first payment is due. The trial period begins on the first day of the month after the notice date, unless the date is after the 15th; then the effective date is the first day of the following month.

For example, if the TPP notice is dated January 15 (or earlier in the month), then the trial period will begin, and the first payment will be due, on February 1. If the TPP notice is dated January 16 (or later in the month), then the trial period will begin, and the first payment will be due, on March 1.

The plan is an offer from the lender to the borrower, but the borrower does not sign and return it. The borrower accepts the TPP by making the first trial period payment. If the borrower does not make the first payment by the end of the month when due—the TPP deadline—the offer expires. So long as a payment reaches the lender by the last day of the month when due, the TPP stays current. Otherwise, it terminates, and the permanent modification will not take effect.

> **TIP**
> It's absolutely essential for the borrower to make the trial period payments on time. Failure to do so will result in cancellation of the loan modification.

Payments during the trial period satisfy the trial modification requirements and suspend any pending foreclosure sale. They do not satisfy the promissory note. There are two consequences: (1) if the modification fails to become permanent, the difference between the trial payment and the regular monthly payment will be due; and (2) because the full contract payment is not being made, the trial payment might be reported by the lender to credit bureaus as delinquent.

If borrowers have submitted the documentation suggested in this book, they may be asked for updates. If they have not already, borrowers will be asked to submit a complete signed Request for Mortgage Assistance (RMA) form, income verification (pay stubs, tax return, etc.), and deposit and investment account statements.

If you think that your TPP is inconsistent with the rules, miscalculated, or otherwise in error, proceed with caution. Examine the offer carefully for compliance with the guidelines. Compare it with the calculations and what you want. Discuss any discrepancy with the lender. Emphasize compliance with the guidelines. Use the escalation process if necessary.[1]

Making the first trial period payment triggers the "one modification rule" for that HAMP tier. If borrowers change their minds about its terms or the final modification, or fail to complete the TPP, it's considered to be the one modification allowed under the applicable HAMP tier.

If borrowers receive a Trial Period Plan, the lender has determined that, for the lender, modification is more beneficial than foreclosure, which likely means that modification is more beneficial than a short sale or deed in lieu of foreclosure. Borrowers need to make the same determination regarding the benefits for them. Know your maximum tolerance. What is the largest payment your budget can accommodate? How much negative equity are you willing to carry into the future? How strong is the attachment you (and your family) have to this particular property?

Lender Initiative

The Trial Period Plan might be in response to the inquiry or proposal, or it might arrive unsolicited. From information on file, lenders can profile borrowers and mortgages that are likely to be eligible for modification. They know which loans entail recent or impending rate changes, negative amortization, or delinquency, whether originally secured by owner-occupied or rental properties, and if within loan eligibility limits.

The guidelines suggest that a lender might actually prepare and send a Trial Period Plan to a borrower before receiving current hardship, income, and occupancy information; they give no explanation how trial period payments might be ascertained before receiving such information. Afterward, the lender would receive the needed details from the borrower, verify them, and then determine the terms of a final modification.

Despite the inconsistency, some lenders are beginning to initiate the HAMP modification process. Many obtain information from borrowers—by telephone or online forms—before making substantive efforts to modify payments. An overture to a borrower typically occurs after one or two missed payments, often by mail, and mixed confusingly with collection activity. I have not yet heard of *any* lender initiative before delinquency.

The problem for lenders: without hardship details and current income, eligibility cannot be determined conclusively. The NPV test cannot accurately predict the advantage of modification over foreclosure, and the payment calculation sequence can only guess the reduction needed to approach the target ratio.

The problem for borrowers: without some initiative of their own, distressed borrowers are likely to be overlooked, overwhelmed, and unprepared.

Other Provisions

Temporary Suspension of Foreclosure

The lender must suspend foreclosure during the trial period. Suspension of foreclosure proceedings continues while payments remain current. Final modification brings the loan current and effectively ends the threat of foreclosure.

Request Suspension of Collection Activities

Though not included in the guidelines, make this request in writing with the RMA, verbally to the single point of contact, and again in writing after receiving the TPP notice. Some lenders respond to a request made by phone. Others might respond to a letter mailed to the address that appears on collection correspondence sent to the borrower.

A few lenders seem unwilling or unable to interrupt their automated collection program once it has been turned loose on the borrower. Borrowers' tendency might be to ignore phone calls and mailings. Be conscious of anything unusual. A notice of default, pending litigation, or scheduled foreclosure should be sent to the borrower by certified mail, but stay alert regardless. Such documents might inform borrowers whether and when to expect a foreclosure sale.

Due-on-Sale Provision

Mortgages that can be assumed by a buyer must be modified to be due when the borrower sells the property.

Escrow Account

An escrow account, sometimes called an "impound account," receives borrower's monthly payments and then provides for periodic property tax and insurance payments when due. If one does not currently exist, a monthly escrow amount will be determined and an escrow account established. Payments then will include the escrow amount. If the TPP ends without final modification, the escrow account remains.

Mortgage Insurer Approval

If a mortgage is subject to mortgage insurance, the mortgage insurer must approve the modification. Many home loans start with mortgage insurance, in which borrowers pay a monthly premium to the insurer, usually with their payment to the lender. Some insurers delegate authority to approve modifications to the loan servicer. However, most loans don't start with mortgage insurance, but many end up in pools of loans that are insured. The pool insurers and reinsurers have been under severe financial stress and regulatory scrutiny. This multilayered loss mitigation labyrinth may complicate the approval process in opaque and time-consuming ways.

Failure to Complete the Trial Period

The trial period may end early due to intervening ineligibility or for such noncompliance as failure to make timely payments, to furnish requested documentation, or to return the final Modification Agreement. Also, for example, if the property were no longer the borrower's primary residence (Tier 1 eligibility), or the borrower's total debt or income changed beyond the lender's limits (underwriting), the lender would not offer final modification. When this happens, the guidelines instruct a lender to consider other foreclosure prevention alternatives.

The term "foreclosure alternatives" usually refers to modifications, short sales, and deeds in lieu of foreclosure. Depending on the reason for ineligibility, however, a borrower might qualify for HAMP Tier 2 modification or for the lender's proprietary modification program.

Summary

The trial period confirms that a borrower is ready, willing, and able to make the lower modified mortgage payments. It also gives the lender time to calculate final Modification Agreement terms using verified income and amounts capitalized in the principal balance. It begins on the first day of the month after the lender mails the TPP notice. It lasts three months, ending on the modification effective date.

The TPP notice states payment amounts and due dates during the trial period. The payments approximate the final modified payment, including principal, interest, and a monthly escrow amount. The borrower accepts the plan by mailing the first TPP payment. The lender may consider an offer to have expired after the TPP deadline if the first payment is not received before the end of the month when due.

Modification

Learning Points:

- When modification becomes permanent.
- Difference between Trial Plan Period (TPP) and final payments.
- Credit reporting after modification.
- Additional incentives for on-time payments.

The final Modification Agreement amends the original mortgage. It permanently changes certain terms and conditions of the original promissory note, while leaving other provisions of the loan unchanged. The underlying security does not change, so the real estate (home or rental property) that served as collateral for the loan before modification continues to secure the modified loan.

During the trial period, the lender updates supporting documentation from the borrower and recalculates the principal balance, accounting for trial period payments, the new interest rate, amortization term, and the resulting monthly mortgage payments. These terms are written into the Modification Agreement, which a lender typically sends to a borrower after receiving the second of three trial period payments.

The borrower must comply with the terms of the TPP. Generally, a borrower must produce requested documentation, notify the lender of material changes in circumstance, and make timely payments during the month when due.

Taking Effect

The Modification Agreement becomes effective on the first day of the month following completion of the TPP. When effective, the modification is final and permanent. Once modified under HAMP, a mortgage may not be modified again within the same HAMP tier. If the final TPP payment is late, the modification effective date may be delayed for a month; if it remains due on the modification effective date, the modification will not take effect and may be canceled by the lender.

The Modification Agreement must be signed by all borrowers who signed the original loan documents, unless a borrower is deceased or the borrowers are divorced. If a divorce settlement transferred the property to one spouse, then the other spouse with no ownership interest in the property is not required to sign. Lenders may evaluate such other circumstances as mental incapacity or incarceration on individual merits but are expected to accommodate a borrower absent due to military deployment.

A new borrower may be added. The guidelines do not elaborate, especially whether the new borrower's qualifications are to be considered for eligibility and underwriting. Because the new borrower would be equally responsible as another borrower for the entire loan, one should exercise caution before taking on an already distressed situation.

A fair assumption is that the new borrower's qualifications would be included, in which case the new borrower must submit comprehensive documentation. An added borrower's income, expenses, assets, and liabilities would influence underwriting. HAMP underwriting means evaluating the risk of imminent default, net present value, the modification waterfall sequences to reduce payments, and the total debt-to-income ratio.

Payments

The lender calculates a final modified monthly payment amount that accounts for any changes in the borrower's financial circumstances and payments made during the TPP. The calculated monthly mortgage payment includes principal and interest, property tax and insurance, and homeowner association fees, if any.

In addition to principal and interest—what we usually call the mortgage or loan payment—the "monthly mortgage payment" includes a monthly escrow or impound amount equivalent to one-twelfth the annual property tax and insurance premium. It doesn't include homeowner association fees, which the borrower pays directly. The lender must manage the escrow account and make tax and insurance payments when due.

The monthly payment is fixed for the first five years. The interest rate then may increase by 1 percent annually until it reaches the interest-rate cap, as determined in the modification waterfall sequence. As the interest rate increases, the payment increases proportionately.

The monthly payment also may increase or decrease if the escrow amount changes. For example, an increase in assessed property value may result in an increase in property tax. Any such change will pass through to the monthly mortgage payment. Stay informed about the escrow items, and contact the lender when a change occurs.

For example, assume a property tax rate of 1 percent: If the property's assessed value increases by 20 percent from $300,000 to $360,000, the tax will increase by $600 from $3,000 to $3,600 per year. The escrow impounds, and thus the monthly mortgage payment, will adjust up by $50. A decline in assessment value will result in a downward adjustment in the escrow impounds.

Also, check whether the lender requires hazard insurance coverage for the loan amount or for the current value of improvements (value excluding land). Whichever is less results in a lower premium payment.

Payoff

The remaining principal balance comes due when the loan is refinanced, ownership of the property transfers, or the original unmodified loan term expires. A buyer may not assume the modified loan, which is due on sale, regardless of provisions in the original loan to the contrary.[1]

The principal balance equals the capitalized principal reduced by the principal portion of monthly mortgage payments made after modification. The capitalized principal balance includes unpaid principal and escrow amounts at the time of modification, together with late interest, but not late fees and penalties. Interest-only payments and negative amortization are not allowed under HAMP.

If the amortization period was extended beyond the original loan term to reduce monthly payments, for example from 30 to 40 years, then a balance will remain when the original 30-year term expires. For those few who may face this issue so far in the future, the remaining balance will be due in a lump-sum balloon payment.

The remaining term is likely to be long. As a practical matter, value appreciation and principal payments will be sufficient to make refinancing the balloon payment feasible with a new mortgage. If the original loan involved a short-range balloon payment (e.g., a 30-year amortization due in 10 years), notice whether the modification eliminates or extends it.

Property values declined significantly after the subprime bubble burst. The resulting "negative equity" means the loan amount is greater than the property value. Virtually everyone who attempts to modify a loan shares this predicament. It affects long-term owners less than owners wanting or needing to transfer by sale, gift, or bequest.

The lingering dilemma: When will property values rise enough to reach the mortgage amount? If the time to sell arrives first, the modified loan is a short sale waiting to happen.[2] Even so, in the meantime, modification offers affordable housing and peace of mind.[3]

Credit Reporting

Credit reporting for HAMP first changes during the TPP and then changes again after the modification effective date. Previous payment history remains unchanged. Delinquencies leading up to the TPP stay on the credit report, but the cumulative effect of late payments should stop. When the TPP begins, lenders report the borrower as paying under a partial or modified payment agreement and payments as current if received by the end of the month when due.

My experience, however, suggests caution. TPP payments are uniformly less than the pre-modified regular monthly (contract) payment. Lenders don't credit TPP payments until they total the full contract payment amount, usually reached with the second payment. Some lenders, despite HAMP instructions to the contrary, report the first TPP month as delinquent.

Especially if you are current going into the TPP, make the second payment before the end of the first month. Then, a portion of the second payment added to the first payment equals the total contract payment, which is credited and current during the month due. Then, repeat by making the third payment before the end of the second month. The loan becomes current on the modification effective date. Afterward, payments equal the new modified contract amount, and are reported as full payments when received.

After modification, the credit report continues to show an open account with the same loan, the same account number, and the same original date the account was opened. Other elements might change, however; for example, the original loan amount will equal the capitalized principal balance, less principal reductions (if any) when they occur; the modified payment and loan term duration; and the payment status category.

Credit reporting to all major credit repositories continues at the end of every month throughout the modification process in accordance with the Fair Credit Reporting Act and credit bureau requirements of the Consumer Data Industry Association.

The Consumer Data Industry Association has created a reporting category—*loan modified under a federal government plan*—specifically for HAMP. On the modification effective date, the lender moves the loan into this category, reports it current, and then going forward reports account activity as for any other credit account. Past delinquencies remain but stop accumulating. Payments received before the end of the month when due are reported as current, and a borrower's credit begins to heal.

"Default" defined by HAMP

Three monthly payments are due and unpaid on the last day of the third month.

Default after Modification

A loan is in default, according to guidelines, when a payment reaches 90 days late—when payments remain unpaid for three consecutive months. If a borrower defaults, the loan loses "good standing" for HAMP purposes. Once lost, good standing cannot be restored, even if the borrower subsequently cures the default and brings the loan current.

When a loan loses good standing, borrower, servicer, and investor incentives immediately cease, as does any unapplied future Principal Reduction Alternative. A lender may begin foreclosure proceedings after, but not until, a HAMP modified loan loses good standing.

As before a modification, lenders must work with borrowers to cure the default. If that is not feasible, then, before starting foreclosure proceedings, the lender must determine whether the borrower qualifies for any other loss mitigation, including HAMP Tier 2 for those defaulting under HAMP Tier 1.

HAMP endeavors to give ready, willing, and able borrowers an opportunity to avoid, but is not a guarantee against, default and foreclosure.

Financial Incentives

Borrowers and servicers are eligible for incentive compensation under HAMP Tier 1. Investors are eligible for incentive compensation under HAMP Tier 1 and Tier 2. Incentives are subject to servicer participation, certain participation caps, and reporting requirements, as well as a final executed Modification Agreement.

Borrower Incentives

Pay for Performance. Borrowers can earn an annual credit against the principal balance of the loan if the monthly mortgage payment was reduced by 6 percent or more. The credit equals one-half of the annual payment reduction up to $1,000 during each of the first five years after modification.[4] However, reduce the amount proportionately for every month the payment is more than 30 days late. If the loan fails to remain in good standing (see above), the incentive ends, and any amount accrued during that year is lost.

For example, assume the monthly mortgage payment is modified to $2,700 from $3,000. The reduction of 10 percent exceeds the 6 percent minimum, so the modification qualifies for the incentive. The reduction is $300 per month. The annual reduction is $3,600, one-half of which is $1,800. If all 12 of 12 payments were on time, then no proportionate reduction occurs ($1,800 times 12 divided by 12 equals $1,800). If only 9 of 12 payments were on time, then a proportionate reduction occurs ($1,800 times 9 divided 12 equals $1,350). However, since both exceed the maximum credit, loan principal balance will be credited (reduced by) $1,000 at the end of this year. The process repeats for five years or until the loan loses good standing.

Servicer Incentives

Pay for Success. If the borrower earns a credit, the lender earns an incentive payment equal to the credit, but for only the first three years after modification and not subject to proportionate reductions for late payments. Like the borrower, the lender loses the incentive payment if the loan fails to remain in good standing. The preceding example applies to the lender, as well as to the borrower, except the amount is a payment, not a credit; is not affected by late payments unless the loan loses good standing; and continues for only three years, not five.

Servicers also receive incentive payments for completed modifications. Amounts depend on the delinquency status of the modified loan, ranging from $400 for loans more than 240 days since last payment to $1,200 for loans less than 240 days since last payment and $1,600 for loans less than 150 days since last payment.

Investor Incentives

The importance to borrowers of servicer and investor incentives is the relationship between reward, priorities, and motivation. Investors receive the following incentives: *Payment Reduction Cost Share* (Tier 1 and Tier 2) to reimburse some of the monthly mortgage payment reduction, *Current Borrower* (Tier 1) for borrowers at risk of imminent default, *Home Price Decline* (Tier not specified) to protect against possible future deterioration of property values, and *Principal Reduction Alternative* (Tier 1 and Tier 2) partial reimbursement proportional to the loan-to-value (LTV) ratio.

Incentive Limitations

For borrowers, servicers, and investors to receive federal incentives, the servicer must execute a servicer participation agreement, which also limits the amount available for incentive compensation. The amount of funds allocated to each lender reflects the total number of modifications that lender will perform—by federal estimate. And once a lender reaches its limit, HAMP pays no further incentives, effectively ending the mandatory program at that lender.

This detail could affect borrowers who procrastinate. The federal estimate of the total number of modifications may overlook potentially millions of eligible borrowers. This is the "monster under the bed." The estimated number of modifications to be performed by the lender may fall dreadfully short.

Borrowers who were not "profiled" by their lender may be missing from the estimated number and excluded from that lender's outreach. Do not risk losing valuable incentives that benefit you and motivate your lender. Do not wait for your lender to contact you.

Re-modification

After a loan receives a permanent HAMP modification, a servicer may not re-modify it until the loan loses good standing or until five years after the earlier modification effective date. Because HAMP began in 2009 and ends in 2015, the likelihood of Tier 1 re-modification of any loan seems remote.

Be aware, however, after failing a Tier 1 modification, that a loan might be eligible for a Tier 2 modification. Otherwise, discuss with the lender other loss mitigation possibilities.[5]

Summary

The final permanent modification takes effect after the TPP. Monthly payments should remain very close to the trial payments with small adjustments for principal paid and interest unpaid during the TPP. Modification brings the loan current. Though it cannot change past delinquent credit reporting, it gives a fresh start going forward. Move over, borrowers and lenders alike receive financial incentives for successful modifications.

Non-approval: Required Disclosures and Remedies

Learning Points:

- What to do if you're turned down.
- When and how to dispute a negative net present value (NPV) result.
- What to do about an incorrect property value.

What happens when a lender declines a modification request? A letter usually follows a phone call—but sometimes arrives unexpectedly—that explains with little detail the reasons for non-approval and much more detail about ways to leave the property short of foreclosure.

Inconsistencies in disclosing the reasons and how to appeal decisions have added to homeowners' frustrations and mistrust. Guidelines now require timely notification that specifically identifies reasons for denial. Lenders must disclose results of the mysterious NPV test input values to borrowers, who then may dispute the values through a standardized procedure.

Far and away, the most common reason for non-approval is "incomplete information" or failure to submit requested documentation on time. Most are "soft" declines, which can be corrected by responding quickly and thoroughly or submitting an updated application. Redundant and irritating? Yes, but do it anyway.

Other common reasons involve too much or too little income, ineligibility, and, sometimes, negative NPV outcomes. If you disagree, then prepare and state your claims in a dispute, commonly referred to as an appeal. Failing a satisfactory conclusion, you may escalate your dispute through a process described in the chapter 12, "Escalation: Challenging Noncompliance," page 97.

Non-approval Notices

When a lender fails to approve a trial period or final modification, it must provide the borrower with a non-approval notice. The notice lists the primary reasons for the denial.[1] In addition, every notice must clearly and specifically include the following:

- Toll-free servicer contact capable of giving details about the notice and reasons for non-approval.
- Access to U.S. Department of Housing and Urban Development–approved housing counselors and Making Home Affordable (MHA) at no charge.
- Whether or not the borrower is eligible for HAMP.
- Availability of foreclosure alternatives, such as other modification programs, short sale, and deed in lieu of foreclosure.
- How a borrower can be considered for such alternatives or, if preapproved, what a borrower must do to participate.
- For an NPV test, if run, the input fields and the values used.
- Servicer e-mail and mailing addresses where a borrower may lodge a dispute.

The borrower faces several options: They may dispute one or more of the reasons for non-approval directly or through a third-party counselor with supporting evidence. The borrower may participate, if qualified, in an internal non-HAMP modification or foreclosure alternative. The borrower may reapply for a HAMP or other modification, if changes in eligibility or qualifications occurred during the lender's months-long decision process. Some resign themselves to the small comfort of not making payments while foreclosure runs its course.

The lender may not conduct a foreclosure sale within 30 days after the notice, or during an active appeal, if the mortgage and property are HAMP eligible and the borrower has not rejected a Trial Period Plan or failed a permanent HAMP modification.

Appealing Non-approval

Reasons for non-approval fall into three general areas: eligibility, income qualifications (modification waterfall), and NPV outcome. Later sections address in detail how to appeal negative NPV outcomes. The non-approval notice must disclose eligibility issues. Though not required, lenders usually disclose some detail for non-approval because of too little or too much income. Most will discuss their calculations.

Eligibility opens the door to HAMP evaluation, and, without it, a borrower's initial package goes nowhere. You should know your eligibility before bothering to complete the Request for Mortgage Assistance and assembling even the minimal documentation to initiate the HAMP process.[2] Often, lenders lean on ineligibility to dismiss a file with inadequate or stale documentation; don't be discouraged by this tactic.

With the expanded Tier 2, some question may arise about which eligibility criteria apply. Start with Tier 1, when possible, because of its superior modification terms. Ineligibility for Tier 1 automatically triggers consideration for Tier 2. Though guidance in this book should reduce uncertainty, confusion most likely would arise around the Tier 1 monthly mortgage payment ratio threshold and previous attempts to complete a Trial Period Plan or permanent HAMP modification. The eligibility ratio (31 percent) does not apply to Tier 2.

After deeming borrowers eligible, HAMP subjects their qualifications to the modification waterfall and the Base NPV Model. A borrower earning too much income almost certainly would fail Tier 1 eligibility's minimum monthly mortgage payment ratio of 31 percent of gross income. A borrower earning too little income bumps into excessive forbearance in the fourth waterfall step and final chance to reduce the monthly payment to meet the required ratio.

Therefore, check the numbers yourself. Ensure that your pre-modification mortgage payment exceeds 31 percent of your gross income and that a realistic post-modification ratio equals 31 percent. If your lender used incorrect gross income, or income and expenses not stipulated by HAMP guidelines, then state your case and appeal.

How to Verify an NPV Outcome

To comply with the Dodd-Frank Act, the U.S. Department of Treasury released a self-service Web-based NPV calculator at CheckMyNPV.com.[3] It allows borrowers and their authorized advisors to independently predict potential NPV eligibility for HAMP. After receiving a non-approval notice, borrowers also can enter the NPV input values used by the servicer and itemized in the notice to verify the servicer's NPV evaluation.

Data input fields (categories) and values coincide with those used by servicers. Despite its intent for uniformity, the U.S. Treasury warns that because a borrower using CheckMyNPV.com may not use exactly the same data used by the servicer, the NPV calculator provides only an estimated outcome.

If you think your "data" is better than the servicer's, and your result is positive, then appeal based on the differences.

NOTE

If an NPV evaluation was performed, the lender must disclose the NPV input fields and values, even if the outcome was positive and not a reason for non-approval. MHA recommends evaluation of all other eligibility criteria before running the NPV test to avoid such disclosure. As a result, there are many declines for ineligibility and inadequate documentation.

Disputed NPV Input

Giving details about the NPV input allows a borrower to correct information that might have led to an erroneous result. If denied because of a negative NPV evaluation, a borrower may dispute the results only once by requesting an NPV reevaluation within 30 calendar days. The 30-day response period begins when the non-approval notice is dated, not when it's received. Borrowers must support claims of inaccuracies with written evidence of values as of the NPV date. When disputing more than one value, a borrower must address all disputed values at one time.

If the borrower submits valid evidence relevant to the NPV outcome, the servicer must perform the NPV calculation with the corrected input values. Following reevaluation, the servicer must provide the updated NPV outcome and input values to the borrower. Keep in mind that input values must be those current on the original NPV date when the first test was run.

Alternatively, before contacting the servicer, a borrower may ask MHA to evaluate whether the disputed NPV inputs would change the NPV outcome from negative to positive. Using the corrected input values offered by the borrower, MHA conducts a preliminary NPV reevaluation and provides the borrower with printed results. Then, the borrower includes the printed results with other evidence submitted to the servicer when requesting a formal reevaluation. The borrower's third-party advisor may request the preliminary reevaluation from the HAMP Solution Center (HSC).

TIP

You must act quickly to appeal a non-approval notice. You have only 30 days from the date on the notice—not from the date of receipt of the notice.

Prepare thoroughly and quickly. Borrowers and their trusted advisors may request only one NPV reevaluation from MHA or HSC. If the reevaluation performed by MHA, HSC, *or the servicer* returns a negative NPV result, the borrower is not eligible for additional appeals of other NPV inputs. Seeking assistance from MHA or HSC does not extend the response period; the borrower must still make the written request to the servicer within 30 calendar days from the date of the non-approval notice.

Property Value[4]

Suppose a borrower is not approved for a Trial Period Plan or permanent modification because of a negative NPV evaluation. The borrower suspects that the property value used by the servicer differs from the actual fair market value of the property on the NPV date when the model was initially run. The borrower may request an NPV reevaluation.

Within 30 calendar days from the date of the non-approval notice, the borrower must provide the servicer with a recent estimate of the property value supported by reasonable evidence. Keep in mind that any other disputed NPV value inputs must be addressed at the same time and, if they alone justify approval, will make reconsideration of property value unnecessary.

Supporting evidence includes anything available to the public—for example, recent sales published in a newspaper or an online service like zillow.com, trulia.com, or a local multiple listing service (no recommendations intended). The lender might have a value estimator on its website. Include a survey of similar properties sold nearby with actual selling prices adjusted for differences in location, size, condition, amenities, and so forth. Photos might help but are not required.

Give some thought to the impact of changing the value. In the totality of a borrower's qualifications, a higher value means more equity (less negative equity), suggests owner commitment, and supports a positive NPV outcome. It also means lower loss from foreclosure and supports a negative NPV outcome. Though difficult to predict, probably best would be a value high enough to encourage commitment but low enough to discourage foreclosure. Use CheckMyNPV.com.

Look at the modification waterfall results and the magnitude of changes needed to arrive at the 31 percent monthly mortgage payment ratio. View it in light of how deeply underwater the house has sunk. The further the borrower must stretch, the less feasible a modification becomes. Be objective; the Base NPV Model removes emotions from the equation.

Upon receipt of the written request, the servicer must perform a preliminary NPV reevaluation using the borrower's estimate of property value, together with any other disputed inputs. If the changed value results in a positive NPV result, the servicer may use it or allow the borrower to request an appraisal. The same applies if MHA or HSC conducts the reevaluation, as noted above.

An appraisal at the borrower's expense is required to complete the final NPV reevaluation. It establishes fair market value of the property on the original NPV date. Within 15 calendar days after the preliminary reevaluation, the borrower pays a $200 deposit toward the full cost of the appraisal.[5] The servicer should give instructions in its notification of the positive NPV result. The balance of the actual appraisal cost will be added to loan arrearages.

Upon receipt of the appraisal, the servicer must perform a final NPV reevaluation using the appraised value and any other disputed NPV input values. The servicer must provide the final NPV outcome and input values to the borrower, together with a copy of the appraisal, and then proceed in accordance with program guidelines.

To summarize, if you think the servicer used an inaccurate property value, you may dispute it by providing supporting evidence within standard time frames. If your estimate of value changes the NPV outcome, then a formal appraisal must be conducted at your expense—$200 now, the remainder of the cost later. If the appraisal confirms your estimate of value and results in a positive NPV, the servicer proceeds according to HAMP guidelines.

NOTE

If reevaluation of other disputed input values results in a positive NPV outcome without changing the property value, or if the servicer chooses to use the borrower's estimate of value, then an appraisal is unnecessary.

Reevaluation

Except those NPV input values disputed by the borrower and determined by the lender to materially affect the outcome, the input values remain the same as those used on the NPV date, when the original evaluation occurred. A reevaluation again uses the NPV model used for the earlier decision, even if new versions have been released in the meantime. In other words, the test must be identical to the original except for the successfully disputed input values.

Alternative to Appeal or Dispute

If circumstances have changed, whether during or after the servicer's decision process, borrowers may reapply. Even minor changes might make a difference. Submit a new version of the Request for Mortgage Assistance and current documentation. Take heart—many of my clients came to me after non-approval and ended up with an affordable modified loan. Persistence.

Summary

If your lender declines your application for a modification, called "non-approval," look for reasons in three areas: eligibility, qualification, and NPV results. You may dispute almost any non-approval within 30 days after notification, during which time any foreclosure activity remains suspended.

When declined for negative NPV results, guidelines mandate a specific procedure to appeal based on disputed input values. The next chapter explains what to do if your appeal fails.

Escalation: Challenging Noncompliance

Learning Points:

- What to do if your lender ignores your dispute.
- Resources that might help you to overcome non-approval.

Early and persistent failure by some servicers to implement the Making Home Affordable (MHA) program in good faith forced the U.S. Department of Treasury to renew efforts aimed at correcting errors, delays, and redundancies by lenders. The process escalates disputes arising primarily from interpretation of guidelines, eligibility decisions, property valuation, notification deadlines, and human error.

Initiated by the borrower or borrower's representative, escalation begins and ends within the servicer's loss mitigation hierarchy, subject to initiative and review by federal MHA personnel. Escalation endeavors to remedy mistakes, ironically, by using the same information that led to the dispute. The servicer alleged to have made the mistake is expected to correct it. Aggrieved borrowers may advocate for themselves or call upon third-party nonprofit or private counselors, according to a defined procedure.

Most important, the rules prohibit foreclosure sales during the escalation process. For modifications, CheckMyNPV.com attempts to remove some of the mystery surrounding the most common conflict, the complex net present value (NPV) test.

Resources

Those inquiring about mortgage relief will hear from their lender about a free 24-hour telephone help line operated by the nonprofit Homeownership Preservation Foundation. The HOPE Hotline[1] directs callers to U.S. Department of Housing and Urban Development (HUD)–approved housing counselors, who provide homeowners with free foreclosure prevention information. They are not employees of the foundation, HUD, or Making Home Affordable (MHA). They give borrowers a preliminary assessment of their eligibility for MHA programs and refer them to MHA for detailed program or non-approval questions. Collectively, these resources are called MHA Help, and borrowers access them directly.

Another resource is the HAMP Solution Center (HSC), which manages escalated cases exclusively from housing counselors, government offices, professional advisors, and other third parties acting on behalf of a borrower (more about third-party escalation later in this chapter).

Escalated Case

Borrower inquiries and disputes that rise to the level of an "escalated case" usually involve the following issues:

- Whether servicer assessed the borrower for the correct MHA program(s).
- Whether non-approval, or servicer's written explanation, were incorrect.
- Whether servicer started or continued foreclosure contrary to guidelines.

An escalated case might begin in the federal hierarchy. Then, the HSC or MHA Help refers the case to the servicer.

A borrower or authorized third party initiates the case, usually after failing to solicit a satisfactory response to the issues from established loss mitigation contacts. Whoever escalates the case is thereafter called the "requestor." It might refer to the borrower, a nonprofit housing counselor, a real estate professional, an attorney, an elected official or staff, MHA Help, HSC, or U.S. Treasury personnel.

Servicers must have written procedures and adequate personnel in place to provide timely and appropriate responses to escalated cases. Hypothetically, with oversight from MHA, servicers decide the outcome, thereby correcting their own mistakes. If the loan and other facts of an inquiry are "substantially similar" to a previously resolved case, however, the servicer may refuse to review it.

Resolution and steps to implement it are communicated within ten days to the borrower and requestor, if different. When HSC or MHA Help concurs with the resolution and the first implementation step occurs, the servicer closes the escalated case.

When enlisting the services of a third party to challenge non-approval, be wary of scams and phonies, particularly if they require up-front payment.

Third-Party Escalation

The world of mortgage relief divides borrowers' representatives into "for-profit" private advisors and "not-for-profit" MHA Help counselors, government representatives, and nonprofits sometimes sanctioned by HUD. When authorized by a borrower, any can serve as a requestor, though MHA Help requires for-profits to act pro bono.

Most servicers refer to them all together as third-party advocates or representatives, and almost everybody cautions against phonies and scams.[2]

To justify opening an escalated case, a claim must contend that the servicer did not assess the borrower for the correct MHA program(s) or failed to comply with program guidelines. Whether you are using an authorized third party or you are advocating for yourself, if you believe that a servicer incorrectly interpreted MHA guidelines, follow these steps:

Step 1: If working through normal contacts and channels at the servicer does not resolve the issue, elevate your concern by asking to speak with a senior manager. Some examples of valid reasons for Step 1 escalation arise when the servicer does any of the following:

- Refuses to stop a scheduled foreclosure sale while evaluating a borrower.
- Charges up-front fees.
- Instructs the borrower to miss a payment.
- Claims that the U.S. Treasury (MHA) is causing the delay.
- Advises a borrower to intentionally misrepresent information.
- Claims nonparticipation when Fannie Mae or Freddie Mac owns the loan.
- Incorrectly denies the borrower's request.

Step 2: If Step 1 does not resolve the issue, then contact the appropriate escalation team:

- If Fannie Mae owns the loan (www.knowyouroptions.com/loanlookup), then call 1-800-7FANNIE (732-6643) or e-mail resource_center@fanniemae.com.
- If Freddie Mac owns the loan (https://ww3.freddiemac.com/loanlookup/), then call 1-800-FREDDIE (373-3343) or e-mail borrower_outreach@freddiemac.com.
- If neither Freddie nor Fannie owns the loan, then contact the HSC at 1-866-939-4469 or e-mail escalations@hmpadmin.com.
- Property owners can call 888-995-HOPE (4673).

NOTE Also use these contacts when a servicer incorrectly claims that its mortgage investor does not participate in HAMP—for example, if Fannie Mae, Freddie Mac, or other government affiliate owns or guarantees the loan.

To assist a borrower, a counselor must provide written authorization from the borrower to the servicer granting permission to share the borrower's mortgage and personal financial information. Until the escalation team receives written authorization, no information can be disclosed. Standard forms are available at https://www.hmpadmin.com/portal/resources/docs/counselor/mha_third_party_authorization_form.doc, or ask the lender. To ensure acceptance, obtain signatures from all borrowers. Ask the lender for specific requirements.

The following information is usually sufficient if borrowers don't have a form. Also, have it handy when contacting the servicer:

- Borrower's(s') name(s).
- Borrower identification (last four digits of Social Security number).
- Property address.
- Servicer name.
- Servicer loan number.
- Third-party name.
- Third-party organization.
- Third-party e-mail.
- Third-party phone.
- Third-party relationship to borrower.
- Date of most recent (if applicable) notice of acceleration, notice of default, or scheduled foreclosure auction.

Be aware that signing the Request for Mortgage Assistance or the MHA Hardship Affidavit authorizes the servicer to disclose personally identifiable information about eligibility, qualifications, and terms of MHA agreements. Despite having no choice when applying for an MHA program—and even though use of the released information is primarily for statistical and beneficial purposes—the authorization granted is nevertheless very broad.

NOTE

At most servicers, the escalation staff is independent from the staff that conducted the initial review of the loan modification request. Consequently, borrowers may be asked to submit the same information or answer the same questions again.

Borrowers' information may be shared with related mortgage servicers, investors, and insurers of both senior and junior mortgages; the U.S. Treasury, Fannie Mae, Freddie Mac, and subcontractors in MHA-related roles; and HUD-approved mortgage counselors.

Be fully informed about the disputed issue. If it involves income and expense numbers or ratios, compare those submitted with any more current and confirm the calculations. If it involves property value, be ready to provide precise comparables, special characteristics, and written documentation. Prepare to overcome the servicer's assumption that it's right and the borrower is wrong. Review the relevant chapters in this book.

Servicer Compliance

Within five business days of receiving an escalated case, the servicer must give the requestor and borrower written acknowledgment of the inquiry with a case reference, a toll-free telephone number for contacting escalation staff, and the resolution date. The resolution date, by which the servicer decides and communicates the outcome to the requestor and borrower, must be within 30 calendar days of the inquiry. However, failure to comply means only that servicers must provide status then, and update every 15 days afterward until resolution—more like a courtesy than accountability.

Guidelines call for adequate trained staff to manage the escalation caseload. Escalation personnel at most major servicers function independently from those who first decided the borrower's eligibility and qualifications. They access relevant borrower documentation directly, which reduces redundancy. They tend to be knowledgeable about program guidelines, familiar with internal procedures, and empowered with authority to achieve resolution. Borrowers and their authorized representatives are given direct access by telephone and e-mail to escalation staff.

Though written as mandatory requirements, enforcement lacks authority and compliance depends on lenders' willingness and temperament.

Resolution

For each escalated case, escalation staff reviews the information and documentation used by loss mitigation personnel to arrive at the original disputed decision or action. To determine the accuracy of the dispute or inquiry, the analyst may review input values, obtain related property and personal information, recalculate the investor's present value return, and contact the investor directly. The borrower or third-party advocate needs to be sufficiently familiar with guidelines to validate the outcome.

An escalated case is considered to be resolved when the servicer does the following:

- Decides either to not change the original decision or to take "corrective action."
- Records the proposed resolution and resolution date in its system.
- Gives requestor and borrower written notification of the proposed resolution and next steps for implementation, within 10 business days after the resolution date.
- Takes the first action to implement the resolution.

If referred by HSC or MHA Help, then it must concur with the proposed resolution.

Corrective actions fall within one or more of the following categories:

- Borrower receives
  - HAMP or 2MP Trial Period Plan.
  - HAMP or 2MP permanent modification.
  - alternative proprietary non-HAMP modification.
  - payment or forbearance plan.
- Lender brings loan current.
- Lender extinguishes the loan balance.
- Short sale or deed in lieu of foreclosure.

- Lender initiates or continues foreclosure.
- Foreclosure is completed.
- Action discontinued during pending bankruptcy.
- Issues are not MHA related.
- No change in original determination.

Suspension of Foreclosure Sale

If a servicer receives an escalated case before midnight of the seventh business day prior to a scheduled foreclosure sale, it must suspend the sale until resolution of the case.

NOTE

Do not count the foreclosure date. Count back seven *business* days, not including weekends and bank holidays. Submit before midnight of that day—precisely according to the lender's escalation process and to the correct office, which might be different from where you previously submitted documentation. Check with the single point of contact relationship manager for details.

The dilemma: When non-approval occurs less than seven business days before the scheduled foreclosure sale, escalate the dispute directly to the HSC or MHA Help.

If not already in foreclosure, the loan may not be referred to foreclosure until the escalated case is resolved. If already begun, foreclosure proceedings may continue, but the sale may not occur. Actual cancellation of the sale usually happens only after completion of the corrective action—for example, final modification or short-sale closing.

The servicer must instruct the attorney or trustee, which actually conducts the foreclosure process, to postpone. This might occur well in advance but often happens within days or hours before the scheduled sale. Each postponement adds an expense, and some lenders refuse to incur the expense until the last minute. Excessive caseloads also delay postponements, adding stress to an already difficult situation.

At this end stage of foreclosure proceedings, communicate with both the lender and the attorney or trustee conducting the foreclosure. Ensure that instructions have been given by the servicer *and* received by the attorney or trustee. Otherwise, an unexpected and unwarranted sale might mistakenly take place.

To repeat, so long as an escalated case remains unresolved, the lender may not conduct a foreclosure sale, nor may a foreclosure conclude while a complete and current HAMP application or a short sale notice is active. Therefore, if "resolution" brings no change—or if you choose not to escalate non-approval—you may reapply for a modification whenever your circumstances change. Often, income, expenses, property value, or other elements change during the several months while the servicer processes, then ultimately declines, the modification request. For example, if insufficient income improves or excessive income declines, either might change the outcome and justify reapplying.

It's easy to become discouraged under such pressure and stress. However, persistence can pay off. Many of my clients, after non-approval, have escalated or reapplied while under the threat of foreclosure. By responding to every request on time and maintaining a current and complete application file, clients repeatedly postponed scheduled foreclosure sales, resulting finally in successful modifications.

Summary

Even if your lender did not approve your application, it must review its decision if you question its compliance with MHA procedures. If needed, look for help through qualified nonprofit housing counselors, real estate professionals, attorneys, elected officials or their staff, MHA Help, HSC, or U.S. Treasury personnel. By meeting time requirements, you can further postpone foreclosure until resolution.

Paper Trail: Documentation

Learning Points:

- Supporting documentation that you will need.
- How to use documentation to your advantage.
- What you should not volunteer unless asked.
- Information your lender needs to make a decision.

Submitting complete and timely information helps to avoid delays in an already long, tedious, and redundant process. Though the official "application" starts with the initial package, the lender keeps a data file full of information about borrowers and their loan and supplements it with whatever is added during telephone conversations and personal interviews. Be prepared.

In addition to conversations, information arrives in standard forms that borrowers complete and in supporting documentation. The forms were discussed in chapter 3, "Getting Started: Initial Package," page 23, so here we focus on documentation. As a reminder, the HAMP application is called the initial package, and it consists of the Request for Mortgage Assistance (RMA) form, IRS form 4506-T or 4506T-EZ, and evidence of income. Visit MakingHomeAffordable.gov or the lender's website for forms and instructions.

Organizing the Documentation

Despite the minimalist approach to the initial package, my experience suggests that it serves little more than to enter the borrower into the lender's system sufficiently to send an automated request for complete supporting documentation. I recommend starting with full documentation, organized in the following order, which roughly tracks the order in which eligibility and underwriting requirements appear in HAMP guidelines.

As applicable and detailed later in this chapter:

- Fax or submission cover sheet that lists the following items.
- RMA form.
- Hardship explanation.
- IRS form 4506-T or 4506T-EZ.
- Proof of income.
- Household expenses.
- Personal federal tax return.
- Proof of occupancy.
- Deposit and investment account statements.
- Rental property leases.
- Non-borrower cohabitant contribution.
- Alimony and child support.
- Other documentation.

All documentation requirements apply to all borrowers. Regarding the subject matter contained in these documents—versus the physical document itself—refer to earlier chapters on eligibility, hardship, delinquency not required, reducing the payment, and debt burden.

Check the lender's specific instructions, usually available on its website link to "home retention," "home preservation," "trouble making your mortgage payment," or another programmatic euphemism—and probably lacking much about Tier 2. Most include a worksheet for personal and financial information. Be thorough. Follow instructions despite any resistance. Anticipate special or unusual circumstances that might raise questions—for example, one-time income that appears on a tax return, overtime, bonus, or change in employment. Then, in advance, answer them in the hardship statement or separate explanation letter and supply supporting documentation to avoid delays later.

Refer to appendix K, "Documentation List," page 181, for a comprehensive list. Organized primarily according to borrower characteristics, the list should be used when actually gathering the documents. Most expire after 90 days, so expect to update them, as a modification decision almost certainly will take longer, and the trial period itself adds three months.

Lenders may use information that borrowers furnish either in writing or verbally. Stop and plan before calling a lender or transmitting information by mail, by delivery service, by facsimile, or electronically. Assemble paperwork, complete forms, calculate ratios, know what you want and what you qualify for, and then take a breath and be sure.

Submitting Information

HAMP guidelines refer to three milestones in the information gathering process: solicitation, eligibility, and Trial Period Plan (TPP). I would add a fourth: preparation of the Modification Agreement. To solicit a borrower's HAMP participation, a lender may rely on verbal financial information obtained from the borrower but often uses computer modeling to find candidates for modification.

However, a lender must use written documentation to verify the borrower's eligibility and income before preparing a TPP and, commonly, again before preparing the Modification Agreement. Information, whether written or verbal, must be current within 90 days or less of the decision or determination milestone. So, as you receive current versions of pay stubs, bank statements, and other periodic documents, save them so you can voluntarily submit them every month or respond immediately to a lender's inevitable request.

A good rule of thumb for income: If you list income from any sources in your financial statement or RMA, then document it. It can be proof of actual receipt (pay stubs, vouchers, bank deposits, account statements) or of the right or entitlement to receive it (lease, annuity statement, social security letter, spousal and child support). For some income, lenders want both proof of entitlement and actual receipt of payment—wait to be asked.

TIP

Lenders require a large number of documents from the borrower. Always keep copies and maintain a log of when you submitted them to the lender. Late or missing documentation is a frequent reason for non-approval.

Once the TPP begins, many lenders expect a borrower to update financial information while they decide the final modification, though HAMP guidelines are vague. In the past, I suggested that a borrower should furnish fresh documents whether or not they are asked. Now, I recommend waiting for the lender's specific request, during the TPP, to avoid unnecessary reevaluation and new issues. Be prepared, though, because the final Modification Agreement depends on information less than 90 days old.

Guidelines encourage lenders to assist borrowers, when necessary, in assembling required documents. If you don't understand a request, ask for clarification. The job description for the single point of contact includes this kind of help. Don't wait; misunderstanding causes delay.

A borrower may furnish the lender written documentation at any time. It should be clearly identified—by borrower's name, loan account number, and date. Always include the loan account number in the upper-right corner of every page. Failure to comply with a lender's request for documentation within the given time is the single most common reason for non-approval that I see. It's called a "soft" decline and can be reversed by submitting the documentation and requesting reinstatement. Some require an entire new package; if so, copy, sign, and redate what you originally used.

TIP

Take the initiative to update documentation. Whenever you receive a more recent version of a document that was already submitted, lay it aside. Check for consistency with earlier versions and prepare to explain significant differences.

Attachments and Enclosures

Except those supplied by the lender that need your signature—RMA and TPP offer, for example—do not submit original documents (e.g., tax returns, pay stubs, bank statement, and utility bills). Copy *everything* that you submit. If you submit a copy, keep a copy. If you submit by fax, keep the fax or a copy of it. The idea is to maintain a complete file for reference when communicating with the lender and as a record. By submitting and keeping copies, you can then refile the originals for safekeeping. I scan and keep electronic or digital copies.

At the end of each month during the modification process, submit all of the updates with explanations if needed. When properly identified, they will be added to your file, already there for the analyst's review without asking and waiting for current versions.

A lender may *not* require a borrower to make an up-front payment to be considered for HAMP modification. Though not specified by the guidelines, this prohibition applies to missed principal and interest payments, tax, and insurance, even if the lender advanced those amounts on the borrower's behalf. The prohibition extends to the servicer's collection department, which might incorrectly tell you that a payment, *any* payment, will help you get the modification. Late fees and administrative or processing costs must be waived on completion of the modification. Trial period payments are the only exception.

Mortgage

Obviously, the lender should have as much information about a mortgage as a borrower has. Actual loan documents may be elusive, considering the number of times a single loan might be transferred from one servicing agent to another or sold by one investment pool to another.

This is fodder for "forensic loan audits," a cottage industry rivaling "foreclosure consultants" and "loan modification experts." An audit looks for errors and omissions in loan documentation, predatory lending practices, and related activities that might gain concessions from a lender in a modification or foreclosure. The term "forensic" simply means "for use in legal proceedings" and implies that you might end up in a lawsuit. If you are trying to modify a loan, a forensic audit might transfer it out of underwriting into the lender's legal department, and modification would become a way to settle the lawsuit.

CAUTION

Submitting false information, or other attempts to mislead a lender, may disqualify a modification. Correct mistaken information and resubmit it immediately, accompanied by a written explanation. Intentional misrepresentation by a borrower or borrower's representative may be fraud and subject to civil, criminal, or professional license sanctions.

The extreme loan audit outcome would be nullification or rescission of the loan, which might bring sanctions against the lender, but also might oblige borrowers to pay back the money received from the improper loan. Some mistakes are so common that lenders simply ignore them until a pattern and a class action lawsuit loom. If you suspect loan or lender abuse, find—and talk directly to—an attorney specifically qualified in secured real estate lending.

> **TIP**
>
> Glance through each of the following categories (Mortgage, Occupancy Status, etc.) and income subcategories. When one applies to you or a co-borrower, focus attention on it. Use the explanation to assemble, expand, or limit information and to present copies of it to your lender.

Avoid bulking up the file with unnecessary loan documents like disclosures, promissory notes, and monthly statements. Exceptions: (1) written promises by a lender to improve the situation, which have not materialized, and (2) a lawyer's opinion letter, if a legal analysis has uncovered discrepancies in required disclosures or other operative elements of the loan.

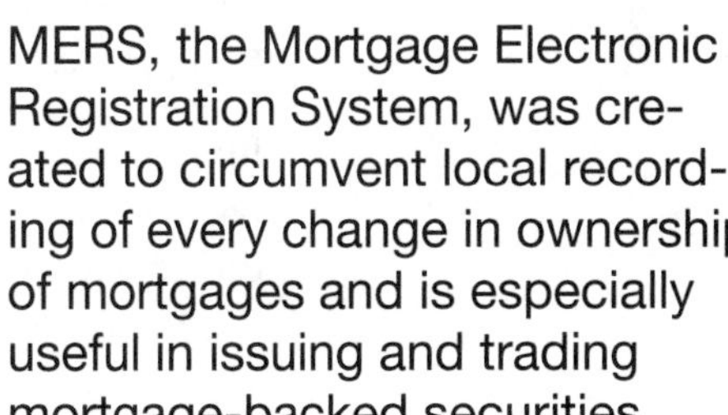

> **CAUTION**
>
> MERS, the Mortgage Electronic Registration System, was created to circumvent local recording of every change in ownership of mortgages and is especially useful in issuing and trading mortgage-backed securities.

Many borrowers believe—are led to believe—that MERS is a villain and that unrecorded and undocumented changes in ownership of their mortgages might relieve them from their obligation to repay. Courts have consistently ruled in favor of MERS, so make sure yours is really (and truly) a unique case, or save yourself some legal fees.

Occupancy Status

Occupancy affects eligibility in the following ways: The property securing the loan to be modified must be occupied as the borrower's principal residence for Tier 1 eligibility and for Tier 2 imminent risk of default eligibility. Servicers rely primarily on a credit report to verify owner occupancy.

For Tier 2 eligibility, the property may be the borrower's principal residence or a rental property. If a rental property, it must be vacant and available for rent or occupied by a tenant or by the borrower's legal dependent, parent, or grandparent. If occupied, it must be the occupant's principal residence.

In addition to the credit report obtained by the lender, proof of occupancy depends on documentation addressed to the occupant at the property address. Examples include pay stubs, account statements, tax documents, or other third-party items, such as utility bills. Up to three corroborating items might be required as reasonable evidence of full-time permanent residence. Guidelines leave the decision to a servicer's good business judgment.

Most files already contain sufficient verification for owner occupancy. Note that Home Affordable Foreclosure Alternatives short-sale relocation assistance requires similar verification. I've encountered problems with post office and private mailboxes, which made establishing a physical address more difficult.

Income

The guidelines break down income into seven categories and, in all cases, require a signed copy of the most recently filed personal federal income tax return (IRS Form 1040), including all schedules and forms available. *Signed copy*. After copying, *sign and date* page 2. This is the most commonly overlooked requirement and may delay a decision on the file.

Also, in all cases, sign and submit IRS Form 4506-T (Request for Transcript of Tax Return) or 4506T-EZ, which may be found on the lender's websites or requested if not part of the modification paperwork. It permits comparison between the copy of the tax returns submitted to the lender and those actually on file at the IRS. It is also used if tax returns are unavailable or incomplete and may be used randomly to audit files. Do not tamper with tax returns.

Income Categories

From HAMP guidelines, plus one that I have added:[1]

Employment income. Includes any compensation from an employer, including regular salary and wages, and items that may be regular or irregular, such as overtime, bonuses, tips, and commission.

If pay stubs accurately reflect employment income, both regular gross (total) and net (after withholdings), then pay stubs covering the most recent two-month period usually are sufficient. If you are paid biweekly, pay stubs for five pay periods are needed to cover two calendar months. Check to ensure that year-to-date gross and net totals are included, or supply them separately.

Irregular items (commission bonus or overtime for example), if they are expected to continue, need separate verification from an employer or a reliable third party, though borrowers can start with their own explanation letter. If income has changed during the year—furlough or reduced hours for example—then include a written explanation and employer's notification or signed confirmation. Also include the most recent Form W-2, and explain any difference from current income.

Self-employment income. Must be substantiated by the most recent quarterly or year-to-date profit-and-loss statement.[2] The size and complexity of the business may influence whether a full year-to-date version is required and whether it must be prepared or reviewed by a third-party accountant or bookkeeper. Otherwise, a format that indicates record keeping contemporaneous with the income or expense event (QuickBooks or other business accounting software) may be sufficiently reliable and should be notated on the statement.

Entitlement income. Includes income from such sources as Social Security, disability or death benefits, or a pension. An entitlement letter, a benefits statement, or other documentation acceptable to a lender must state the amount, frequency, and duration of the benefit and must indicate that the income will continue for at least three more years. The guidelines are unclear when the three-year remaining duration begins, whether from decision, TPP, or modification effective date.

Public assistance. Includes unemployment benefits, among other programs. An entitlement letter, exhibits, a benefits statement, or other documentation must state the amount, frequency, and duration of the benefit and must indicate that the income will continue for at least nine months.

Real estate rent. Add to the one-year requirement the second-most-recent year of personal federal income tax returns—*signed*. Make certain to include Schedule E, Supplemental Income and Loss, and use net rental income plus noncash depreciation expense. Otherwise, to determine net rental income, HAMP subtracts 25 percent of gross rent for vacancy loss and maintenance expenses. The remaining 75 percent may be further reduced by mortgage interest, property tax, and insurance expenses. If rents have changed, then also include current leases and calculate HAMP ratios using current rents.

Investments. These are not covered in the guidelines. Use the approach for real estate rent. Interest and dividends, deferred compensation, royalties, retirement distributions, and other returns on investments may be shown with the second year of tax returns and Schedule E. Include periodic statements covering at least three months (quarterly or annual should suffice). Point out changes in income, which are relevant to hardship and qualification. Changes in investment asset value are secondary but relevant.

Alimony or child support. The guidelines do not require borrowers to disclose alimony and child support received. As a general rule, minimize income to minimize the modified monthly mortgage payment. Do not disclose these amounts, unless you need the income either to help you qualify to make the modified payment or to reduce an excessive overall debt-to-income ratio. It will depend on the lender's specific criteria.

If you voluntarily disclose such income, then provide copies of the settlement and custody agreements that state the award amount and remaining duration, which must be at least three years. Furthermore, full, regular, and timely payments must be shown with reasonably reliable evidence, such as deposit slips, bank statements, or *signed* federal income tax returns.

CAUTION

Decide whether you want to disclose alimony and child support *before* calling your lender or submitting financial information. When unsure, start by excluding it, then adding it if needed.

Non-borrower cohabitant contributions. The guidelines do not require borrowers to disclose income earned by a spouse or partner who cohabits but is not a borrower and is not obligated on the promissory note. Nor do the guidelines require disclosure of amounts received from non-borrower occupants, such as children or a renter living in the principal residence. As a general rule, do not disclose these amounts, unless such income helps you qualify to make the modified payment or to reduce an excessive overall debt-to-income ratio.

To use a spouse or partner's income, supply the same documentation as for the borrower. Room-and-board income needs a written agreement, probably supported by bank statements showing regular deposits.

Excluded income. A servicer may not add the following items to income, so a borrower should not submit related documentation: income tax refunds; non-borrower non-household income (friends or family members who are not borrowers and who do not occupy the borrower's home may not contribute income for qualifying purposes); grants, including mortgage-assistance payments; severance payments; unemployment benefits; and payments from non–Making Home Affordable unemployment assistance programs.

Cash Reserves

Generally, the term "liquid assets" or "liquid monetary assets" are synonymous. Cash reserves include assets such as cash, savings, money market funds, marketable stocks, or bonds (excluding retirement accounts and assets that serve as an "emergency fund").

By requesting two months of cash-reserve account statements, lenders can see unusual activity. One lender wants four months for personal and business accounts of a self-employed business owner. Transferring or spending large chunks of cash is a red flag. Especially if the amounts impact allowable cash-reserve maximums, add a written explanation. For example, advances to purchase materials inflated a plumbing contractor's deposit accounts, so a six-month average explained the fluctuations.

Be aware of a discrepancy between HAMP guidelines and Fannie Mae's interpretation of "emergency fund." HAMP permits up to three months of total debt payments, including all mortgages, other obligations, and a living-expense allowance. It is more liberal than Fannie Mae, which permits up to three months of mortgage payments, including only those expenses associated with the senior loan.

The importance of this distinction is the amount of liquid funds the borrower may have available at completion of the modification process. For a borrower, the more the better. If borrowers qualify with less than three months' cash reserve, that reserve may disappear during the three-month trial period. It may have already vanished after 90 to 120 days waiting for the lender to give the initial provisional response.

Considering the length of time lenders take to process modification proposals, delay may actually give a more accurate picture of current circumstances. Submitting other documentation, but waiting to submit deposit account statements, might avoid disclosure of unusual transfer or payment activity and will reflect a smaller balance as the account is spent down.

During a prolonged wait, any cash exceeding the three-month reserve should be used to pay down credit accounts, especially lines of credit that can be preserved for the future and drawn against in an emergency. An inflated checking or savings account might disqualify the modification, but a lower credit balance will have little impact.

Federal Tax Forms

The requirement to submit personal federal income tax returns and Form 4506-T (or 4506T-EZ) is discussed above. Do not include state tax returns unless the lender specifically requests them. To repeat, copies of tax returns must be *signed and dated* at the bottom of page 2. They must be *signed* to affirm and place responsibility for their accuracy.

If income has changed during or after the tax year reported, attach a written explanation. A hardship explanation addresses such changes, but specifics in context may help.

If you, the borrower, have significant ownership interest in a business that files its own tax returns, you might be asked to submit two years of corporate or partnership returns. Wait until asked and then confirm this requirement with the lender before submission, to avoid confusion, bulk, and unnecessary disclosure. The same applies to Form K-1 or similar reports of individual allocations of profit and loss.

Other Required Documentation

Alert the lender with a reference at the front of the initial package when including such items as a divorce decree, property settlement, child-custody agreement, rental-property lease, entitlement letter, and insurance declaration page. I usually place the referenced items at the end of a submission.

Later, when submitting additional requested documentation, use a cover sheet to list included items. The cover sheet can be an e-mail with attachments, a fax transmittal, or a cover letter for mail or delivery service. Most lenders prefer fax; if by attachment to e-mail, use PDF format only.

Summary

For you to qualify for a modification, lenders eventually must substantiate all your stated information with supporting written or printed documentation. Except the hardship and other letters of explanation, the personal and financial information presented in the RMA requires third-party verification.

Without volunteering anything more than necessary, borrower initiative helps to move decision making forward faster. Information given verbally in a phone conversation with the lender also must be verified. Prepare in advance so your conversation and documentation align to your best advantage.

Working with Your Lender

Learning Points:

- How to deal effectively with your lender.
- What to do before talking to your lender.
- How to submit information.
- Questions to ask your lender.

When calling a lender, I always try to multitask to avoid wasting time while enduring the automated phone answering systems. Borrowers and their advisors have spent endless minutes and countless hours wading through repetitive and irrelevant selections before speaking to a real person. To address this problem at the larger participating lenders, Making Home Affordable (MHA) requires

TIP

You're likely to encounter people at your lender with an imperfect understanding of HAMP. To the degree possible, master the details of the program and the particulars of your situation prior to speaking with your lender.

assignment of a "relationship manager" to serve as the borrower's single point of contact. More about that later; first some quick advice.

General Contact

Terminology varies and escalates as customer service transfers to home retention, which transfers to loss mitigation, which transfers to settlement, which transfers to recovery, which transfers to liquidation. You get the point. And beware the confounding mantra: "We are a debt collector. Any information you give may be used for that purpose, but we're here to help you."

Know your eligibility, your qualifying information, and your objectives before talking with the lender, whether the servicer initiates the call or you make first contact. Summarize major points in writing for your reference. These "talking points" will enable you to obtain more information from customer service people and to insist on continuing the conversation through to its conclusion. You may need to talk with several different people to draw a complete picture of what the lender wants and what you want. Clarifying your part in advance will strengthen your communications.

Your information is retrieved by loan account number and Social Security number. Anyone you speak with has access to your electronic loan file and makes detailed notes. Keep two factors in mind: First, personnel are mostly interchangeable, and everyone accesses the same information about your loan, its status, and related activities and conversations. Second, *not* everyone has a full understanding of the information, HAMP guidelines, and the lender's use of the guidelines. So, we must endure inconsistency, repetition, and redundancy.

If any conversation or result contradicts the guidelines and the suggestions in this book, then call again and yet again if necessary. It may take two or three tries before connecting with someone who grasps and appreciates your individual circumstances, and understands how to accomplish your objective.

Finally, if you are not prepared, do not guess. Explain that you are not ready to talk about those details, ask when you can call back, and insist on it. Don't allow yourself to be pressured.

Single Point of Contact

If you are even potentially eligible, your servicer must assign a relationship manager, who acts as your single point of contact until resolution of your MHA process, whether it is HAMP, Home Affordable Foreclosure Alternatives, other MHA program, an internal alternative, or foreclosure. The assignment starts when loan payments become delinquent or when a borrower requests mortgage relief.

The relationship manager stays informed about the individual borrower's loan status and communicates information about options for delinquency relief and how to be considered for them. This single point of contact coordinates documentation, tracks progress of your request, informs you of a decision, and explains actions needed after a decision is rendered: if positive, then steps needed for final resolution; if negative, then available alternatives.

Equally important, the relationship manager maintains direct and immediate access to other servicer personnel with the authority to stop foreclosure proceedings. If a borrower expresses interest in appealing or escalating an adverse decision, the relationship manager assists in contacting appropriate internal staff and directing the borrower to MHA for assistance.

Be aware, however, of several limitations: This requirement applies only to larger lenders, specifically those servicing more than $75 million of potentially eligible loans. A single point of contact might change as personnel come and go or workloads shift. When the relationship manager is unavailable, you might transfer to another customer service representative who can update information and status, or you might be left to the mercy of voice mail. Some lenders expect relationship managers to initiate periodic contact with borrowers, but consistency varies. The situation has improved very much at some lenders, and very little at others.

Many lenders appoint a relationship manager who interacts with other staff working on your loan. Keep that person informed about any difficulties you have in moving the evaluation process forward and if you intend to appeal a negative decision.

Twelve Questions to Ask Your Lender

1. Does your lender participate in the MHA program?[1]
2. For your specific loan, does the "investor" also participate?
3. If either or both do not participate, or if your loan is ineligible, what proprietary or "in-house" alternatives are available for your specific situation?
4. If not already, must your payments be delinquent to be considered for mortgage relief, and what about imminent risk of default?
5. If delinquent, what is the present status of your loan?
6. If not yet referred to foreclosure, how much longer until such referral? If already referred to foreclosure, when? Has a foreclosure sale been scheduled and, if so, when? If not, what is the likelihood and when?
7. How can the foreclosure process be suspended or postponed?
8. Did the servicer send or receive your (borrower's) correspondence about participating in the MHA program?
9. How can you initiate HAMP Tier 1 or Tier 2 or other mortgage relief? Specifically, what forms and information are needed and where can you find them? Ask for specific instructions to find the forms online or for a package to be delivered to you.
10. What is the best way—with specific fax number or e-mail address—to submit forms, correspondence, and documentation?
11. Who is your single point of contact (a.k.a. relationship manager), and what is his/her specific contact information? If not, when will one be assigned, and what is the most direct way—and phone number—to check status? Note the person's name and use it during the conversation.

12. What is your servicer's typical turnaround time for entering information and arriving at a decision? Business or calendar days?

+1. If you are considering a short sale, how can you initiate a short sale?[2]

In response, you might get the verbal equivalent of a blank stare. Most customer service representatives are well trained and informed. If necessary, though, rephrase and ask again, call back and talk with someone else, or speak to a supervisor.

Submitting Information

If you do nothing else, include your name and loan account number on every piece of paper submitted. Some clients merge the information onto sheets of self-adhesive address labels, and then apply a label near the upper right corner of each page. I scan all documents into PDF format, add loan number, borrower name, and date as a header (and footer) on every page, and then submit electronically whenever possible.

NOTE

Many lenders emphasize the hardship letter for narrative explanations or special requests. Use it to communicate what you want, as well as to explain your hardship circumstances, or write a separate letter or summary.

Use your lender's fax or cover sheet, which are common components in application or documentation request packages. Otherwise, create your own for all your written communications. Identify the lender and loan number, the individual recipient and contact information, the borrower (you), and property address. As a record, consider adding a list of the attached or transmitted items. Keep copies of everything and don't send originals except signed forms.

The HAMP Solution Center for third-party advocates wants the following information on incoming correspondence, which is a good summary:

- Borrower's name.
- Property address.
- Servicer name.
- Servicer loan number.
- Foreclosure date (if applicable).
- Counselor name and organization.
- Counselor e-mail.
- Counselor phone.
- Counselor relationship to homeowner.

If Declined[3]

If declined, find out the reason(s). Is the mortgage ineligible, or did your financial circumstances disqualify you? If the non-approval letter isn't clear, then get details. Be persistent. Understand what you are being told. Ask again. Call back. Do not let someone's impatience distract or discourage you. This happens less than one might assume but can be intimidating when it does.

Once you have a clear understanding of the issues that resulted in your application's denial, review those areas of this book. Prepare a response. Before you call, take notes. Outline the points you want to make. A computer generates many decisions relayed by a human being who may not understand the criteria and formula that produced the result. Make that person an ally by persuasively, persistently, and patiently discussing how your situation varies from the computer assumptions. Try to lay emotions aside for the moment.

We gain nothing by frustration with the lender's employees, deserved or not. Direct their attention to the "computer model." Point out that your *calculations* produce different results than those produced by the *computer*. If it involves financial qualifications, ask to compare each component of the calculation. If it involves eligibility, ask how to correct the deficiency or implement Tier 2 if applicable. If you agree to pursue a modification alternative, ask how to qualify. Ask to speak to a supervisor when necessary.

Third-Party Advocates

Nonprofit and for-profit counselors are generically referred to as "third-party advocates." Many lenders have organized separate units to work with third parties advising borrowers. Real estate brokers, and closing agents or attorneys, almost always serve as the intermediaries in short sales and fall within the general category.

Borrowers must authorize servicers and MHA offices to release their loan information, which is confidential, to any third party. Some have their own forms; others accept the counselor's or agent's form. Check into the requirements early. It often takes several days to receive the form and then several more for the authorization to appear in the servicer's system. Make sure it's there ahead of any emergency.

Summary

Whatever your lender says, its first responsibility is not to help delinquent borrowers. Its first responsibility (and legal duty) is to its shareholders and mortgage investors whose loans they service by collecting payments from you. Most customer service personnel are courteous, knowledgeable, and interchangeable. Their job is to pass along to decision makers whatever information you give them.

Your job, then, is to give them the most beneficial information possible. They will not help you; you must figure it out for yourself. They definitely have the advantage, but you should expect to receive accurate answers to your questions and full disclosure about their decisions. Identify every piece of paper you submit with your name and loan number and keep a copy. Above all else, preparation, patience, and persistence pay off.

Circumstances and Consequences

Learning Points:

- Deficiency liability and how to avoid it.
- Tax consequences and how to avoid them.
- Effect on credit reports.
- How special situations are handled.

Modification, short sale, or strategic default? Whatever your chosen course, attention to the following will improve your outcome. Much applies generally to all Making Home Affordable (MHA) programs. Most specifics draw from HAMP guidance, which underlies other MHA programs like Home Affordable Foreclosure Alternatives (HAFA). Otherwise, I've tried to rely on universal legal concepts with some small reference to California, where I practice.

Deficiency Liability

Your home or rental property serves as collateral for your real estate loan. You pledged it by giving a security interest to your lender with the right to foreclose if you default on your loan payments. When a loan is not paid in full—short sale, deed in lieu, or foreclosure—a deficiency results. Then, when the title

Check the laws in your state regarding deficiency liability if you elect a short sale or deed in lieu or are foreclosed in order to avoid personal liability for the unpaid balance of the loan. State laws vary.

passes to someone else and you no longer own the property, it no longer secures the loan, and any deficiency becomes a personal obligation.

Try to avoid such an outcome. When the property transfers voluntarily in a short sale or by tender of a deed in lieu of foreclosure, the lender must consent by releasing its security interest. Terms and conditions are negotiable. Ensure that the lender's consent includes a release of liability and waiver of its right to seek recovery of the deficiency from you personally. If the lender won't agree, then get professional advice and consider withdrawing the transaction and letting the property go to foreclosure.

Ultimately, to collect, the lender would sue the borrower for the deficiency amount. If the lender wins, then the court enters a deficiency judgment, which may be enforced as any other award of the court. State foreclosure statutes might release borrowers from deficiency liability by law or might prohibit the foreclosing lender from commencing a separate lawsuit. State laws vary. Get competent legal advice in the jurisdiction where the property is located.

Some states, like California, restrict the lender to a "single action," meaning the choice to foreclose is the single or only legal shot at the borrower and extinguishes any further obligation. Because a short sale or deed in lieu is negotiated, the single (legal) action remains, allowing any available collection activities, including a lawsuit.

In California, after approving a short sale, state law prohibits a lender from seeking a deficiency judgment. So, by statute, the deficiency is no longer a personal liability—known as nonrecourse—and is not subject to debt forgiveness tax, which the next section explains in more detail.

Tax Liability

If the lender forgives the deficiency, the deficiency amount may be subject to debt forgiveness taxation. Whether from foreclosure, tendering a deed in lieu of foreclosure, a short sale, principal reduction, or settlement of the mortgage for less than its unpaid principal balance, the lender's loss is considered income to the released borrower.

In California after a short sale, state law extinguishes personal liability for the deficiency, and the IRS has ruled that debt forgiveness tax does not apply. Whether this affects state tax or other states with similar laws has yet to be determined.

NOTE

Do not confuse this with the mortgage interest deduction, either for homeowners or as an expense for rental properties. The interest portion of the modified monthly payments continues as an itemized deduction, which you report as occurring before the modification for as long as you own the property.

The following comes directly from IRS publications, available through the IRS or at MortgageBriefing.com. It is general guidance only. *It is not tax or legal advice. Do not rely* solely on what is written here or elsewhere in this book for making decisions that might affect federal, state, or local income or other tax. State and local laws may differ from federal laws and IRS regulations and might impose additional tax on debt forgiveness. Consult a professional financial, tax, or legal advisor.

Canceled Debt

If a lender discounts (reduces) the principal balance of a loan because you pay it off early or agrees to a loan modification (a "workout") that includes a reduction in the principal balance of a loan, the amount of the discount or the amount of principal reduction is canceled debt. However, if the debt is nonrecourse and you did not retain the collateral, you do not have cancellation of the debt income. The amount of the canceled debt must be included in income unless one of the exceptions or exclusions described later applies.[1]

Principal Residence Exemption. Normally, forgiven debt results in taxable income. Certain "qualified debt" that is reduced by mortgage restructuring (principal reduction by modification) or forgiven in connection with a foreclosure (short sale or deed in lieu of foreclosure) might be excluded.[2]

Qualified Debt. Qualified debt (1) was used to buy, build, or substantially improve the taxpayer's principal residence; (2) was secured by that residence; and (3) did not exceed $2 million ($1 million for a married person filing a separate return). Debt used to refinance qualified debt is also eligible for the exclusion but only up to the amount of the old mortgage principal, just before the refinancing. (Cash-out or equity loans, therefore, would not qualify.)[3]

CAUTION

The Principal Residence Exemption expired December 31, 2012, and was extended by Congress through 2013. At this writing, legislation to extend the exemption to cover 2014 and 2015 has been moved from committee to the Senate and House of Representatives for consideration. Refer to Senate Bill 2260.

Reporting Debt Forgiveness. Borrowers whose debt is reduced or eliminated receive a year-end statement (Form 1099-C) from their lender. Lenders are required to furnish this form to borrowers by January 31. By law, this form must show the amount of debt forgiven and the fair market value of any property given up through foreclosure. (Refer disputes to the lender and, for HAFA, the HAMP Solution Center.) In most cases, eligible homeowners need to report the amount and then, for the exemption, complete and attach Form 982, Reduction of Tax Attributes Due to Discharge of Indebtedness.[4]

Insolvency. Debt forgiven on second homes, rental property, business property, credit cards, or car loans does not qualify for the homeowner tax-relief exemption.

In some cases, however, other kinds of tax relief, based on insolvency for example, may be available.[5]

Do not include canceled debt in reported income to the extent that you were insolvent immediately before the cancellation.[6]

Here, "insolvent" means that the total of all liabilities exceeded the fair market value of all assets, meaning the value of everything you own. This includes assets that serve as collateral for debt. It includes exempt assets, which are beyond the reach of creditors under the law, such as interest in a pension plan and the value of a retirement account.[7]

Liabilities include the entire amount of recourse (personal) debts, and the amount of nonrecourse (secured) debt that does not exceed the fair market value of the property securing such debt. Excluded are debts discharged in Title 11 bankruptcy and qualified principal residence indebtedness (see above).[8]

Generally, if you exclude canceled debt from income under one of these provisions, you must also reduce your tax attributes (certain credits, losses, and basis of assets). Consult a tax advisor.[9]

Bankruptcy. Debt canceled in a Title 11 bankruptcy case is not included in income.[10]

NOTE

If your primary asset is an underwater home, you have a car loan or lease, and you carry credit card balances, then you might be "insolvent" by IRS standards, despite making ends meet.

Credit Score

If a borrower was *delinquent* before the trial period, the lender will continue to report the appropriate level of delinquency. If a borrower was *current* at the start of the trial period and makes each trial period payment on time, the lender will continue to report such payments as current. Either way, the lender reports both as "paying under a partial or modified payment agreement."

After modification, the lender reports account activity as for any other credit account. The report continues to show an open account with the same loan, the same account number, and the same original loan amount and date but with changes to principal balance, loan term, and payment amount according to terms of the modification.

On the modification effective date, the lender reports the account as current and as a "loan modified under a federal government plan." Subsequently, status depends on timely payments. Modification will not change delinquencies reported prior to the Trial Period Plan (TPP).

The lasting impact of reporting a mortgage under a partial or modified payment agreement remains unclear. However, the sheer volume eventually will neutralize, to some degree, the derogatory implications of a modification and, possibly, the preceding hardship delinquencies. And, finally, the credit bottom has been reached, and the climb out, though arduous, can begin.

Short Sales. Credit reporting for short sales falls into one of two categories, depending on whether the lender forgives the deficiency. When the deficiency is forgiven, the lender reports the loan as "paid in full for less than the full balance." Translation: Though less than the full remaining loan balance at the time of the short sale, the minimum net was accepted by the lender in full satisfaction of the debt. The report shows the account closed with a zero balance and nothing past due. It ends any further reporting on the loan.

When the deficiency is not forgiven, the lender reports the account as "collateral released by creditor with balance owing." Translation: The lender released the lien so clear title could pass to the short-sale buyer but did not waive the deficiency liability. The report continues to show an open account with the same loan, the same account number, and the same original loan amount and date.

Going forward, the lender reports account activity as for any other credit account. The short sale reduced the outstanding balance by the amount of the minimum net, resulting in a new balance equal to the deficiency amount. Other changes depend on agreement between lender and borrower. They might include extending the loan-term duration, changing the monthly payment, or forbearing payments or interest for a period of time. The lender reports the original or changed terms and on-time payments as current or late payments as delinquent. Reporting on the account continues until paid or moved to another status like charged off, discharged in bankruptcy, or deficiency judgment.

> **CAUTION**
>
> There's little advantage of utilizing a short sale if the lender will not waive the deficiency liability. In those circumstances, foreclosure may be a better option.

In either case, whether the deficiency is waived or not, any derogatory reports for late payments before closing the short sale will remain on the borrower's credit record.

Needless to say, an open deficiency poses ongoing liability and credit difficulties. A foreclosure might offer an alternative that brings a conclusion to the account and a foundation for healing credit. If the primary senior lender refuses to waive deficiency liability in a short sale, consider canceling the sale and proceeding to foreclosure.

Divorce

Hardship. In virtually every instance, divorce changes household financial circumstances unfavorably and, therefore, qualifies as an eligibility hardship. By extension, each party encounters temporary or permanent reduced income and increased expense. In most cases, cash reserves decline, and credit and other obligations rise. Add emotional distress and everybody experiences every event listed in the Hardship Affidavit.

Borrower. If the property that secures the mortgage transfers to one party during the trial period, that person (borrower) is obliged to inform the lender. The lender then must determine, and inform the borrower, whether (1) to continue the TPP and convert to a permanent modification, (2) to terminate the TPP and reevaluate that person separately, or (3) to terminate the TPP and consider other loss mitigation options.

Co-borrower. Assume the property that secures the mortgage transfers to one borrower by divorce and property settlement, or an ongoing divorce is contested. Whether the non-occupant borrower must participate in the MHA process or sign related paperwork is left to the servicer's discretion and mortgage investor requirements.

It is possible, therefore, that the non-occupant-transferring co-borrower would not sign the Modification Agreement or be obligated by it. Guidelines do not specifically address whether the Modification Agreement, in effect, releases the transferring party from unaltered obligations in the underlying promissory note.

> **NOTE**
>
> Typically, the spouse who transfers the house wants to be removed from the loan and its related liability. Though desirable, it usually entails refinancing by the other spouse, which is often difficult for a single person. As a coincidental effect, modification might accomplish this release from liability.

The Modification Agreement alters the fundamental terms and conditions of the promissory note. Those and all other provisions are secured by the property now owned by one former spouse. As for the transferring spouse, a compelling argument can be made that such a release may be implied, with no ownership interest in the property or liability on the promissory note. Ask the lender to include a release and waiver of liability for the transferring spouse—unlikely, but ask anyway.

Identical Borrowers

Borrowers must be the same for the Modification Agreement as for the underlying promissory note. Exceptions are divorce (see above), death, mental incapacity, excused absence (e.g., military deployment), and the addition of a new borrower. The circumstances of any such exception may qualify as a hardship, though a new borrower's income may improve financial conditions sufficiently to justify the modification.

Borrowers must be "natural persons," which excludes such entities as corporations, limited and general partnerships, and limited liability companies.

New Borrower

A borrower may be added, but not subtracted, except as mentioned above. If the current borrower(s) cannot pass the net present value test (meaning that modification is less beneficial to the lender than foreclosure) or cannot verify sufficient income to meet monthly gross expenses, then adding a borrower and the new borrower's net income may save the modification.

This might also be accomplished by using a contribution from a non-borrower occupant, like a child or partner.

The new borrower becomes liable for the entire mortgage obligation, just as any other borrower would be, and it is risky business, considering the preexisting distress of the borrower and mortgage. If the original borrower can modify the mortgage, only a very special reason would explain adding a borrower—for example, marriage or an anticipated partial or full transfer of title.

Title Held in Trust

For estate-planning purposes, many owners transfer title into a living or testamentary trust. Usually, it's an inter vivos revocable trust, which means that the person making the trust (trustor) may revoke the trust anytime during his/her lifetime (inter vivos). Such a property held in trust is eligible under HAMP if the borrower is the trustor and signs the modification in that capacity and as an individual.

Typically, however, when completing a new financing (refinance or equity loan), a transfer to trust since the original financing must be reversed, individuals—not the trust—will sign the recorded security instrument (mortgage or trust deed) and other loan documents. After closing the new loan, and recording the security instrument, the title again is transferred into the trust. If the trust or other title change occurred after the loan, then such a procedure might be necessary to modify it.

Ineligible Mortgages

The logic of MHA applies to all loans, eligible or not. The same procedure, analysis, formulas, and conclusions that apply to eligible mortgages should apply to ineligible mortgages and properties. If modification benefits a lender more than foreclosure, then modification makes sense. Otherwise, a short sale makes more sense than foreclosure, and should be used with or without MHA sanction and incentives.

> **NOTE**
> Ultimately, the loan servicer and the investor decide whether to modify a loan or proceed with foreclosure. They must be convinced that the benefits of modification outweigh the consequences of foreclosure.

Whether common sense prevails depends on the lender—both loan servicer and mortgage investor. Individual mortgages—yours and mine—back securities owned by investment pools. An agreement with the investor, together with its due diligence and fiduciary duties, dictates the servicer's response to change any loan, eligible or ineligible. Behind the scenes, will servicers and investors work to apply MHA principles to all loans? Possibly, eventually, when evidence shows undeniably that the benefits of MHA outweigh foreclosure.

Summary

If your modification reduces the loan amount, then you might owe income tax on the canceled debt. The IRS might exempt the canceled debt from taxation, if you used the loan to buy, build, or remodel your home, assuming Congress extends the provision from its 2013 deadline. Another exemption, which has not expired, is "insolvency," a technical term better explained by qualified tax counsel. State or local taxes might apply, and a deficiency that remains after a short sale or foreclosure might become a personal liability depending on state laws.

Be aware when owners or borrowers have changed since originating the mortgage to be modified. If you divorced, want to add or remove another borrower, or hold the property in trust, you will encounter special requirements. If ineligible for HAMP, your loan still might qualify for a proprietary modification and other mortgage relief.

Short Sale: Modification Alternative

Learning Points:

- Definition of a short sale and when and how to use it.
- Relationship of short sales to HAMP.
- Home Affordable Foreclosure Alternatives (HAFA) short-sale alternative to HAMP.

Short sales offer an important alternative to modifying a mortgage. They dominate large segments of the residential real estate marketplace, which has been littered in the past with debris from failed and frustrated transactions. Many underwater owners face years of negative equity, and some are staring down the barrel of impending foreclosure.

Another reason for addressing short sales in connection with modifications is the close relationship between HAMP and the federal HAFA program.[1] HAFA depends heavily on HAMP. It regulates short sales for participating servicers and lenders and, like HAMP, is intended to become the industry standard.

First, some of the broad issues that distressed borrowers face when deciding whether to modify or sell. Then, an introduction to using HAFA to complete a successful short sale and benefit from its incentives.

What Is a Short Sale?

When a lender agrees to accept less than the full amount owed, it's called a "short payoff." A short sale is a conventional sale that results in a short payoff when the net proceeds—price minus costs—are less than the loan balance.

The loan to be repaid consists of two parts. The promissory note creates the loan and the obligation for a borrower to repay it. The security instrument (lien, mortgage, or deed of trust) pledges the property as collateral and gives the lender a contingent interest in the property.

In a short sale, the lender agrees to accept less than the full amount owed, and releases its lien so the title passes unencumbered to the buyer. The question remains whether the lender will also release the borrower from the unpaid portion of the loan, from the shortfall or deficiency. If so, the lender forgives the debt, and the borrower owes nothing more. Otherwise, the unpaid portion becomes a personal liability of the borrower, and the lender reserves a right to sue for recovery of the deficiency.

The borrower still owns the property during a short sale and, therefore, is the seller. As the seller, the borrower selects the real estate agent and lists the property for sale. As in any sale of a mortgaged property, the lender must approve the loan payoff. Historically, the selling price has been sufficient to fully pay the outstanding loan principal, and the lender's approval was routine. The difference between conventional and short sales is the short payoff, which depends on the lender's approval criteria and decision.

Like a loan modification, a short sale is an alternative to foreclosure. Some mistakenly assume that the lender is the seller, which occurs only after a lender acquires the property through foreclosure. This misperception arises understandably from the lender's significant involvement in approving the seller's circumstances and the property's value. Though not a party to the transaction, the lender plays a pivotal role in the success or failure of the sale.

CAUTION

If you're involved in a short sale, be certain that the lender is "forgiving" the difference between the amount borrowed and amount received by the lender to ensure the lender does not seek the difference from you following the sale.

Deficiency

When a loan is not paid in full, as in a short sale, a deficiency results. It's the difference between the amount owed by the borrower and the amount received by the lender.

The lender can forgive the deficiency, or the deficiency might be extinguished by statute. Otherwise, the sale of the property "strips" the loan of its collateral—the lien, mortgage, or deed of trust—and the deficiency becomes an unsecured personal liability. The lender then may sue the individual borrower for the deficient amount. If the lender prevails, the court awards a deficiency judgment.

The importance of ensuring that the lender waives its right to seek a deficiency judgment cannot be overemphasized. This is accomplished by statute in some states, including California. When a lender approves the short sale of a one- to four-unit residential property, the law prohibits the lender from seeking a deficiency judgment. The prohibition applies to senior and subordinate lenders alike.

Otherwise, the lender's waiver is voluntary. To be effective, it must happen before closing the short sale. The waiver must be in writing, typically contained in the lender's approval letter and closing instructions, and often needs to be negotiated. Without it, close at your own risk or cancel the sale. The alternatives are foreclosure, which, in some states, extinguishes the liability, or bankruptcy to discharge the deficiency liability. Before deciding to close, or not, get qualified professional advice.

Foreclosure would not extinguish a secondary junior loan. Talk to a professional about two potential complications: (1) whether or not foreclosure in a particular state extinguishes the debt and, (2) if there is a junior loan or lien, whether it could be settled or forgiven in separate negotiations. If all else fails, open deficiencies might be discharged in bankruptcy; consult qualified legal counsel.

The objective—debt forgiveness—can lead also to tax liability, which is covered elsewhere in this book. Exemptions might be available. Consult a professional tax advisor.

Considerations

When advising my clients, I hear several common themes. Significant personal reasons compel homeowners to stay with the property and modify the loan: family, friends, neighborhood, schools, sweat equity, pride of ownership, prospect of regaining lost equity, sentimental and emotional attachments, affordability of a modification, expense of moving and renting, deficiency liability and tax, credit record, a sense of responsibility, and similar considerations.

Others want out. The loan is unaffordable and the lender won't cooperate. The value has declined, equity is long gone, and the lender won't participate by reducing principal. Frustration has led to despair. They want a fresh start, even with damaged credit and spent resources. Knowing that a short sale harms credit much less than a foreclosure, they hope to reenter the market near the bottom, rather than carrying the burden of a house purchased near the top.

Whether you stay or leave, try to set aside emotions and make an objective evaluation of your current circumstances and your short- and long-range goals. You have a choice among modification, short sale, strategic default, or doing nothing. Modification brings your loan current and gives housing affordability, even if you expect to move in a few years and still face a short sale then.

A short sale now might offer several advantages. Especially after declining a modification, some lenders and HAFA pay incentives for selling rather than proceeding to foreclosure. While awaiting a short sale—or modification—the foreclosure process might continue, but the actual foreclosure sale usually can be postponed, though not until shortly before the auction. Most already delinquent borrowers do not resume loan payments, and, after starting foreclosure, many lenders accept nothing less than the entire amount due.

Keep in mind that you are selling your property and must endure a lockbox, showings, appointments, finding a professional real estate agent, listing, selling, and qualifying for the short payoff. Also, reorient your attitude regarding price. A short sale means that you have no equity, so a higher or lower price doesn't affect you. Find a price that satisfies your lender and try to get over your loss and what the market has done to the value of your property. A few prefer foreclosure despite the stress and credit impact.

Most lenders do not consider a modification and a short sale simultaneously, though HAFA no longer prohibits it. Personal financial documentation for a modification usually covers what's required for a short sale, making a switch from modification to short sale easier than vice versa. If you can't decide, start with a modification and convert to a short sale. Find a real estate broker with short sale and HAFA experience and ask your agent for guidance.

Timing is important because the debt forgiveness tax exemption for purchase loans secured by a borrower's principal residence (refer to the section on canceled debt in chapter 15) expired at the end of 2013. Uncertainty about further extension by Congress has slowed short-sale activity. Talk with a qualified tax professional about the exemption, whether it will be extended, and how it might affect the decision to sell. Also, ask whether the insolvency exemption would substitute. And then, include your real estate agent in the strategy for closing accordingly.

Home Affordable Foreclosure Alternatives[2]

The HAFA program consists of guidelines and financial incentives for loan servicers (lenders) and borrowers to encourage a short sale or a deed in lieu to avoid foreclosure. Both alternatives reduce the need for potentially lengthy and expensive foreclosure proceedings while preserving the condition and value of the property. The program began on April 5, 2010.

Significant changes occurred effective June 1, 2012, consistent with expansion and extension of HAMP and other Making Home Affordable programs. HAFA now includes one- to four-unit residential rental properties (which may be vacant), allows relocation assistance for tenants as well as homeowners, and increases the permissible payment to a subordinate mortgage holder to $8,500 from $6,000. Subject to lender discretion, HAFA no longer subjects borrowers to maximum income limits, though financial hardship still must be claimed.

Deed in Lieu of Foreclosure

Deed in lieu of foreclosure, euphemistically referred to as "handing over the keys," is shortened to "deed in lieu" or simply "DIL" for convenience. Lenders accept a deed in lieu of foreclosure and take the title to the property subject to other liens and claims by subordinate lenders, the IRS, the local tax assessor, and other creditors. Most prefer foreclosure, which extinguishes all such claims. Otherwise, both HAFA and lenders expect a borrower to clear the title of such encumbrances before the transfer.

Though only a remote possibility, be aware that HAFA theoretically allows lenders to accept a deed in lieu, and then lease back or sell back the property to the defaulting owner.

Summary

A short sale means selling a property at a price that does not fully pay the mortgage. It is an important alternative to foreclosure or modification. The federal HAFA program encourages lenders to cooperate by offering uniform guidelines and incentives, similar to HAMP.

Other Making Home Affordable Programs

Learning Points:

- Other mortgage relief programs that relate to HAMP.
- Programs for second mortgages, principal reduction, and unemployed borrowers.
- Program to allow nondelinquent homeowners to refinance underwater mortgages.

HAMP principles serve increasingly as an industry standard. Though beyond the scope of this book, several other opportunities start from the HAMP eligibility criteria or relate so closely to the subject of distressed mortgages as to warrant a brief mention. Specifically for short sales, refer to the preceding chapter and to the author's book *The ABA Consumer Guide to Short Sales*.

Second Lien Modification Program

Many borrowers who modify a senior mortgage also have a junior mortgage (second lien). Sometimes the second loan helped to purchase the property and reduce the buyer's down payment. Otherwise, the owner "withdrew" equity through a lump-sum loan or revolving line of credit. Delinquency on the junior mortgage usually accompanies default on the senior loan.

To address this problem and coordinate a solution with HAMP, the U.S. Department of Treasury introduced the Second Lien Modification Program (2MP). This option for the junior loan follows permanent HAMP modification of the senior loan. When the servicer of the second lien is a 2MP participant, that servicer must offer either to modify the borrower's second lien or to extinguish it in exchange for a lump-sum payment from the U.S. Treasury. The 2MP offer relies on the financial information provided by the borrower for the HAMP modification and requires no additional evaluation by the second-lien servicer.

The process should occur automatically and transparently according to a predefined protocol. The senior lender reports the modification and borrower's qualifications to a nationwide data repository. In turn, the repository notifies the junior lender. This transfer of information usually takes place internally when the first and second lenders are the same.

If the junior lender participates in Making Home Affordable (MHA), 2MP obliges it to modify the second loan, with or without principal reduction, or to extinguish the loan altogether. Junior lenders that don't participate in MHA, generally, may offer similar loan relief, though without the same MHA incentives.

2MP modification first adds past-due interest and allowable expenses to the loan balance. Then, it reduces the interest rate to 1 percent for loans requiring monthly payments of principal and interest (amortizing) or reduces the interest rate to 2 percent for loans with interest-only payments. Next, the remaining loan term is extended to match the modified term of the senior loan.

Finally, if the senior lender deferred principal through forbearance or forgave principal by permanently reducing the loan balance, the junior lender must defer or forgive the same portion of the second loan over the same period of time. As with HAMP, a trial period precedes permanent modification.

Borrowers, servicers, and investors receive incentives for successful modifications. For full or partial loan extinguishment, investors may receive roughly 20–40 percent reimbursement, or less for seriously delinquent loans.

Home Affordable Refinance Program

The Home Affordable Refinance Program (HARP) applies only to loans owned or guaranteed by Fannie Mae[1] or Freddie Mac[2] and secured by the borrower's primary residence consisting of one to four units. It is intended for nondelinquent "underwater" borrowers whose home values have dropped below their mortgage balances. Unlike a modification, the new loan replaces the existing loan with all the qualifying, closing, and documentation requirements of a conventional loan.

Like a conventional refinance, a new loan replaces the old loan. However, the new loan amount, based on a lower property value, is less than the old loan. It is a "short refinance," and the old lender must accept less than the remaining loan balance. Here, the loan is owned or guaranteed by a government-sponsored enterprise, which apparently takes the hit. The borrower must meet income and credit qualifications, and the loan to be refinanced must be current with no more than one 30-day late payment during the preceding 12 months and none during the last six months.

The program enables homeowners without financial hardship to benefit from lower mortgage interest rates despite significant declines in property values. The loan to be refinanced must be greater than 80 percent but not more than 125 percent of the home's current market value. The objective is a more affordable mortgage, and "cash-out" is not allowed.

Principal Reduction Alternative[3]

Hypothetically, this might solve the residential mortgage and real estate crisis. However, lenders have decided, for all but the most egregious loans, that forgiving principal for a few might upset the many underwater homeowners who continue to make timely payments.

Briefly, the program alters the standard HAMP modification waterfall. If the eligible loan principal balance exceeds 115 percent of the current property value, then servicers must evaluate modification using the Alternative Modification Waterfall, which adds a step after Step 1. The step reduces the capitalized principal balance to 115 percent of the current property value before applying the remaining Standard Modification Waterfall steps. The effect for such loans is to evaluate them twice; once for the full capitalized principal balance, and once for the reduced principal balance.

Any principal reduction begins with forbearance of the amount. The lender then forgives one-third at the end of each of the first three years, so long as the borrower remains current on payments. The alternative calculation is required; using it is optional. Keep in mind that the lender will report principal reduction as income during each of the years when debt was forgiven.

> **NOTE** Mortgages insured by the Federal Housing Administration (FHA) are eligible for modifications under circumstances slightly different from the HAMP program. If the loan is FHA insured, contact the lender for details.

The Principal Reduction Alternative (PRA) depends entirely on the investor's discretion and largesse. Thus, I rarely see it. One exception includes servicers obliged under the U.S. Department of Justice's $26 billion global settlement for mortgage abuses by the five largest lenders. The other involves defective loans usually assumed in bulk by a solvent servicer from an insolvent one at a deep discount or guaranteed return. It occurs infrequently even after several years of jawboning.

Unemployment Program

This variation on HAMP provides temporary mortgage relief for homeowners who lose their jobs. It directly addresses the financial hardship imposed by unemployment; the homeowner must be eligible for unemployment benefits and actually collecting them on the Unemployment Program (UP) effective date. Mortgages secured by rental properties are not eligible.

Also referred to as "unemployment forbearance," relief consists of reduced or suspended monthly payments through forbearance by the lender. Such forbearance continues for a minimum of 12 months, or longer if the servicer and investor allow, but only until reemployment.

If you lose your job, you may be eligible for mortgage relief. Contact your lender as soon as you apply for unemployment insurance.

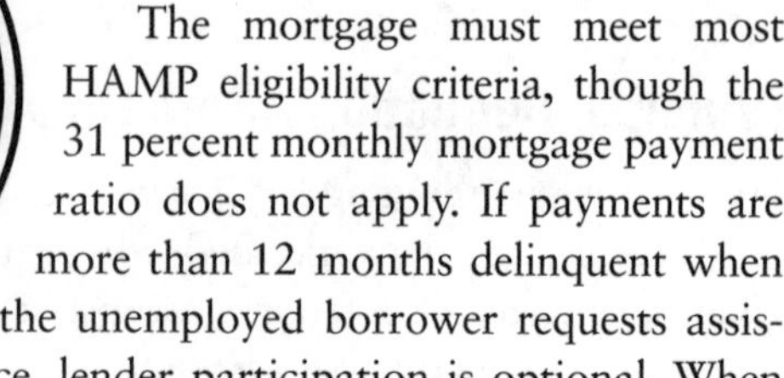

The mortgage must meet most HAMP eligibility criteria, though the 31 percent monthly mortgage payment ratio does not apply. If payments are more than 12 months delinquent when the unemployed borrower requests assistance, lender participation is optional. When assistance ends, the servicer evaluates the borrower for a HAMP modification based on income from new employment. If unemployment continues, the evaluation excludes benefit payments, and the lender must consider the borrower for Home Affordable Foreclosure Alternatives and for proprietary foreclosure alternatives.

The HAMP UP relieves unemployed homeowners from the fear of losing their homes to foreclosure while finding new employment. Lenders may not begin or continue foreclosure during the forbearance period. UP then offers an opportunity to arrange a permanent solution based on reemployment income. Be proactive with the lender. Make contact soon after applying for unemployment insurance and before missing several payments. Ask the lender whether it participates and what you must provide. This can contribute some stability to an otherwise unpredictable time.

FHA-HAMP

The FHA implemented a program during the summer of 2009 to modify FHA-insured mortgages in a manner complementary to HAMP. Similar to HAMP, the program calculates an affordable monthly mortgage payment equal to 31 percent of the borrower's monthly gross income. It requires the borrower to complete a trial period before permanently modifying the loan.

The loan servicer must be FHA approved. It files a partial claim on the insured loan, and can recover up to 12 months of past-due payments, pre-foreclosure costs, and principal reduction in connection with the modification. This reimbursement suggests that FHA-insured loans might have a better chance than conventional loans for a principal reduction.

Unlike HAMP, which considers loans when in imminent risk of default, FHA's version requires that at least one, but not more than 12, payment must be past due. If the borrower had available funds to make mortgage and other debt payments without hardship, FHA considers the default to be intentional and the borrower to be ineligible. In effect, this parallels HAMP hardship requirements but is stated differently.

If the FHA-insured mortgage loan meets standard HAMP eligibility criteria, the borrower is eligible for pay-for-performance compensation and the servicer is eligible for pay-for-success compensation from the U.S. Treasury.[4]

If the loan is FHA insured and the first payment was due more than a year ago, contact the lender (servicer) for details.

FHA Short Refinance Option

Intended for nondelinquent underwater borrowers whose home values have dropped below their mortgage balances, this short refinance consists of a new FHA-insured loan with an amount that is less than the old loan amount. The old lender accepts a "short payoff" similar to a short sale and forgives the difference.

However, unlike a short sale, the loan to be paid must be current to qualify. So, the old lender voluntarily gives up a performing asset and converts it to a written-down loss—counterintuitive for servicers and mortgage investors alike. This optional program will need better incentives than offered so far to gain much traction.

Briefly, loan payments must be current and the borrower must meet FHA income and credit qualifications. This is not an alternative for someone seeking a modification, which presumes financial hardship and delinquency or imminent risk of default. For the same reasons, the short refinance option won't compete with short sales.

FHA's new loan cannot exceed 97.75 percent of current property value, and the old lender must forgive at least 10 percent (accept no more than 90 percent) of the remaining balance to be paid by the refinancing. This is the least painful scenario for the current lender and means a property value slightly less than 109 percent of the current loan balance. More than 10 percent underwater, then the lender must make up the difference.

Next, the FHA refinance option prohibits the new senior loan plus an existing second loan from exceeding 115 percent of current market value. If the junior loan or line of credit exceeds 17.25 percent of current value, the junior lender must forgive the difference.

Such write-downs occur daily in short sales, serious defaults, and foreclosures, but these loans are current. What's the motivation? To write off a performing asset, despite the noble gesture and admission of complicity, sounds to a bank like fingernails on a blackboard. The original FHA press release estimated help for four million homeowners. Despite such optimism, the real value of the program seems limited.

Summary

Several federal programs related to HAMP can provide relief to both delinquent and current homeowners. There are similar modification programs for junior mortgages and for mortgages insured by FHA and other federal agencies. There are refinance programs for underwater owners not experiencing financial hardship.

As mentioned earlier in this book, Fannie Mae and Freddie Mac do not participate in HAMP but offer equivalent programs. Though not covered in this book, most features are identical, some are very similar, and only a few are significantly different from HAMP.

Conclusion

What appeared in the beginning to be a catastrophe actually turned out to be worse. From various data in 2009, Making Home Affordable estimated three to four million "at-risk homeowners" who might benefit from mortgage payment relief. As statistics in the introduction suggest, the current problem touches many, many more in altogether unanticipated ways. That we have grown accustomed and jaded to the calamity does not diminish its magnitude.

Borrower Initiative: The Problem

The bigger problem—the monster under the bed—is borrowers whose rates have not exploded, principal balances have not increased, payments have not gone delinquent, but whose lives are upside down or whose mortgages are underwater.

The early estimates drew from borrowers' information that lenders already knew: loan applications, payment adjustments, interest-rate projections, credit histories, voluntary borrower communications, and computer modeling based on statistical generalizations. They do not—cannot—take into account changes in financial, employment, family, and other personal and fluid circumstances of people's lives.

HAMP eligibility is not limited to the kinds of events that lenders can predict. Hardship need not be limited to the effects of lousy loans or the extremes of delinquency. If you experience financial hardship, you meet other criteria reviewed earlier in this book, and your lender participates, your lender must reduce your monthly mortgage payment.

Hardship comes in many forms: reduced or lost income, changed household financial circumstances, increased monthly expenses including mortgage payments, insufficient cash reserves, excessive monthly credit payments, or other events that disrupt your ability to make mortgage payments. My point is that too many people give up before starting or give in too soon. Don't be a casualty of lender overwhelm or a victim of your own fear.

Borrower Initiative: The Solution

The choice: Do nothing (yes, that's a *choice*). Wait, let your stress rise and your resources dwindle, and hope that the lender will find you and take care of you. Or take the most responsible action available under the circumstances and get in the game. Be a spectator or a player. For spectators, here's what the game looks like. For players, here are the actions to take.

Prepare mentally and emotionally. Tell somebody you trust about the problem. Don't leave it locked up in your head. Except in extreme cases, where payments have not been made for many months, you have plenty of time. Lenders must follow a legally defined procedure to foreclose. Unless you have buried your head deeply in the sand, you will not arrive home one day and find your furniture in the front yard. Neither are your personal assets likely to be in jeopardy.

Finally, despite the old adage that "misery loves company," we seem to suffer alone. Take comfort. Millions of individuals and families share your predicament. "So what?" you ask. Lenders are overwhelmed and are neither interested nor equipped to pick you out of the crowd for special treatment, bad or good. Drop the shame, the fear, and false hope long enough to *do something*.

Prepare your financial information. You now know about the monthly mortgage payment ratio and how to calculate it by using the resources in this book. Run the numbers before calling your lender. Many will take your financial information by phone. If not ready, you might tend to estimate and paint an inaccurate picture. If you are ready, though, you might speed up the process. Eventually, all numbers will need to be documented anyway, so gather them together for review before the call.

Prepare to talk with your lender. Briefly, review your hardship, gather your current income and expense information, compare it to your pre-hardship situation, and understand the HAMP guidelines. Review your calculations. Know what you want and what you qualify for and then get ready to insist on it.

Find out if your lender participates. Go to MakingHomeAffordable.gov. Scroll over Get Started, and click on Contact Your Mortgage Company in the drop-down box. Use the phone number shown. Otherwise, call the customer service number on your monthly statement, or visit your lender's website.

Call your lender. Have available the loan or account number, your Social Security number, and the property address. Tell them you want to modify your mortgage. Ask whether the servicer and investor participate in HAMP and how to submit an initial package. Refer to 12 Questions to Ask Your Lender, page 117. They might want details about your situation, so be prepared before calling.

Tell them what you want to tell them and that you don't want to answer questions if you're unprepared. Ask for what you want. Do not take no for an answer. If necessary, call again, then again, until you talk to someone who "gets it." For nonparticipating lenders, ask about non-HAMP proprietary programs.

Cooperate. Try to put emotions (and logic) aside. Find out how to submit information, whether to use the lender's forms and where to find them, what processes your proposal will go through, and how long it will take.

Expect to hear unfamiliar terms, so prepare to ask for explanations. Also, expect circular and redundant requests for more or updated information. Though guidelines accept periodic items like pay stubs and bank statements up to 90 days old, some lenders say 60 days or even 30 days. Whatever the lender's preference, expect to be asked for recent versions of such items, so routinely resubmit copies monthly.

Final Words

This is the user's manual for homeowners, landlords, and their professional advisors to get the most out of the federal Home Affordable Modification Program. If your lender subscribes to the program (or not), then your chances to modify your mortgage have improved as a result of reading this book and following its guidance.

If you have not yet missed a payment, but the probability is unmistakable, then do not wait for the inevitable. Do not spend all of your savings or draw down your retirement funds or borrow from family or friends to make ends meet. If you want to stay in your home and can afford a portion of your mortgage payment, then inform your lender and get busy on a modification proposal. You hold that power in your hands.

Do not wait for your lender to contact you. When your lender tells you, "we're here to help," don't use that as an excuse to neglect your responsibility. If you need help, embolden yourself and insist on it. My advice for everyone trying to stay ahead of a mortgage and mounting obligations: overcome the fear and sense of isolation long enough to take action.

Wishing you peace of mind and a bright future.

Eligibility Comparison

Criteria	Tier 1	Tier 2
Loan origination	Senior mortgage originated on or before January 1, 2009	Same
Loan previously modified	Not modified previously under HAMP	Not modified previously under Tier 2
Delinquency	Payments are delinquent (60 days) or default is reasonably foreseeable	Payments are delinquent or, for owner-occupied properties only, default is reasonably foreseeable
Property	Property is "single family" (1–4 units)	Same
Occupancy	Principal residence	Principal residence or rental
Condition	Not condemned, may be vacant	Same
Hardship	Financial hardship, insufficient liquid assets	Same
Payments	Pre-modification PITIA greater than 31% gross income	Post-modification PITIA 25–42% gross income, payment reduced 10% or more

(continued)

Criteria	Tier 1	Tier 2
Escrow account	Required for property taxes and insurance	Same
Loan limits	1 unit $729,750 2 units $934,200 3 units $1,129,250 4 units $1,403,400	Same
Program expiration	Request by December 31, 2015; complete by September 30, 2016	Same
Servicer participation	"Servicer Participation Agreement" subject to mortgage investor limitations	Same

Modification Waterfall with Principal Reduction Alternative (PRA)

		Tier 1	Tier 2
Step 1	Loan Amount	Capitalize remaining principal, delinquent interest, and allowable lender costs	Same
Step 1 A	*Reduce Principal*	*Reduce loan amount to 115% of current market value*	*Same*
Step 2	Interest Rate	Reduce to as low as 2%	Adjust to current conforming 30-year fixed rate plus risk adjustment (0% as of May 2014)
Step 3	Extend Loan Term	Amortize up to 480 months	Change to 480 months
Step 4	Forbearance	Reduce interest-bearing principal	Reduce interest-bearing principal to 115% of current market value

Modification Worksheet Tier 1

Modification Waterfall

Step 1: Capitalize: Determine the adjusted unpaid principal balance. ______________

Current Unpaid Principal Balance (UPB) ______________

Plus: Accrued Interest + ______________

Exclude: Past Due Principal (included in UPB) ______________

Plus: Escrow and Servicing Advances + ______________

Exclude: Late & Administrative Fees ______________

Estimated Capitalized Principal Balance = ______________

Step 1a: Alternative: Principal Reduction Alternative (PRA)

Estimated Capitalized Principal Balance ______________

Minus: Property Value × 115% – ______________

If Less Than or Equal to Zero, Skip This Step = ______________

If Greater Than Zero, Then Use	
Property Value × 115%	________
Principal Reduction Alternative (PRA) Balance	= ________

Step 2: Reduce the Interest Rate: Interest rate floor is 2.000%.

Gross Income	________
Target Monthly Mortgage Payment Ratio	× 31% ________
Target Monthly Mortgage Payment	= ________
Minus: Property Tax	– ________
Minus: Hazard Insurance	– ________
Minus: Flood Insurance	– ________
Less: Homeowner Association Fee	– ________
Target Monthly Principal & Interest	= ________
Remaining Term to Maturity	________ months
Estimated Capitalized Principal Balance (Step 1)	________
Over the remaining term to Maturity	________ months
Interest Rate to Reach Target Monthly Principal & Interest	________ %
***If less than 2.00%,** then continue to Step 3.*	________

***PRA Balance** (Step 1a)*	
Interest Rate to Reach Target Monthly Principal & Interest	________ %
rounded up to nearest 0.125%	________
***If less than 2.00%,** then continue to Step 3.*	

***If greater than 2.00%,** round up to nearest 0.125%; and*	
Fixed for first five years,	+/– ________ %
Recalculate Target Monthly Principal & Interest	
Followed by 1% annual increases, Year 6 + 1%	________ %
Year 7 + 1%	________ %
Year 8 + 1%	________ %
Year 9 + 1%	________ %
Until rate reaches the Interest Rate Cap,*	
then fixed for the remaining loan term.	________ %

***Interest Rate Cap means Freddie Mac Weekly**

Primary Mortgage Market Survey (PMMS) Rate ____________

Rounded up/down to the nearest 0.125% ____________ %

Adjusted to the Modification date. ____________ %

Step 3: Extend the Term and Re-amortize

Target Monthly Principal & Interest ____________

Interest Rate to Reach Target Payment (Step 2) 2.000% ____________

Estimated Capitalized Principal Balance (Step 1) ____________

Extended Term to Reach Target Payment ____________ months

If more than 480 months, then go to Step 4. ____________

Balloon payment is required at maturity. ____________

PRA Balance (Step 1a)

Extended Term to Reach Target Payment ____________ months

If more than 480 months, then go to Step 4.

Balloon payment is required at maturity.

If less than 480 months, STOP.

Step 4: Principal Forbearance: A portion of principal with no interest or monthly payment due

Target Monthly Principal & Interest ____________

Interest Rate to Reach Target Payment (Step 2) 2.000% ____________

Extended Term to Reach Target Payment (Step 3) 480 months ____________

Interest-Bearing Principal calculated on these terms ____________

Estimated Capitalized Principal Balance (Step 1)

Interest-Bearing Principal to Reach Target Payment ____________

Remainder: Non-Interest-Bearing Principal Forbearance = ____________

Unless forgiven under PRA, this amount will be due and payable upon the earliest of (a) transfer of the property, (b) payoff of the interest bearing unpaid principal balance, or (c) maturity of the mortgage loan.

Summary: Modified Loan Terms

STEP 1: Estimated Capitalized Principal Balance ____________

STEP 1a: Principal Reduction Alternative Balance ____________

STEP 2: Interest Rate to Reach Target Payment ____________ %

STEP 3: Extended Term to Reach Target Payment ____________ months

STEP 4: Principal Forbearance to Reach Target Payment	__________
STEP 4: Interest-Bearing Principal Amount	__________
MODIFIED PAYMENT:	
Target Monthly Principal & Interest	__________
Plus: Escrow (impound) Expenses	+ __________
Target Monthly Mortgage Payment	= __________
(Greater than 31% × gross income)	

Modification Worksheet Tier 2

Modification Waterfall

Step 1: Capitalize: Determine the adjusted unpaid principal balance.

Current Unpaid Principal Balance (UPB)	________
Plus: Accrued Interest	+ ________
Exclude: Past Due Principal (included in UPB)	________
Plus: Escrow and Servicing Advances	+ ________
Exclude: Late & Administrative Fees	________
Estimated Capitalized Principal Balance	= ________

Step 2: Adjust the Interest Rate

Current PMMS Rate	________ %
Found at http://www.freddiemac.com/ lower left.	
Round up or down to nearest 0.125%	________ %
Plus: Risk Adjustment (as of 04/22/2014)	+ 0.000% ________
Use this Interest Rate	= ________

Step 3: Extend the Term

Extended the Amortization Term 480 months

Step 4: Principal Forbearance: A portion of principal with no interest or monthly payment due

Estimated Capitalized Principal Balance ______________(A)

Estimated Property Value ______________

Property Value × 115% ______________*(B)*

If (A) is Greater Than (B), Then

Interest Bearing Principal equals (B), and ______________

Non-Interest Bearing Principal equals (A) − (B) ______________

If (A) is Less Than (B), Then

Interest Bearing Principal equals (A), and ______________

Non-Interest Bearing Principal equals *- 0 -* ______________

Calculate Payment

Interest Bearing Principal (Step 4) ______________

Interest Rate (Step 2) ______________ %

Amortization Term (Step 3) 480 months

Calculate Target Monthly Principal & Interest ______________

Principal Forbearance

Non-Interest-Bearing Principal (Step 4) ______________

Unless forgiven under PRA, this amount will be due and payable upon the earliest of (a) transfer of the property, (b) payoff of the interest bearing unpaid principal balance, or (c) maturity of the mortgage loan.

Summary: Modified Loan Terms

STEP 1: Estimated Capitalized Principal Balance ______________

STEP 2: Interest Rate PMMS rounded plus 0.000% ______________ %

STEP 3: Extended Term 480 months

STEP 4: Interest Bearing Principal ______________

MODIFIED PAYMENT:

Monthly Principal & Interest ______________

Plus: Monthly Escrow + ______________

Equals: Monthly Mortgage Payment = ______________

Divided by: Gross Monthly Income / ______________

Equals: Monthly Mortgage Payment Ratio = ______________

Ratio must equal 25–42%

Income and Expense

Date				
Borrower				
Lender				
Loan #				
Monthly Income	**Gross**	**Less**	**Net**	
Income/Salary from all Sources				
Investment Income				
Other:				
Gross Monthly Income				**A**
Minus: Deductions				B
Net Monthly Income		A – B =		C
Monthly Expenses	**Itemized**	**Categorized**	**Totals**	
Food				
Groceries				
Dining out				
Other:				

(continued)

(continued)

Monthly Expenses	Itemized	Categorized	Totals	
Total Food				D
Utilities				
Laundry				
Gas/electricity				
Water				
Garbage				
Phone (inc. long distance)				
Cell phone				
Internet access				
TV				
Other:				
Total Utilities				E
Auto Transportation				
Public transit				
Car insurance				
Maintenance				
Parking				
Gas				
Other:				
Total Auto Transportation				F
Insurance				
Health/Medical				
Disability				
Life				
Dental				
Other Real Estate				
Total Insurance				G
Personal Care				
Medical & Dental (uninsured)				
Prescriptions (uninsured)				
Toiletries & Cosmetics				
Services (haircut, etc.)				
Clothing new				
Clothing care				
Health club				
Other:				
Total Personal Care				H
Miscellaneous				

Tuition				
Subscriptions				
Charity				
Gifts				
Entertainment				
Other:				
Total Miscellaneous				I
Household Expenses		**D + E + F + G + H + I =**		**J**
Credit				
Credit Cards				
Car Loan / Lease				
Equity Loan / Line this property				
Mortgages other property				
Personal Loan / Line				
Education Loans				
Other				
Total Credit				K
Monthly Expenses		**J + K =**		**L**
Subject Property				
Principal and/or Interest				
Property Tax				
Property Insurance				
HOA				
Total Housing				M
Total Expenses		**L + M =**		**N**
Surplus/(Deficit)				
before Modification		**C − N =**		
After Modification				
Modified Principal & Interest				
Property Tax				
Property Insurance				
HOA				
Total Housing				O
Total Expenses after modification		**L + O =**		**P**
Surplus				
after Modification		**C − P =**		

Profit and Loss

Simple record for small business owners and sole proprietors. Detail may be required. Use your own record-keeping format when possible.

Business Name			
Year			
Borrower			
Lender			
Loan #			
	Income	**Expense**	**Profit (Loss)**
January 1–31			
February 1–28			
March 1–31			
April 1–30			
May 1–31			
June 1–30			

(continued)

(continued)

	Income	Expense	Profit (Loss)
July 1–31			
August 1–31			
September 1–30			
October 1–31			
November 1–30			
December 1–31			
TOTALS			
Signature		Date	
Signature		Date	

Financial Statement

Following is a comprehensive financial statement of income, expenses, and liquid monetary assets, which includes all line items mentioned in the HAMP guidelines, plus a few for clarification and completeness.

Not all line items apply to everyone. Skip those that do not apply to you. Use only the "Combined" column to calculate simple ratios and to track income and expenses provided to your servicer.

MONTHLY INCOME	Borrower 1	Borrower 2	Combined
Employment Income			
Salary & Wages			
Regular Overtime, Bonus & Allowance			
Commission			
Tips & Other Personal Service			
Equals: Gross Employment Income			
Less: Withholdings & Deductions			
Net Employment Income			

continued

MONTHLY INCOME	Borrower 1	Borrower 2	Combined
Self-Employment Income			
Net Profit (Loss) from Active Participation			
Sole Proprietor (Schedule C, IRS form 1040)			
Corporation (principal shareholder)			
Partner or JV (Schedule K-1, IRS form 1065)			
Shareholder (Schedule K-1, IRS form 1120s)			
Other:			
Net Self-Employment Income			
Non-Employment Income			
Investments			
Interest, Dividends, Passive K-1			
Retirement Account Distribution			
Net Rental Income (positive)			
Other:			
Entitlements			
Pension, Profit Sharing (distribution)			
Annuities, Insurance, Royalties (received)			
Social Security benefits			
Leave of absence, disability, death benefits			
Public Assistance			
Other:			
Other			
Alimony & Child Support (received)			
Beneficiary (Schedule K-1, IRS form 1041)			
Other:			
Total Non-Employment Income			
Total Income			

MONTHLY EXPENSES & OBLIGATIONS	Outstanding Balance	Monthly Payment
Expense Payments This Property		
Primary Expenses		
1st Mortgage Principal & Interest ^ *		
Property Tax		
Hazard Insurance		
Flood Insurance		
Homeowner Assoc. Fees		
Delinquent & Escrow Shortage Capitalization		
Equals: Primary Property Liability & Expense		
Secondary Expenses		
2nd Mortgage Principal & Interest ^ **		
Other Liens (e.g. tax, mechanics)		
Special Assessments, Bonds		
Mortgage Insurance		
Equals: Other Property Liability & Expense		
Total Property Liability & Expense		
Credit Payments		
Fixed-Term (Installment) Debt		
Vehicle Loan(s)		
Vehicle Lease Payment(s)		
Other (10+ payments remain)		
Open-End Debt		
Open-End (line of credit) Accounts		
Revolving (credit card) Accounts		
Personal Debt:		
Total Credit Expense		
Other Expenses		
Net Rental Loss for Investment Real Estate ^		
Alimony & Child Support (10+ mos remain)		
Net Property Expense for Second Home ^		
Other:		
Allowance for Living Expenses		
Total Other Expenses		
Monthly Gross Expenses & Obligations		

^ Mortgage Balance. * Maximum Scheduled Payment. ** May Apply to Equity Line of Credit.

CASH RESERVE BALANCES	Borrower 1	Borrower 2	Combined
Liquid Assets			
Checking & Savings Accounts			
Certificates of Deposit (all maturities)			
Stocks & Bonds			
Mutual & Money Market Funds			
Other:			
Total Liquid Assets			
Nonliquid Assets			
Retirement: Other-Administered (employer)			
Retirement: Self-Admin (IRA, 401k, etc.)			
Deferred Compensation			
College Funds			
Other Restricted Funds			
Other:			
Total Non-Liquid Assets			

Request for Mortgage Assistance (RMA)

The following seven-page form is for information and reference only. An interactive form to be completed for submission to a servicer in the initial package may be found at https://www.hmpadmin.com/portal/programs/docs/hamp_borrower/rma_english.pdf.

Note: Making Home Affordable, program names, logos and designs are trademarks belonging to the U.S. Department of the Treasury.

Making Home Affordable Program
Request For Mortgage Assistance (RMA)

If you are experiencing a financial hardship and need help, you must complete and submit this form along with other required documentation to be considered for foreclosure prevention options under the Making Home Affordable (MHA) Program. You must provide information about yourself and your intentions to either keep or transition out of your property; a description of the hardship that prevents you from paying your mortgage(s); information about **all** of your income, expenses and financial assets; whether you have declared bankruptcy; and information about the mortgage(s) on your principal residence and other single family real estate that you own. Finally, you will need to return to your loan servicer (1) this completed, signed and dated Request for Mortgage Assistance (RMA); and (2) completed and signed IRS Form 4506-T or 4506T-EZ; and (3) all required income documentation identified in Section 4.

When you sign and date this form, you will make important certifications, representations and agreements, including certifying that all of the information in this RMA is accurate and truthful.

SECTION 1: BORROWER INFORMATION

BORROWER		CO-BORROWER	
BORROWER'S NAME		CO-BORROWER'S NAME	
SOCIAL SECURITY NUMBER	DATE OF BIRTH (MM/DD/YY)	SOCIAL SECURITY NUMBER	DATE OF BIRTH (MM/DD/YY)
HOME PHONE NUMBER WITH AREA CODE		HOME PHONE NUMBER WITH AREA CODE	
CELL OR WORK NUMBER WITH AREA CODE		CELL OR WORK NUMBER WITH AREA CODE	
MAILING ADDRESS		MAILING ADDRESS (IF SAME AS BORROWER, WRITE "SAME")	
EMAIL ADDRESS		EMAIL ADDRESS	

Has any borrower filed for bankruptcy? ☐ Chapter 7 ☐ Chapter 13

Filing Date: __________ Bankruptcy case number: __________

Has your bankruptcy been discharged? ☐ Yes ☐ No

Is any borrower a servicemember? ☐ Yes ☐ No

Have you recently been deployed away from your principal residence or recently received a permanent change of station order? ☐ Yes ☐ No

How many single family properties other than your principal residence do you and/or any co-borrower(s) own individually, jointly, or with others? ______

Has the mortgage on your principal residence ever had a Home Affordable Modification Program (HAMP) trial period plan or permanent modification? ☐ Yes ☐ No

Has the mortgage on any other property that you or any co-borrower own had a permanent HAMP modification? ☐ Yes ☐ No If "Yes", how many? ______

Are you or any co-borrower currently in or being considered for a HAMP trial period plan on a property other than your principal residence? ☐ Yes ☐ No

SECTION 2: HARDSHIP AFFIDAVIT

I (We) am/are requesting review under MHA.
I am having difficulty making my monthly payment because of financial difficulties created by (check all that apply):

☐ My household income has been reduced. For example: reduced pay or hours, decline in business or self employment earnings, death, disability or divorce of a borrower or co-borrower.

☐ My expenses have increased. For example: monthly mortgage payment reset, high medical or health care costs, uninsured losses, increased utilities or property taxes.

☐ lI am unemployed and (a) I am receiving/will receive unemployment benefits or (b) my unemployment benefits ended less than 6 months ago.

☐ My monthly debt payments are excessive and I am overextended with my creditors. Debt includes credit cards, home equity or other debt.

☐ My cash reserves, including all liquid assets, are insufficient to maintain my current mortgage payment and cover basic living expenses at the same time.

Other:

Explanation (continue on a separate sheet of paper if necessary):

SECTION 3: PRINCIPAL RESIDENCE INFORMATION

(This section is required even if you are not seeking mortgage assistance on your principal residence)

I am requesting mortgage assistance with my principal residence ☐ **Yes** ☐ **No**

If "yes", I want to: ☐ **Keep the property** ☐ **Sell the property**

Property Address: ______ Loan I.D. Number: ______

Other mortgages or liens on the property? ☐ Yes ☐ No Lien Holder / Servicer Name: ______ Loan I.D. Number: ______

Do you have condominium or homeowner association (HOA) fees? ☐ Yes ☐ No If "Yes", Monthly Fee $______ Are fees paid current? ☐ Yes ☐ No

Name and address that fees are paid to: ______

Does your mortgage payment include taxes and Insurance? ☐ Yes ☐ No If "No", are the taxes and insurance paid current? ☐ Yes ☐ No

Annual Homeowner's Insurance $______

Is the property listed for sale? ☐ Yes ☐ No If "Yes", Listing Agent's Name: ______ Phone Number: ______

List date? ______ Have you received a purchase offer? ☐ Yes ☐ No Amount of Offer $ ______ Closing Date: ______

Complete this section ONLY if you are requesting mortgage assistance with a property that is not your principal residence.

Principal residence servicer name: ______ Principal residence servicer phone number: ______

Is the mortgage on your principal residence paid? ☐ Yes ☐ No If 'No", number of months your payment is past due (if known): ______

SECTION 4: COMBINED INCOME AND EXPENSE OF BORROWER AND CO-BORROWER

Monthly Household Income		**Monthly Household Expenses/Debt (*Principal Residence Expense Only)**		**Household Assets**	
Monthly Gross wages	$	First Mortgage Principal & Interest Payment*	$	Checking Account(s)	$
Overtime	$	Second Mortgage Principal & Interest Payment*	$	Checking Account(s)	$
Self employment Income	$	Homeowner's Insurance*	$	Savings / Money Market	$
Unemployment Income	$	Property Taxes*	$	CDs	$
Untaxed Social Security / SSD	$	HOA/Condo Fees*	$	Stocks / Bonds	$
Food Stamps/Welfare	$	Credit Cards/Installment debt (total min. payment)	$	Other Cash on Hand	$
Taxable Social Security or retirement income	$	Child Support / Alimony	$		
Child Support / Alimony**	$	Car Payments	$		
Tips, commissions, bonus and overtime	$	Mortgage Payments other properties****	$		
Gross Rents Received ***	$	Other	$	Value of all Real Estate except principal residence	$
Other	$			Other	$
Total (Gross income)	$	**Total Debt/Expenses**	$	**Total Assets**	$

**** Alimony, child support or separate maintenance income need not be disclosed if you do not choose to have it considered for repaying your mortgage debt.**

***** Include rental income received from all properties you own EXCEPT a property for which you are seeking mortgage assistance in Section 6.**

****** Include mortgage payments on all properties you own EXCEPT your principal residence and the property for which you are seeking mortgage assistance in Section 6.**

Required Income Documentation (Your servicer may request additional documentation to complete your evaluation for MHA)	
All Borrowers	☐ Include a signed IRS Form 4506-T or 4506T-EZ
☐ Do you earn a wage? Borrower Hire Date (MM/DD/YY) ________ Co-borrower Hire Date (MM/DD/YY)________	☐ For each borrower who is a salaried employee or hourly wage earner, provide the most recent pay stub(s) that reflects at least 30 days of year-to-date income.
☐ Are you self-employed?	☐ Provide your most recent signed and dated quarterly or year-to date profit and loss statement.
☐ Do you receive tips, commissions, bonuses, housing allowance or overtime?	☐ Describe the type of income, how frequently you receive the income and third party documentation describing the income (e.g., employment contracts or printouts documenting tip income).
☐ Do you receive social security, disability, death benefits, pension, public assistance or adoption assistance?	☐ Provide documentation showing the amount and frequency of the benefits, such as letters, exhibits, disability policy or benefits statement from the provider and receipt of payment (such as two most recent bank statements or deposit advices).
☐ Do you receive alimony, child support, or separation maintenance payments?	☐ Provide a copy of the divorce decree, separation agreement, or other written legal agreement filed with the court that states the amount of the payments and the period of time that you are entitled to receive them. AND ☐ Copies of your two most recent bank statements or deposit advices showing you have received payment. **Notice: Alimony, child support or separate maintenance income need not be disclosed if you do not choose to have it considered for repaying your mortgage debt.**
☐ Do you have income from rental properties that are not your principal residence?	☐ Provide your most recent Federal Tax return with all schedules, including Schedule E. ☐ If rental income is not reported on Schedule E, provide a copy of the current lease agreement with bank statements showing deposit of rent checks.

SECTION 5: OTHER PROPERTIES OWNED

(You must provide information about all properties that you or the co-borrower own, other than your principal residence and any property described in Section 6 below. Use additional sheets if necessary.)

Other Property #1

Property Address: ________________ Loan I.D. Number: ________

Servicer Name: ________________ Mortgage Balance $ ________ Current Value $ ________

Property is: ☐ Vacant ☐ Second or seasonal home ☐ Rented Gross Monthly Rent $ ________ Monthly mortgage payment* $ ________

Other Property #2

Property Address: ________________ Loan I.D. Number: ________

Servicer Name: ________________ Mortgage Balance $ ________ Current Value $ ________

Property is: ☐ Vacant ☐ Second or seasonal home ☐ Rented Gross Monthly Rent $ ________ Monthly mortgage payment* $ ________

Other Property #3

Property Address: ________________ Loan I.D. Number: ________

Servicer Name: ________________ Mortgage Balance $ ________ Current Value $ ________

Property is: ☐ Vacant ☐ Second or seasonal home ☐ Rented Gross Monthly Rent $ ________ Monthly mortgage payment* $ ________

*** The amount of the monthly payment made to your lender – including, if applicable, monthly principal, interest, real property taxes and insurance premiums..**

SECTION 6: OTHER PROPERTY FOR WHICH ASSISTANCE IS REQUESTED

(Complete this section **ONLY** if you are requesting mortgage assistance with a property that is not your principal residence.)

I am requesting mortgage assistance with a rental property. ☐ **Yes** ☐ **No**

I am requesting mortgage assistance with a second or seasonal home. ☐ **Yes** ☐ **No**

If "Yes" to either, I want to: ☐ **Keep the property** ☐ **Sell the property**

Property Address: ______________________ Loan I.D. Number: __________

Do you have a second mortgage on the property ☐ Yes ☐ No If "Yes", Servicer Name: __________ Loan I.D. Number: __________

Do you have condominium or homeowner association (HOA) fees? ☐ Yes ☐ No If "Yes", Monthly Fee $ ________ Are HOA fees paid current? ☐ Yes ☐ No

Name and address that fees are paid to: ______________________

Does your mortgage payment include taxes and insurance? ☐ Yes ☐ No If "No", are the taxes and insurance paid current? ☐ Yes ☐ No

Annual Homeowner's Insurance $ __________ Annual Property Taxes $ __________

If requesting assistance with a rental property, property is currently:
☐ Vacant and available for rent.
☐ Occupied without rent by your legal dependent, parent or grandparent as their principal residence.
☐ Occupied by a tenant as their principal residence.
☐ Other ______________________

If rental property is occupied by a tenant: Term of lease / occupancy ___/___/___ -- ___/___/___ Gross Monthly Rent $ __________
MM / DD / YYYY MM / DD / YYYY

If rental property is vacant, describe efforts to rent property: ______________________

If applicable, describe relationship of and duration of non-rent paying occupant of rental property: ______________________

Is the property for sale? ☐ Yes ☐ No If "Yes", Listing Agent's Name: __________ Phone Number: __________

List date? __________ Have you received a purchase offer? ☐ Yes ☐ No Amount of Offer $ __________ Closing Date: __________

RENTAL PROPERTY CERTIFICATION

(You must complete this certification if you are requesting a mortgage modification with respect to a rental property.)

☐ By checking this box and initialing below, I am requesting a mortgage modification under MHA with respect to the rental property described in this Section 6 and I hereby certify under penalty of perjury that each of the following statements is true and correct with respect to that property:

1. I intend to rent the property to a tenant or tenants for at least five years following the effective date of my mortgage modification. I understand that the servicer, the U.S. Department of the Treasury, or their respective agents may ask me to provide evidence of my intention to rent the property during such time. I further understand that such evidence must show that I used reasonable efforts to rent the property to a tenant or tenants on a year-round basis, if the property is or becomes vacant during such five-year period.

   Note: The term "reasonable efforts" includes, without limitation, advertising the property for rent in local newspapers, websites or other commonly used forms of written or electronic media, and/or engaging a real estate or other professional to assist in renting the property, in either case, at or below market rent.

2. The property is not my secondary residence and I do not intend to use the property as a secondary residence for at least five years following the effective date of my mortgage modification. I understand that if I do use the property as a secondary residence during such five-year period, my use of the property may be considered to be inconsistent with the certifications I have made herein.

   Note: The term "secondary residence" includes, without limitation, a second home, vacation home or other type of residence that I personally use or occupy on a part-time, seasonal or other basis.

3. I do not own more than five (5) single-family homes (i.e., one-to-four unit properties) (exclusive of my principal residence).

Notwithstanding the foregoing certifications, I may at any time sell the property, occupy it as my principal residence, or permit my legal dependent, parent or grandparent to occupy it as their principal residence with no rent charged or collected, none of which will be considered to be inconsistent with the certifications made herein.

This certification is effective on the earlier of the date listed below or the date the RMA is received by your servicer.

Initials: Borrower ______ **Co-borrower** ______

SECTION 7: DODD -FRANK CERTIFICATION

The following information is requested by the federal government in accordance with the Dodd-Frank Wall Street Reform and Consumer Protection Act (Pub. L. 111-203). **You are required to furnish this information.** The law provides that no person shall be eligible to begin receiving assistance from the Making Home Affordable Program, authorized under the Emergency Economic Stabilization Act of 2008 (12 U.S.C. 5201 et seq.), or any other mortgage assistance program authorized or funded by that Act, if such person, in connection with a mortgage or real estate transaction, has been convicted, within the last 10 years, of any one of the following: (A) felony larceny, theft, fraud, or forgery, (B) money laundering or (C) tax evasion.

I/we certify under penalty of perjury that I/we have not been convicted within the last 10 years of any one of the following in connection with a mortgage or real estate transaction:

(a) felony larceny, theft, fraud, or forgery,
(b) money laundering or
(c) tax evasion.

I/we understand that the servicer, the U.S. Department of the Treasury, or their respective agents may investigate the accuracy of my statements by performing routine background checks, including automated searches of federal, state and county databases, to confirm that I/we have not been convicted of such crimes. I/we also understand that knowingly submitting false information may violate Federal law. This certification is effective on the earlier of the date listed below or the date this RMA is received by your servicer.

SECTION 8: INFORMATION FOR GOVERNMENT MONITORING PURPOSES

The following information is requested by the federal government in order to monitor compliance with federal statutes that prohibit discrimination in housing. **You are not required to furnish this information, but are encouraged to do so. The law provides that a lender or servicer may not discriminate either on the basis of this information, or on whether you choose to furnish it.** If you furnish the information, please provide both ethnicity and race. For race, you may check more than one designation. If you do not furnish ethnicity, race, or sex, the lender or servicer is required to note the information on the basis of visual observation or surname if you have made this request for a loan modification in person. **If you do not wish to furnish the information, please check the box below.**

BORROWER	☐ I do not wish to furnish this information	CO-BORROWER	☐ I do not wish to furnish this information
Ethnicity:	☐ Hispanic or Latino	*Ethnicity:*	☐ Hispanic or Latino
	☐ Not Hispanic or Latino		☐ Not Hispanic or Latino
Race:	☐ American Indian or Alaska Native	*Race:*	☐ American Indian or Alaska Native
	☐ Asian		☐ Asian
	☐ Black or African American		☐ Black or African American
	☐ Native Hawaiian or Other Pacific Islander		☐ Native Hawaiian or Other Pacific Islander
	☐ White		☐ White
Sex:	☐ Female	*Sex:*	☐ Female
	☐ Male		☐ Male

To be completed by interviewer		***Name/Address of Interviewer's Employer***
This request was taken by:	*Interviewer's Name (print or type) & ID Number*	
☐ Face-to-face Interview ☐ Mail	*Interviewer's Signature* *Date*	
☐ Telephone ☐ Internet	*Interviewer's Phone Number (include area code)*	

SECTION 9: BORROWER AND CO-BORROWER ACKNOWLEDGEMENT AND AGREEMENT

1. I certify that all of the information in this RMA is truthful and the hardship(s) identified above has contributed to submission of this request for mortgage relief.

2. I understand and acknowledge that the Servicer, the U.S. Department of the Treasury, the owner or guarantor of my mortgage loan, or their respective agents may investigate the accuracy of my statements, may require me to provide additional supporting documentation and that knowingly submitting false information may violate Federal and other applicable law.

3. I authorize and give permission to the Servicer, the U.S. Department of the Treasury, and their respective agents, to assemble and use a current consumer report on all borrowers obligated on the loan, to investigate each borrower's eligibility for MHA and the accuracy of my statements and any documentation that I provide in connection with my request for assistance. I understand that these consumer reports may include, without limitation, a credit report, and be assembled and used at any point during the application process to assess each borrower's eligibility thereafter.

4. I understand that if I have intentionally defaulted on my existing mortgage, engaged in fraud or if it is determined that any of my statements or any information contained in the documentation that I provide are materially false and that I was ineligible for assistance under MHA, the Servicer, the U.S. Department of the Treasury, or their respective agents may terminate my participation in MHA, including any right to future benefits and incentives that otherwise would have been available under the program, and also may seek other remedies available at law and in equity, such as recouping any benefits or incentives previously received.

5. I certify that any property for which I am requesting assistance is a habitable residential property that is not subject to a condemnation notice.

6. I certify that I am willing to provide all requested documents and to respond to all Servicer communications in a timely manner. I understand that time is of the essence.

7. I understand that the Servicer will use the information I provide to evaluate my eligibility for available relief options and foreclosure alternatives, but the Servicer is not obligated to offer me assistance based solely on the representations in this document or other documentation submitted in connection with my request.

8. I am willing to commit to credit counseling if it is determined that my financial hardship is related to excessive debt.

9. If I am eligible for assistance under MHA, and I accept and agree to all terms of an MHA notice, plan, or agreement, I also agree that the terms of this Acknowledgment and Agreement are incorporated into such notice, plan, or agreement by reference as if set forth therein in full. My first timely payment, if required, following my servicer's determination and notification of my eligibility or prequalification for MHA assistance will serve as my acceptance of the terms set forth in the notice, plan, or agreement sent to me.

10. I understand that my Servicer will collect and record personal information that I submit in this RMA and during the evaluation process, including, but not limited to, my name, address, telephone number, social security number, credit score, income, payment history, government monitoring information, and information about my account balances and activity. I understand and consent to the Servicer's disclosure of my personal information and the terms of any MHA notice, plan or agreement to the U.S. Department of the Treasury and its agents, Fannie Mae and Freddie Mac in connection with their responsibilities under MHA, companies that perform support services in conjunction with MHA, any investor, insurer, guarantor, or servicer that owns, insures, guarantees, or services my first lien or subordinate lien (if applicable) mortgage loan(s) and to any HUD-certified housing counselor.

11. I consent to being contacted concerning this request for mortgage assistance at any e-mail address or cellular or mobile telephone number I have provided to the Servicer. This includes text messages and telephone calls to my cellular or mobile telephone.

The undersigned certifies under penalty of perjury that all statements in this document are true and correct.

Borrower Signature	Social Security Number	Date of Birth	Date
Co-borrower Signature	Social Security Number	Date of Birth	Date

HOMEOWNER'S HOTLINE

If you have questions about this document or the Making Home Affordable Program, please call your servicer.
If you have questions about the program that your servicer cannot answer or need further counseling, you can call the Homeowner's HOPE™ Hotline at 1-888-995-HOPE (4673).

The Hotline can help with questions about the program and offers free HUD-certified counseling services in English and Spanish.

NOTICE TO BORROWERS

Be advised that by signing this document you understand that any documents and information you submit to your servicer in connection with the Making Home Affordable Program are under penalty of perjury. Any misstatement of material fact made in the completion of these documents including but not limited to misstatement regarding your occupancy of your property, hardship circumstances, and/or income, expenses, or assets will subject you to potential criminal investigation and prosecution for the following crimes: perjury, false statements, mail fraud, and wire fraud. The information contained in these documents is subject to examination and verification. Any potential misrepresentation will be referred to the appropriate law enforcement authority for investigation and prosecution. By signing this document you certify, represent and agree that: "Under penalty of perjury, all documents and information I have provided to my Servicer in connection with the Making Home Affordable Program, including the documents and information regarding my eligibility for the program, are true and correct."

If you are aware of fraud, waste, abuse, mismanagement or misrepresentations affiliated with the Troubled Asset Relief Program, please contact the SIGTARP Hotline by calling 1-877-SIG-2009 (toll-free), 202-622-4559 (fax), or www.sigtarp.gov and provide them with your name, our name as your servicer, your property address, loan number and the reason for escalation. Mail can be sent to Hotline Office of the Special Inspector General for Troubled Asset Relief Program, 1801 L St. NW, Washington, DC 20220.

Beware of Foreclosure Rescue Scams. Help is FREE!

- **There is never a fee to get assistance or information about the Making Home Affordable Program from your lender or a HUD-approved housing counselor.**
- **Beware of any person or organization that asks you to pay a fee in exchange for housing counseling services or modification of a delinquent loan.**
- **Beware of anyone who says they can "save" your home if you sign or transfer over the deed to your house. Do not sign over the deed to your property to any organization or individual unless you are working directly with your mortgage company to forgive your debt.**
- **Never make your mortgage payments to anyone other than your mortgage company without their approval.**

IRS Form 4506-T

http://www.irs.gov/pub/irs-pdf/f4506t.pdf

Form **4506-T**
(Rev. September 2013)
Department of the Treasury
Internal Revenue Service

Request for Transcript of Tax Return

▶ **Request may be rejected if the form is incomplete or illegible.**

OMB No. 1545-1872

Tip. Use Form 4506-T to order a transcript or other return information free of charge. See the product list below. You can quickly request transcripts by using our automated self-help service tools. Please visit us at IRS.gov and click on "Order a Return or Account Transcript" or call 1-800-908-9946. If you need a copy of your return, use **Form 4506, Request for Copy of Tax Return.** There is a fee to get a copy of your return.

1a Name shown on tax return. If a joint return, enter the name shown first.	**1b First social security number on tax return, individual taxpayer identification number, or employer identification number (see instructions)**
2a If a joint return, enter spouse's name shown on tax return.	**2b Second social security number or individual taxpayer identification number if joint tax return**

3 Current name, address (including apt., room, or suite no.), city, state, and ZIP code (see instructions)

4 Previous address shown on the last return filed if different from line 3 (see instructions)

5 If the transcript or tax information is to be mailed to a third party (such as a mortgage company), enter the third party's name, address, and telephone number.

Caution. *If the tax transcript is being mailed to a third party, ensure that you have filled in lines 6 through 9 before signing. Sign and date the form once you have filled in these lines. Completing these steps helps to protect your privacy. Once the IRS discloses your tax transcript to the third party listed on line 5, the IRS has no control over what the third party does with the information. If you would like to limit the third party's authority to disclose your transcript information, you can specify this limitation in your written agreement with the third party.*

6 **Transcript requested.** Enter the tax form number here (1040, 1065, 1120, etc.) and check the appropriate box below. Enter only one tax form number per request. ▶ ____________

a **Return Transcript,** which includes most of the line items of a tax return as filed with the IRS. A tax return transcript does not reflect changes made to the account after the return is processed. Transcripts are only available for the following returns: Form 1040 series, Form 1065, Form 1120, Form 1120A, Form 1120H, Form 1120L, and Form 1120S. Return transcripts are available for the current year and returns processed during the prior 3 processing years. Most requests will be processed within 10 business days . . . . ☐

b **Account Transcript,** which contains information on the financial status of the account, such as payments made on the account, penalty assessments, and adjustments made by you or the IRS after the return was filed. Return information is limited to items such as tax liability and estimated tax payments. Account transcripts are available for most returns. Most requests will be processed within 10 business days . ☐

c **Record of Account,** which provides the most detailed information as it is a combination of the Return Transcript and the Account Transcript. Available for current year and 3 prior tax years. Most requests will be processed within 10 business days . . . . ☐

7 **Verification of Nonfiling,** which is proof from the IRS that you **did not** file a return for the year. Current year requests are only available after June 15th. There are no availability restrictions on prior year requests. Most requests will be processed within 10 business days . . ☐

8 **Form W-2, Form 1099 series, Form 1098 series, or Form 5498 series transcript.** The IRS can provide a transcript that includes data from these information returns. State or local information is not included with the Form W-2 information. The IRS may be able to provide this transcript information for up to 10 years. Information for the current year is generally not available until the year after it is filed with the IRS. For example, W-2 information for 2011, filed in 2012, will likely not be available from the IRS until 2013. If you need W-2 information for retirement purposes, you should contact the Social Security Administration at 1-800-772-1213. Most requests will be processed within 10 business days . ☐

Caution. *If you need a copy of Form W-2 or Form 1099, you should first contact the payer. To get a copy of the Form W-2 or Form 1099 filed with your return, you must use Form 4506 and request a copy of your return, which includes all attachments.*

9 **Year or period requested.** Enter the ending date of the year or period, using the mm/dd/yyyy format. If you are requesting more than four years or periods, you must attach another Form 4506-T. For requests relating to quarterly tax returns, such as Form 941, you must enter each quarter or tax period separately. ____________ ____________ ____________ ____________

Check this box if you have notified the IRS or the IRS has notified you that one of the years for which you are requesting a transcript involved **identity theft** on your federal tax return . . . . ☐

Caution. Do not sign this form unless all applicable lines have been completed.

Signature of taxpayer(s). I declare that I am either the taxpayer whose name is shown on line 1a or 2a, or a person authorized to obtain the tax information requested. If the request applies to a joint return, at least one spouse must sign. If signed by a corporate officer, partner, guardian, tax matters partner, executor, receiver, administrator, trustee, or party other than the taxpayer, I certify that I have the authority to execute Form 4506-T on behalf of the taxpayer. **Note.** *For transcripts being sent to a third party, this form must be received within 120 days of the signature date.*

Phone number of taxpayer on line 1a or 2a

Sign Here

▶ **Signature** (see instructions) Date

▶ **Title** (if line 1a above is a corporation, partnership, estate, or trust)

▶ **Spouse's signature** Date

For Privacy Act and Paperwork Reduction Act Notice, see page 2. Cat. No. 37667N Form **4506-T** (Rev. 9-2013)

Section references are to the Internal Revenue Code unless otherwise noted.

Future Developments

For the latest information about Form 4506-T and its instructions, go to *www.irs.gov/form4506t.* Information about any recent developments affecting Form 4506-T (such as legislation enacted after we released it) will be posted on that page.

General Instructions

CAUTION. *Do not sign this form unless all applicable lines have been completed.*

Purpose of form. Use Form 4506-T to request tax return information. You can also designate (on line 5) a third party to receive the information. Taxpayers using a tax year beginning in one calendar year and ending in the following year (fiscal tax year) must file Form 4506-T to request a return transcript.

Note. If you are unsure of which type of transcript you need, request the Record of Account, as it provides the most detailed information.

Tip. Use Form 4506, Request for Copy of Tax Return, to request copies of tax returns.

Automated transcript request. You can quickly request transcripts by using our automated self-help service tools. Please visit us at IRS.gov and click on "Order a Return or Account Transcript" or call 1-800-908-9946.

Where to file. Mail or fax Form 4506-T to the address below for the state you lived in, or the state your business was in, when that return was filed. There are two address charts: one for individual transcripts (Form 1040 series and Form W-2) and one for all other transcripts.

If you are requesting more than one transcript or other product and the chart below shows two different addresses, send your request to the address based on the address of your most recent return.

Chart for individual transcripts (Form 1040 series and Form W-2 and Form 1099)

If you filed an individual return and lived in:	Mail or fax to:
Alabama, Kentucky, Louisiana, Mississippi, Tennessee, Texas, a foreign country, American Samoa, Puerto Rico, Guam, the Commonwealth of the Northern Mariana Islands, the U.S. Virgin Islands, or A.P.O. or F.P.O. address	Internal Revenue Service RAIVS Team Stop 6716 AUSC Austin, TX 73301 512-460-2272
Alaska, Arizona, Arkansas, California, Colorado, Hawaii, Idaho, Illinois, Indiana, Iowa, Kansas, Michigan, Minnesota, Montana, Nebraska, Nevada, New Mexico, North Dakota, Oklahoma, Oregon, South Dakota, Utah, Washington, Wisconsin, Wyoming	Internal Revenue Service RAIVS Team Stop 37106 Fresno, CA 93888 559-456-5876
Connecticut, Delaware, District of Columbia, Florida, Georgia, Maine, Maryland, Massachusetts, Missouri, New Hampshire, New Jersey, New York, North Carolina, Ohio, Pennsylvania, Rhode Island, South Carolina, Vermont, Virginia, West Virginia	Internal Revenue Service RAIVS Team Stop 6705 P-6 Kansas City, MO 64999 816-292-6102

Chart for all other transcripts

If you lived in or your business was in:	Mail or fax to:
Alabama, Alaska, Arizona, Arkansas, California, Colorado, Florida, Hawaii, Idaho, Iowa, Kansas, Louisiana, Minnesota, Mississippi, Missouri, Montana, Nebraska, Nevada, New Mexico, North Dakota, Oklahoma, Oregon, South Dakota, Texas, Utah, Washington, Wyoming, a foreign country, or A.P.O. or F.P.O. address	Internal Revenue Service RAIVS Team P.O. Box 9941 Mail Stop 6734 Ogden, UT 84409 801-620-6922
Connecticut, Delaware, District of Columbia, Georgia, Illinois, Indiana, Kentucky, Maine, Maryland, Massachusetts, Michigan, New Hampshire, New Jersey, New York, North Carolina, Ohio, Pennsylvania, Rhode Island, South Carolina, Tennessee, Vermont, Virginia, West Virginia, Wisconsin	Internal Revenue Service RAIVS Team P.O. Box 145500 Stop 2800 F Cincinnati, OH 45250 859-669-3592

Line 1b. Enter your employer identification number (EIN) if your request relates to a business return. Otherwise, enter the first social security number (SSN) or your individual taxpayer identification number (ITIN) shown on the return. For example, if you are requesting Form 1040 that includes Schedule C (Form 1040), enter your SSN.

Line 3. Enter your current address. If you use a P. O. box, include it on this line.

Line 4. Enter the address shown on the last return filed if different from the address entered on line 3.

Note. If the address on lines 3 and 4 are different and you have not changed your address with the IRS, file Form 8822, Change of Address. For a business address, file Form 8822-B, Change of Address or Responsible Party—Business.

Line 6. Enter only one tax form number per request.

Signature and date. Form 4506-T must be signed and dated by the taxpayer listed on line 1a or 2a. If you completed line 5 requesting the information be sent to a third party, the IRS must receive Form 4506-T within 120 days of the date signed by the taxpayer or it will be rejected. Ensure that all applicable lines are completed before signing.

Individuals. Transcripts of jointly filed tax returns may be furnished to either spouse. Only one signature is required. Sign Form 4506-T exactly as your name appeared on the original return. If you changed your name, also sign your current name.

Corporations. Generally, Form 4506-T can be signed by: (1) an officer having legal authority to bind the corporation, (2) any person designated by the board of directors or other governing body, or (3) any officer or employee on written request by any principal officer and attested to by the secretary or other officer.

Partnerships. Generally, Form 4506-T can be signed by any person who was a member of the partnership during any part of the tax period requested on line 9.

All others. See section 6103(e) if the taxpayer has died, is insolvent, is a dissolved corporation, or if a trustee, guardian, executor, receiver, or administrator is acting for the taxpayer.

Documentation. For entities other than individuals, you must attach the authorization document. For example, this could be the letter from the principal officer authorizing an employee of the corporation or the letters testamentary authorizing an individual to act for an estate.

Signature by a representative. A representative can sign Form 4506-T for a taxpayer only if the taxpayer has specifically delegated this authority to the representative on Form 2848, line 5. The representative must attach Form 2848 showing the delegation to Form 4506-T.

Privacy Act and Paperwork Reduction Act Notice. We ask for the information on this form to establish your right to gain access to the requested tax information under the Internal Revenue Code. We need this information to properly identify the tax information and respond to your request. You are not required to request any transcript; if you do request a transcript, sections 6103 and 6109 and their regulations require you to provide this information, including your SSN or EIN. If you do not provide this information, we may not be able to process your request. Providing false or fraudulent information may subject you to penalties.

Routine uses of this information include giving it to the Department of Justice for civil and criminal litigation, and cities, states, the District of Columbia, and U.S. commonwealths and possessions for use in administering their tax laws. We may also disclose this information to other countries under a tax treaty, to federal and state agencies to enforce federal nontax criminal laws, or to federal law enforcement and intelligence agencies to combat terrorism.

You are not required to provide the information requested on a form that is subject to the Paperwork Reduction Act unless the form displays a valid OMB control number. Books or records relating to a form or its instructions must be retained as long as their contents may become material in the administration of any Internal Revenue law. Generally, tax returns and return information are confidential, as required by section 6103.

The time needed to complete and file Form 4506-T will vary depending on individual circumstances. The estimated average time is: **Learning about the law or the form,** 10 min.; **Preparing the form,** 12 min.; and **Copying, assembling, and sending the form to the IRS,** 20 min.

If you have comments concerning the accuracy of these time estimates or suggestions for making Form 4506-T simpler, we would be happy to hear from you. You can write to:

Internal Revenue Service
Tax Forms and Publications Division
1111 Constitution Ave. NW, IR-6526
Washington, DC 20224

Do not send the form to this address. Instead, see *Where to file* on this page.

IRS Form 4506T-EZ

http://www.irs.gov/pub/irs-pdf/f4506tez.pdf

Form **4506T-EZ**
(Rev. January 2012)
Department of the Treasury
Internal Revenue Service

Short Form Request for Individual Tax Return Transcript

▶ **Request may not be processed if the form is incomplete or illegible.**

OMB No. 1545-2154

Tip. Use Form 4506T-EZ to order a 1040 series tax return transcript free of charge, or you can quickly request transcripts by using our automated self-help service tools. Please visit us at IRS.gov and click on "Order a Transcript" or call 1-800-908-9946.

1a Name shown on tax return. If a joint return, enter the name shown first.	**1b First social security number or individual taxpayer identification number on tax return**
2a If a joint return, enter spouse's name shown on tax return.	**2b Second social security number or individual taxpayer identification number if joint tax return**

3 Current name, address (including apt., room, or suite no.), city, state, and ZIP code (see instructions)

4 Previous address shown on the last return filed if different from line 3 (see instructions)

5 If the transcript is to be mailed to a third party (such as a mortgage company), enter the third party's name, address, and telephone number. The IRS has no control over what the third party does with the tax information.

Third party name	Telephone number
Address (including apt., room, or suite no.), city, state, and ZIP code	

Caution. If the tax transcript is being mailed to a third party, ensure that you have filled in line 6 before signing. Sign and date the form once you have filled in this line. Completing this step helps to protect your privacy. Once the IRS discloses your IRS transcript to the third party listed on line 5, the IRS has no control over what the third party does with the information. If you would like to limit the third party's authority to disclose your transcript information, you can specify this limitation in your written agreement with the third party.

6 **Year(s) requested.** Enter the year(s) of the return transcript you are requesting (for example, "2008"). Most requests will be processed within 10 business days.

________ ________ ________ ________

☐ Check this box if you have notified the IRS or the IRS has notified you that one of the years for which you are requesting a transcript involved **identity theft** on your federal tax return.

Note. *If the IRS is unable to locate a return that matches the taxpayer identity information provided above, or if IRS records indicate that the return has not been filed, the IRS may notify you or the third party that it was unable to locate a return, or that a return was not filed, whichever is applicable.*

Caution. Do not sign this form unless all applicable lines have been completed.

Signature of taxpayer(s). I declare that I am the taxpayer whose name is shown on either line 1a or 2a. If the request applies to a joint return, **either** husband or wife must sign. **Note.** *For transcripts being sent to a third party, this form must be received within 120 days of the signature date.*

Sign Here

		Phone number of taxpayer on line 1a or 2a
▶ **Signature** (see instructions)	Date	
▶ **Spouse's signature**	Date	

For Privacy Act and Paperwork Reduction Act Notice, see page 2. Cat. No. 54185S Form **4506T-EZ** (Rev. 1-2012)

Section references are to the Internal Revenue Code unless otherwise noted.

What's New

The IRS has created a page on IRS.gov for information about Form 4506T-EZ at *http://www.irs.gov/form4506*. Information about any recent developments affecting Form 4506T-EZ (such as legislation enacted after we released it) will be posted on that page.

Caution. Do not sign this form unless all applicable lines have been completed.

Purpose of form. Individuals can use Form 4506T-EZ to request a tax return transcript for the current and the prior three years that includes most lines of the original tax return. The tax return transcript will not show payments, penalty assessments, or adjustments made to the originally filed return. You can also designate (on line 5) a third party (such as a mortgage company) to receive a transcript. Form 4506T-EZ cannot be used by taxpayers who file Form 1040 based on a tax year beginning in one calendar year and ending in the following year (fiscal tax year). Taxpayers using a fiscal tax year must file Form 4506-T, Request for Transcript of Tax Return, to request a return transcript.

Use Form 4506-T to request tax return transcripts, tax account information, W-2 information, 1099 information, verification of non-filing, and record of account.

Automated transcript request. You can quickly request transcripts by using our automated self-help service tools. Please visit us at IRS.gov and click on "Order a Transcript" or call 1-800-908-9946.

Where to file. Mail or fax Form 4506T-EZ to the address below for the state you lived in when the return was filed.

If you are requesting more than one transcript or other product and the chart below shows two different addresses, send your request to the address based on the address of your most recent return.

If you filed an individual return and lived in:	Mail or fax to the "Internal Revenue Service" at:
Alabama, Kentucky, Louisiana, Mississippi, Tennessee, Texas, a foreign country, American Samoa, Puerto Rico, Guam, the Commonwealth of the Northern Mariana Islands, the U.S. Virgin Islands, or A.P.O. or F.P.O. address	RAIVS Team Stop 6716 AUSC Austin, TX 73301 512-460-2272
Alaska, Arizona, Arkansas, California, Colorado, Hawaii, Idaho, Illinois, Indiana, Iowa, Kansas, Michigan, Minnesota, Montana, Nebraska, Nevada, New Mexico, North Dakota, Oklahoma, Oregon, South Dakota, Utah, Washington, Wisconsin, Wyoming	RAIVS Team Stop 37106 Fresno, CA 93888 559-456-5876
Connecticut, Delaware, District of Columbia, Florida, Georgia, Maine, Maryland, Massachusetts, Missouri, New Hampshire, New Jersey, New York, North Carolina, Ohio, Pennsylvania, Rhode Island, South Carolina, Vermont, Virginia, West Virginia	RAIVS Team Stop 6705 P-6 Kansas City, MO 64999 816-292-6102

Line 1b. Enter your employer identification number (EIN) if your request relates to a business return. Otherwise, enter the first social security number (SSN) or your individual taxpayer identification number (ITIN) shown on the return. For example, if you are requesting Form 1040 that includes Schedule C (Form 1040), enter your SSN.

Line 3. Enter your current address. If you use a P.O. box, include it on this line.

Line 4. Enter the address shown on the last return filed if different from the address entered on line 3.

Note. If the address on lines 3 and 4 are different and you have not changed your address with the IRS, file Form 8822, Change of Address.

Signature and date. Form 4506T-EZ must be signed and dated by the taxpayer listed on line 1a or 2a. If you completed line 5 requesting the information be sent to a third party, the IRS must receive Form 4506T-EZ within 120 days of the date signed by the taxpayer or it will be rejected. Ensure that all applicable lines are completed before signing.

Transcripts of jointly filed tax returns may be furnished to either spouse. Only one signature is required. Sign Form 4506T-EZ exactly as your name appeared on the original return. If you changed your name, also sign your current name.

Privacy Act and Paperwork Reduction Act Notice. We ask for the information on this form to establish your right to gain access to the requested tax information under the Internal Revenue Code. We need this information to properly identify the tax information and respond to your request. If you request a transcript, sections 6103 and 6109 require you to provide this information, including your SSN. If you do not provide this information, we may not be able to process your request. Providing false or fraudulent information may subject you to penalties.

Routine uses of this information include giving it to the Department of Justice for civil and criminal litigation, and cities, states, the District of Columbia, and U.S. commonwealths and possessions for use in administering their tax laws. We may also disclose this information to other countries under a tax treaty, to federal and state agencies to enforce federal nontax criminal laws, or to federal law enforcement and intelligence agencies to combat terrorism.

You are not required to provide the information requested on a form that is subject to the Paperwork Reduction Act unless the form displays a valid OMB control number. Books or records relating to a form or its instructions must be retained as long as their contents may become material in the administration of any Internal Revenue law. Generally, tax returns and return information are confidential, as required by section 6103.

The time needed to complete and file Form 4506T-EZ will vary depending on individual circumstances. The estimated average time is: **Learning about the law or the form,** 9 min.; **Preparing the form,** 18 min.; and **Copying, assembling, and sending the form to the IRS,** 20 min.

If you have comments concerning the accuracy of these time estimates or suggestions for making Form 4506T-EZ simpler, we would be happy to hear from you. You can write to:

Internal Revenue Service
Tax Products Coordinating Committee
SE:W:CAR:MP:T:M:S
1111 Constitution Ave. NW, IR-6526
Washington, DC 20224

Do not send the form to this address. Instead, see *Where to file* on this page.

Documentation List

Check your lender's specific requirements before submitting any documentation. **Expect to furnish all items in this first group, and others that apply to your situation.**

Request for Mortgage Assistance (RMA), including personal information:

Social Security number, date of birth, mailing address if other than property, e-mail, phone numbers, and preferred times to reach you.

- Borrower's income.
  - □ Household expenses.
  - □ Hardship explanation.
  - □ Copies of the two most recent statements for checking and savings accounts.
  - □ Utility bill with your name and the property address (proof of occupancy).
  - □ Recent monthly mortgage statement for each loan (primarily for your reference).
  - □ IRS Form 4506-T, Request for Transcript of Tax Return.

Signed copy of most recent *personal federal* income tax return, with schedules and forms.

Employed

- □ Copy of most recent IRS Form W-2.
- □ Copies of the two most recent pay stubs indicating year-to-date earnings.
- □ For additional income such as bonuses, commissions, fees, housing allowances, tips, and overtime, a letter from the employer or other reliable third-party documentation indicating that the income will continue.

Self-Employed

- □ Schedule C and K-1s with *personal federal* tax return.
- □ Most recent profit and loss statement for period since year of provided tax return.
- □ Other reliable third-party documentation supporting net income (e.g., certified public accountant letter).

If business is reported separately, then

- □ *Signed* copy of most recent *business federal* income tax return, with schedules and forms.
- □ Signed IRS Form 4506-T for business.

Other Income

Currently received from entitlements, such as social security, disability, or pension.

- □ Benefits statement or letter with amount, frequency, and duration of at least three years.
- □ Tax reporting forms.

Real Estate Rental Income

- □ Signed copy of the *two* (one additional) most recently filed federal income tax returns, including Schedules E—Supplemental Income and Loss.
- □ Copies of signed rental agreement, if gross rental income has changed significantly from that shown on tax returns.

Monetary Assets

Copies of the most recent statement(s) covering at least two months.

Liquid Assets

Available for withdrawal from a financial institution or brokerage firm.

- □ Certificates of deposit.
- □ Stocks and bonds.
- □ Mutual and money market funds.
- □ Other available funds.

Nonliquid Assets

Subject to age or use restrictions, or to significant tax or other penalties.

- □ Retirement (IRA, Keogh, 401(k)) Accounts
- □ Pension and profit-sharing.
- □ Other retirement investments.
- □ College or similar savings plans.
- □ Beneficiary or trust accounts.
- □ Other restricted funds.

Alimony or Child Support Paid or Received (Optional)

- □ Divorce decree, separation agreement, court decree, or legal written agreement, if the remaining duration exceeds three years.
- □ Evidence of full, regular, and timely payments (e.g., deposit slips, bank statements, or signed federal income tax returns).

Public Assistance

For example, unemployment benefits.

- □ Letters, exhibits, or benefits statement, stating amount, frequency, and remaining duration of at least nine months.

Non-borrower Household Income (Optional)

- □ If you receive income, reimbursement, rent, etc. from someone living in your home (e.g. boarder rental agreement).

Escalation by Third Party

Making Home Affordable HAMP Solution Center

http://www.irs.gov/pub/irs-pdf/f4506tez.pdf

Help for America's Homeowners

Case Submission

Please e-mail this document to **escalations@hmpadmin.com**

Date: ______ *(mm/dd/yyyy)*

HOMEOWNER INFORMATION

Homeowner Name:
Property Address:
Phone:
Email Address:

Last 4 digits of SS#:
MHA Program: choose one

SERVICER INFORMATION

Servicer Name:
Servicer Loan #:
(required to escalate)

Investor Type:
choose one

ESCALATION INFORMATION

Name:
Contact Name:
Contact Phone #:
Contact Email:
Relationship to Homeowner:

Are you charging a fee?
◯ Yes ◯ No
If so, how much?

Case Type: *(choose one)*

- ◯ Servicer did not assess the borrower for the applicable MHA Program according to Program Guidelines
- ◯ Initiation or continuance of foreclosure actions in violation of Program Guidelines, and there is no foreclosure sale scheduled to occur in the next 14 days
- ◯ Initiation or continuance of foreclosure actions in violation of Program Guidelines, and foreclosure is imminent (i.e., sale scheduled to occur in the next 14 days)
- ◯ Inappropriate program denial
- ◯ Other

If other, please describe:

Foreclosure Date *(if applicable)*:
Eviction Date *(if applicable)*:
Description of Concerns:

** If you/the homeowner was denied assistance under the Making Home Affordable Program, please provide a copy of the Non-Approval Notice the homeowner received.

Third Party Authorization Form

Please provide a copy of the authorization form executed by the homeowner that authorizes us to communicate with you about the homeowner's mortgage loan and authorizes you to act on their behalf with respect to assistance on their mortgage loan. The MHA Third Party Authorization Form is available as the 2nd page of this Case Submission form or at http://www.hmpadmin.com under "Programs" - "Home Affordable Modification Program" - "Borrower Documents" - "General Solicitation Offers".
You can send a copy of the Non-Approval Notice and the authorization form as an email attachment or by fax to 1-240-699-3883.
Note: The information requested needs to be sent from your organization's email account, not a public ISP (such as AOL, Yahoo, gmail, etc.). For future communication, please retain the servicer loan number for reference to this case.

Third-Party Authorization

Making Home Affordable HAMP Solution Center

HELPING YOU STAY IN YOUR HOME.

Third-Party Authorization Form

Mortgage Lender/Servicer Name ("Servicer") **[*Account*][*Loan*] Number**

The undersigned Borrower and Co-Borrower (if any) (individually and collectively, "Borrower" or "I"), authorize the above Servicer and the following third parties

[Counseling Agency] **[Agency Contact Name and Phone Number]**

[State HFA Entity] ***[State HFA Contact Name and Phone Number]***

[Other Third Party] **[Third Party *Contact Name and Phone Number*]**

[Relationship of Other Third Party to Borrower and Co-Borrower]

(individually and collectively, "Third Party") to obtain, share, release, discuss, and otherwise provide to and with each other public and non-public personal information contained in or related to the mortgage loan of the Borrower. This information may include (but is not limited to) the name, address, telephone number, social security number, credit score, credit report, income, government monitoring information, loss mitigation application status, account balances, program eligibility, and payment activity of the Borrower. I also understand and consent to the disclosure of my personal information and the terms of any agreements under the Making Home Affordable or Hardest Hit Fund Programs by Servicer or State HFA to the U.S. Department of the Treasury or their agents in connection with their responsibilities under the Emergency Economic Stabilization Act.

The Servicer will take reasonable steps to verify the identity of a Third Party, but has no responsibility or liability to verify the identity of such Third Party. The Servicer also has no responsibility or liability for what a Third Party does with such information.

Before signing this Third-Party Authorization, beware of foreclosure rescue scams!

- It is expected that a HUD-approved housing counselor, HFA representative or other authorized third party will work directly with your lender/mortgage servicer.
- Please visit http://makinghomeaffordable.gov/counselor.html to verify you are working with a HUD-approved housing counseling agency.
- Beware of anyone who asks you to pay a fee in exchange for a counseling service or modification of a delinquent loan.

This Third-Party Authorization is valid when signed by all borrowers and co-borrowers named on the mortgage and until the Servicer receives a written revocation signed by any borrower or co-borrower.

I UNDERSTAND AND AGREE WITH THE TERMS OF THIS THIRD-PARTY AUTHORIZATION:

Borrower

Printed Name

SIGN

Signature

Co-Borrower

Printed Name

SIGN

Signature

Scam Avoidance

Making Home Affordable Statement[1]

Beware of Foreclosure Rescue Scams!

Real Help is Free!

Foreclosure rescue and mortgage modification scams are a growing problem that could cost you thousands of dollars—or even your home.

Scammers make promises that they can't keep, such as guaranteeing to "save" your home or lower your mortgage, usually for a fee, often pretending that they have direct contact with your mortgage servicer—which they do not.

But the federal government provides the help you need for free!

Just call 888-995-HOPE (4673) for information about The Making Home Affordable Program® and to speak with a HUD-approved housing counselor. Assistance is available free, 24/7, in 160 languages.

Tips to Avoid Scams:

1. Beware of anyone who asks you to pay a fee in exchange for counseling services or the modification of a delinquent loan.

2. Beware of people who pressure you to sign papers immediately or who try to convince you that they can "save" your home if you sign or transfer over the deed to your house.
3. Do not sign over the deed to your property to any organization or individual unless you are working directly with your mortgage company to forgive your debt.
4. Never make a mortgage payment to anyone other than your mortgage company without their approval.

What to Do if You Have Been the Victim of a Scam

If you believe you have been the victim of a scam, you should file a complaint with the Federal Trade Commission (FTC). Visit the FTC's online Complaint Assistant or call 877-FTC-HELP (877-382-4357) for assistance in English or Spanish.

StopFraud.gov Statement[2]

To report Mortgage Fraud or Loan Scams:

Federal Bureau of Investigation

Phone: 1-800-CALLFBI (225-5324)

Online Tips: FBI Tips and Public Leads Form

To file a complaint with the FBI, contact the nearest FBI field office. Locations are listed at www.fbi.gov/contactus.htm or https://tips.fbi.gov/, or for major cases, you can also report information by calling the toll-free number 1-800-CALLFBI (225-5324).

Housing and Urban Development (HUD) Office of the Inspector General Hotline

Phone: (800) 347-3735

Fax: (202) 708-4829

E-mail: hotline@hudoig.gov

Address: HUD OIG Hotline (GFI), 451 7th Street, SW, Washington, D.C. 20410

PreventLoanScams.org: A project of the Lawyers' Committee for Civil Rights under the Law

Website: PreventLoanScams.org

Phone: 1-888-995-HOPE

PreventLoanScams.org was launched to serve as a nationwide clearinghouse for loan modification scam information on complaints filed, laws and regulations, and enforcement actions. If you think you've been scammed or approached by a company or individual promising to help you with your foreclosure, report it today.

Federal Trade Commission (FTC): Complaint Assistant

Website (Spanish): https://www.ftccomplaintassistant.gov/Consumer_HomeES.htm

Phone: (for complaints against companies, organizations, or business practices) (877) FTC-HELP

Phone: (for complaints about identity theft) (877) ID-THEFT

E-mail: (for complaints about spam or phishing) spam@uce.gov

The Federal Trade Commission collects complaints about fraud, companies, business practices, identity theft, and episodes of violence in the media.

Mortgage Relief Definitions

Temporary or Short Term

Agreement not to foreclose. Temporarily suspends or delays foreclosure proceedings when a condition of default exists. Typically, an unwritten temporary suspension during a pending modification. A formal proposal would be strengthened by evidence of disclosure or loan closing-document irregularities, or of predatory lending practices.

Forbearance. Reduces or suspends payments with lender's agreement, while negotiating another form of relief or until a temporary difficulty ends.

Reinstatement. Pays by a specific date all back interest and principal owed, in exchange for "reinstating" the loan to its pre-default status. Will take loan out of delinquency status but will not reverse previous delinquency reports to credit bureaus. Typically combined with forbearance and the expectation of a windfall (e.g., bonus, investment, insurance settlement, tax refund).

Repayment plan. Apportions delinquent amounts to subsequent payments until all back interest and principal are current. Usually for short-term financial problems, such as extraordinary medical care or unemployment, making it difficult to pay other expenses in a given month.

Long-Term

Mortgage modification. Changes the original loan terms when delinquent amounts cannot be repaid, a change in circumstances makes the monthly payment unaffordable, and/or a scheduled rate adjustment makes the new payment unaffordable. Typically, such changes include adding delinquent amounts to the loan balance, lowering the interest rate, converting an adjustable to a fixed rate, extending the repayment term, and reinstating the loan to pre-default status.

Forbearance of interest. Waives interest on a portion of the loan principal to reduce monthly payments to an affordable and sustainable level. That portion of principal must be repaid but without interest.

Principal forgiveness. Reduces the outstanding loan amount, thereby reducing the monthly payment. A form of loan modification but very difficult to obtain from lenders.

Short refinance. Replaces the original loan with a new affordable loan. The difference (shortfall) is forgiven, usually resulting in a lower loss to lender than foreclosing. Has the effect of a principal reduction. Complicated by junior liens and judgments, if any.

Claim advance. Brings a delinquent mortgage current with an interest-free loan to a borrower from a mortgage insurance company, which avoids paying a claim to the underlying insured lender.

Permanent

Sale. A conventional sale when mortgage payments become unaffordable and the property value is *greater than the loan balance*. Combine with forbearance for a specific period of time to find a purchaser and close escrow. Remainder of the loan, back interest, and fees are paid and the balance (equity) is preserved.

Pre-foreclosure sale or short payoff. A conventional sale when the net proceeds are *less than the loan balance*. Lender agrees to accept less than the full amount owed and the difference (shortfall) is forgiven. Usually combined with forbearance, agreement not to foreclose, and a nonrecourse agreement. Often called a "short sale."

Deed in lieu of foreclosure. Often simply called "deed in lieu." Borrower voluntarily surrenders ownership of the property to lender, and the debt is forgiven. This option may be unavailable if other liens encumber title to the property (e.g., judgments of other creditors, junior mortgages, and IRS or state tax liens). Sometimes referred to colloquially as "turning over the keys."

Nonrecourse agreement. Lender agrees not to make claims against assets other than the property to compensate for any deficiency.

Bankruptcy. Borrowers may discharge personal liability for a mortgage, but the lender retains the right to foreclose. Typically, this option is viable for a borrower with unsustainable consumer credit, or might be considered after a short sale or foreclosure to discharge deficiency liability. Consult qualified legal and financial counsel.

Making Home Affordable Programs

- Home Affordable Modification Program (HAMP), http://www.makinghomeaffordable.gov/programs/lower-payments/Pages/hamp.aspx
- Principal Reduction Alternative (PRA), http://www.makinghomeaffordable.gov/programs/lower-payments/Pages/pra.aspx
- Second Lien Modification Program (2MP), http://www.makinghomeaffordable.gov/programs/lower-payments/Pages/lien_modification.aspx
- Home Affordable Unemployment Program (UP), http://www.makinghomeaffordable.gov/programs/unemployed-help/Pages/up.aspx
- Home Affordable Foreclosure Alternatives (HAFA) Program, http://www.makinghomeaffordable.gov/programs/exit-gracefully/Pages/hafa.aspx
- Home Affordable Refinance Program (HARP), http://www.makinghomeaffordable.gov/programs/lower-rates/Pages/harp.aspx
- Fannie Mae Home Affordable Modification Program (HAMP), http://knowyouroptions.com/modify/home-affordable-modification-program
- Freddie Mac Home Affordable Modification Program (HAMP), http://www.freddiemac.com/mortgage_help/home_affordable_modification.html
- Housing Finance Agency Fund for the Hardest Hit Housing Markets (HHF), http://www.makinghomeaffordable.gov/programs/unemployed-help/Pages/hhf.aspx

- FHA Home Affordable Modification Program (FHA-HAMP), http://www.makinghomeaffordable.gov/programs/lower-payments/Pages/fha-hamp.aspx
- Second Lien Modification Program for FHA Loans (FHA2LP), http://www.makinghomeaffordable.gov/programs/lower-rates/Pages/fha2lp.aspx
- FHA Refinance for Borrowers with Negative Equity (FHA Short Refinance), http://www.makinghomeaffordable.gov/programs/lower-rates/Pages/short-refinance.aspx
- USDA's Special Loan Servicing, http://www.makinghomeaffordable.gov/programs/lower-payments/Pages/rd-hamp.aspx
- Veteran's Affairs Home Affordable Modification (VA-HAMP), http://www.makinghomeaffordable.gov/programs/lower-payments/Pages/va-hamp.aspx

Payment Constant

A payment constant can be multiplied by any loan amount to find the loan payment (principal and interest) for the corresponding interest rate and loan amortization term. The following table shows *monthly* principal and interest payments per $100,000 for corresponding *annual* interest rates and amortization terms in years. Amortization in months may be estimated as partial years.

For the following examples, assume the loan amount is $427,800.

Loan Amount ÷ 100,000 = Multiplier. The example loan multiplier is 4.278.

Example 1: Interest rate is 5.375%. Term is 30 years. Find unknown *payment amount*:

Years	5.000%	5.125%	5.250%	5.375%	5.500%
29	544.86	552.46	560.10	567.80	575.54
30	536.82	544.49	552.20	559.97	567.79
31	529.39	537.13	544.91	552.75	560.64

Payment = Constant × Multiplier: 559.97 × 4.278 = $2,395.56 per month

Example 2: Payment is $1,473.43. Term is 34 years. Find unknown *interest rate*:

Years	2.000%	2.125%	2.250%	2.375%	2.500%
33	345.16	351.55	358.00	364.52	371.10
34	338.00	344.42	350.91	357.46	364.09
35	331.26	337.71	344.24	350.83	357.50

Payment ÷ Multiplier = Constant: $1,473.43 ÷ 4.278 = 344.42.
Interest rate is 2.125%.

Example 3: Payment is $1,323.79. Interest Rate is 2.125%. Find unknown *amortization term*:

Years	2.000%	2.125%	2.250%	2.375%	2.500
38	313.26	319.81	326.44	333.15	339.93
39	307.90	314.49	321.15	327.89	334.71
40	302.83	309.44	316.14	322.92	329.78

Payment ÷ Multiplier = Constant: $1,323.79 ÷ 4.278 = 309.44.
Term is 40 years.

Years	2.000%	2.125%	2.250%	2.375%	2.500%	2.625%	2.750%	2.875%	3.000%
25	423.85	429.97	436.13	442.35	448.62	454.94	461.31	467.74	474.21
26	411.30	417.44	423.64	429.90	436.21	442.57	448.99	455.46	461.98
27	399.69	405.87	412.11	418.40	424.75	431.15	437.61	444.13	450.70
28	388.93	395.15	401.42	407.75	414.14	420.58	427.09	433.65	440.27
29	378.93	385.18	391.49	397.86	404.29	410.78	417.32	423.93	430.59
30	369.62	375.90	382.25	388.65	395.12	401.65	408.24	414.89	421.60
31	360.92	367.24	373.62	380.06	386.57	393.14	399.78	406.47	413.23
32	352.79	359.14	365.55	372.04	378.58	385.20	391.87	398.61	405.42
33	345.16	351.55	358.00	364.52	371.10	377.76	384.48	391.26	398.11
34	338.00	344.42	350.91	357.46	364.09	370.78	377.54	384.37	391.27
35	331.26	337.71	344.24	350.83	357.50	364.23	371.03	377.91	384.85
36	324.91	331.40	337.96	344.59	351.29	358.07	364.91	371.83	378.82
37	318.92	325.44	332.03	338.70	345.44	352.26	359.15	366.11	373.14
38	313.26	319.81	326.44	333.15	339.93	346.78	353.71	360.72	367.80
39	307.90	314.49	321.15	327.89	334.71	341.61	348.58	355.63	362.75
40	302.83	309.44	316.14	322.92	329.78	336.71	343.73	350.82	357.98

Years	3.000%	3.125%	3.250%	3.375%	3.500%	3.625%	3.750%	3.875%	4.000%
25	474.21	480.74	487.32	493.94	500.62	507.35	514.13	520.96	527.84
26	461.98	468.56	475.19	481.87	488.60	495.39	502.22	509.11	516.05
27	450.70	457.33	464.01	470.74	477.53	484.37	491.26	498.21	505.21
28	440.27	446.94	453.67	460.46	467.30	474.20	481.15	488.15	495.21
29	430.59	437.32	444.10	450.94	457.83	464.78	471.79	478.85	485.97
30	421.60	428.38	435.21	442.10	449.04	456.05	463.12	470.24	477.42
31	413.23	420.05	426.93	433.87	440.87	447.94	455.06	462.23	469.47
32	405.42	412.29	419.22	426.21	433.26	440.38	447.55	454.79	462.08
33	398.11	405.03	412.01	419.05	426.16	433.33	440.56	447.85	455.20
34	391.27	398.23	405.26	412.35	419.51	426.73	434.02	441.37	448.78
35	384.85	391.86	398.94	406.08	413.29	420.57	427.91	435.31	442.77
36	378.82	385.88	393.00	400.19	407.46	414.78	422.18	429.63	437.16
37	373.14	380.25	387.42	394.66	401.97	409.35	416.80	424.31	431.89
38	367.80	374.95	382.17	389.46	396.82	404.25	411.75	419.32	426.95
39	362.75	369.95	377.21	384.55	391.97	399.45	407.00	414.62	422.31
40	357.98	365.23	372.54	379.93	387.39	394.92	402.53	410.20	417.94

Years	4.000%	4.125%	4.250%	4.375%	4.500%	4.625%	4.750%	4.875%	5.000%
25	527.84	534.76	541.74	548.76	555.83	562.95	570.12	577.33	584.59
26	516.05	523.04	530.08	537.17	544.30	551.49	558.73	566.01	573.34
27	505.21	512.26	519.36	526.52	533.72	540.98	548.28	555.64	563.04
28	495.21	502.33	509.49	516.71	523.98	531.30	538.68	546.10	553.57
29	485.97	493.15	500.38	507.66	514.99	522.38	529.82	537.32	544.86
30	477.42	484.65	491.94	499.29	506.69	514.14	521.65	529.21	536.82
31	469.47	476.77	484.12	491.53	498.99	506.51	514.08	521.71	529.39
32	462.08	469.44	476.85	484.32	491.85	499.43	507.07	514.76	522.51
33	455.20	462.61	470.09	477.62	485.21	492.85	500.56	508.32	516.13
34	448.78	456.25	463.78	471.37	479.02	486.73	494.50	502.32	510.20
35	442.77	450.30	457.89	465.55	473.26	481.03	488.86	496.74	504.69
36	437.16	444.74	452.39	460.10	467.87	475.70	483.59	491.54	499.55
37	431.89	439.53	447.24	455.01	462.84	470.73	478.68	486.69	494.76
38	426.95	434.65	442.41	450.24	458.12	466.08	474.09	482.16	490.29
39	422.31	430.06	437.88	445.76	453.71	461.72	469.79	477.92	486.11
40	417.94	425.75	433.62	441.56	449.56	457.63	465.76	473.95	482.20

Years	5.000%	5.125%	5.250%	5.375%	5.500%	5.625%	5.750%	5.875%	6.000%
25	584.59	591.90	599.25	606.65	614.09	621.57	629.11	636.68	644.30
26	573.34	580.72	588.15	595.62	603.14	610.71	618.32	625.98	633.68
27	563.04	570.49	577.99	585.54	593.14	600.78	608.47	616.20	623.99
28	553.57	561.10	568.67	576.29	583.97	591.68	599.45	607.26	615.12
29	544.86	552.46	560.10	567.80	575.54	583.34	591.18	599.07	607.00
30	536.82	544.49	552.20	559.97	567.79	575.66	583.57	591.54	599.55
31	529.39	537.13	544.91	552.75	560.64	568.58	576.57	584.61	592.69
32	522.51	530.31	538.17	546.08	554.04	562.05	570.11	578.22	586.38
33	516.13	524.00	531.92	539.90	547.93	556.01	564.14	572.32	580.55
34	510.20	518.14	526.13	534.17	542.27	550.42	558.62	566.87	575.17
35	504.69	512.69	520.74	528.85	537.02	545.23	553.50	561.82	570.19
36	499.55	507.62	515.73	523.91	532.14	540.42	548.75	557.14	565.58
37	494.76	502.89	511.07	519.31	527.60	535.95	544.35	552.80	561.30
38	490.29	498.48	506.72	515.02	523.38	531.79	540.25	548.77	557.33
39	486.11	494.36	502.66	511.02	519.44	527.91	536.44	545.02	553.64
40	482.20	490.50	498.87	507.29	515.77	524.30	532.89	541.53	550.21

Glossary of Terms[1]

acceleration. A loan in default may be called due, the first step in a foreclosure, regardless of its actual due date. Correcting the default, which can be accomplished by loan modification, ends the threat.

acknowledgement of request for short sale (ARSS). Lender's confirmation of receipt from a borrower of a sales contract that results in a short sale, which initiates the analysis and results in approval, disapproval, or counteroffer.

adjustable rate mortgage. Some loans are designed with an interest rate that changes from time to time. The periodic changes are determined by adding a fixed margin to a variable index rate, which reflects market conditions and allows lenders to maintain a current yield. Changes may be limited by lifetime and period caps, which may be maximums or minimums. All elements—index, margin, caps, and period—are defined in the promissory note.

affidavit. A written statement that affirms that its contents are true and accurate.

agreement not to foreclose. Temporarily suspends or delays foreclosure proceedings when a condition of default exists. Typically, an unwritten temporary suspension during a pending modification. A formal proposal would be strengthened by evidence of disclosure or loan closing-document irregularities or predatory lending practices.

amortization. When loan payments include both interest and principal, each payment reduces the outstanding loan balance. As the loan balance declines, less of the payment goes to interest and more goes to principal, thus accelerating the reduction of the loan balance over time. If it is paid completely, the loan is fully amortizing.

balloon payment. When a loan is not fully amortizing, a principal balance remains at the end of the loan term, and is due in a lump-sum payment. *See* amortization.

bankruptcy. Forgiveness of debt through a judicial process. When bankruptcy is a consideration, its procedures and consequences should always be discussed with qualified legal counsel and financial advisors.

borrower NPV calculator. A Web-based self-service tool for borrowers and their advisors to independently predict potential NPV eligibility for HAMP. Required by Dodd-Frank Act and developed by U.S. Department of Treasury.

capitalized principal balance. Includes the unpaid principal balance of a loan, plus payments advanced by the lender for such expenses as property tax or insurance not paid by a borrower. It might also include the interest portion of missed payments but must exclude late fees or administrative costs if a modification occurs.

cash reserves. Also known as liquid assets; money that can be withdrawn within a short period of time. Obvious examples are checking and savings accounts. Others are sellable stocks, bonds, mutual funds, money market funds, and, for HAMP purposes, certificates of deposit of any maturity. Excluded are retirement accounts, whether self-administered (IRA, 401(k), Keogh, etc.) or other administered (employer, pension), and deferred compensation or stock options. *See also* emergency reserve.

claim advance. If the mortgage is insured, the insurer may consider an interest-free loan to bring the account current, avoiding a lender's claim for a loss from foreclosure or short sale. Full repayment of the interim loan might be delayed for several years.

combined loan-to-value ratio (CLTV). Calculated by dividing the total combined senior and junior loan amounts by the property value. *See* loan-to-value ratio.

current monthly mortgage payment. The mortgage payment including property tax and insurance prior to modification. *See* mortgage payment.

current monthly P&I. Shorthand for "principal and interest." *See* monthly P&I.

debt. As used to calculate the debt coverage ratio, the current principal and interest portion of the current monthly mortgage payment for the loan to be modified.

debt coverage ratio. The relationship of net income to loan payments, indicating the income "cushion" that remains after making those payments. Used in the Fannie Mae and other imminent default screens.

debt-to-income ratio. *See* gross expense-to-income ratio.

deed in lieu of foreclosure. Often simply called "deed in lieu." Borrower voluntarily surrenders ownership of the property to lender, and the debt is forgiven. This option may be unavailable if other liens encumber title to the property (e.g., judgments of other creditors, junior mortgages, and IRS or state tax liens). Sometimes referred to colloquially as "turning over the keys."

deed of trust. Also known as a trust deed, a form of mortgage that allows for enforcement of the lender's claim according to a predefined and streamlined procedure sanctioned by state law. In a foreclosure, the trust deed allows a lender (through a trustee) to sell the underlying property without judicial action but then precludes recourse to borrower's other assets. *See* single action rule.

deficiency judgment. When a loan is not paid in full, a deficiency results. If the lender sues the borrower for the deficit amount and wins, then the court enters a deficiency judgment, which may be enforced as any other award of the court. *See* single action rule.

disposable net income. Income left after payroll deductions, all credit obligations, including housing and living expenses, but excluding the mortgage payment to be modified.

eligibility. Borrower, mortgage, property, and lender must meet a set of criteria before a loan may be considered for modification under HAMP.

emergency reserve. Equal to three times monthly "debt payments," according to HAMP. Fannie Mae limits the reserve to three times monthly "housing expenses," which is a lower cash-reserve amount. *See also* cash reserves.

equity. The difference between the value of property and the encumbrances, liens, loans, and other claims against the property. This net value is the ownership interest in the property. If it is a negative amount, the terms "negative equity" and "underwater" are commonly used.

escalation. The process used by a borrower or advisor to challenge and correct a lender's negative decision.

escrow. A disinterested third party is appointed to hold items of value deposited by one party with instructions to deliver those items to another party on the occurrence of a predetermined event. An example is the sale and purchase of a home. The seller deposits a conveyance deed and the buyer deposits (or arranges for a lender to deposit) funds equaling the purchase price. Each instructs escrow to deliver the deposited items to the other when all the conditions of the sale and purchase are complete.

escrow account. An accumulating amount paid by a borrower monthly and held by the lender to pay annual or semiannual property tax and insurance premium payments. Sometimes referred to as an impound account.

estimated principal balance. The loan amount used to determine the modified payments. Includes the balance at time of modification, plus past due interest and escrow amounts paid by the lender on behalf of the borrower. It may not include late fees and other administrative costs. *See* capitalized principal balance.

extinguishment. A creditor extinguishes a loan by forgiving any remaining principal balance, past due amounts, and fees, effectively terminating the loan and releasing any collateral that secures repayment. For example, extinguishment of a junior mortgage terminates the loan and releases the security (mortgage or trust deed) encumbering the underlying real estate, but does not affect the senior lien.

Fannie Mae. Founded in 1938, one of two government-sponsored enterprises used to underwrite trillions of dollars of mortgages, allowing the private financial markets to fund the American Dream of homeownership. After suffering substantial losses due to deteriorated real estate and mortgage markets, it was placed into conservatorship in September 2008 under the Federal Housing Finance Agency. *See also* Freddie Mac.

Federal Housing Finance Agency (FHFA). The conservator created and appointed to oversee Fannie Mae and Freddie Mac.

forbearance. A reduction or suspension of payments with lender's agreement while negotiating another form of relief or until a temporary difficulty ends.

forbearance of interest. A waiver of interest on a portion of the loan principal to reduce monthly payments to an affordable and sustainable level. That portion of principal must be repaid, but without interest.

foreclosure. A statutory procedure beginning with a borrower's default in payments on a loan and ending with the sale of the property securing the loan. The sale proceeds go first to paying the costs of sale then to paying the loan. If the proceeds are insufficient to satisfy the loan, state law determines whether the borrower may be held personally liable. *See* judicial foreclosure, single action rule, and trustee sale.

foreclosure alternatives. Refer to appendix O, "Mortgage Relief Definitions," page 197, where the alternatives are listed by function. They are listed alphabetically in this glossary.

forgiveness. A permanent reduction of the unpaid principal balance of a loan. *See* principal forgiveness.

Freddie Mac. Founded in 1970, one of two government-sponsored enterprises used to underwrite trillions of dollars of mortgages, allowing the private financial markets to bankroll the American Dream of homeowners. In September 2008, after suffering substantial losses due to deteriorated real estate and mortgage markets, it was placed into conservatorship under the Federal Housing Finance Agency. *See also* Fannie Mae.

government-sponsored enterprise (GSE). *See* Fannie Mae and Freddie Mac.

gross expense-to-income ratio. Compares income from all sources with all credit and most living expenses and measures relative debt burden, overall ability to meet obligations, viability of the loan modification beyond its impact on monthly mortgage payments, and responsible use of borrowed money. Also referred to as the "monthly debt ratio," "debt-to-income ratio," and "back-end ratio."

gross income. All income from any source, before withholdings or deductions, including earnings received from self-employment and nonemployment sources such as pension or public assistance. A component of the monthly mortgage payment ratio; refer to page 60.

Hardship Affidavit. A standardized form for describing the "events" that contribute to a borrower's difficulty making mortgage payments. A central component of eligibility, a borrower must describe the hardship events in writing.

homeowner association (HOA). The governing board for a condominium, planned unit development, or other group of homeowners gathered for a common purpose. Fees are collected from homeowners for administering the group and improving, maintaining, and repairing the property. Unpaid fees may become a lien against the individual owner's property.

housing expense. Occasionally used with the same meaning as monthly mortgage payment. *See* mortgage payment.

imminent risk of default. The likelihood that a borrower, who is current on payments, will be unable to continue making timely payments. Either the lender must find a borrower to be "at risk," or a borrower must be 60 or more days late (seriously delinquent), to be eligible for modification. Also referred to as "reasonably foreseeable default."

impound account. *See* escrow account.

income. *See* gross income.

initial package. Begins the HAMP evaluation process. It consists of the Request for Mortgage Assistance form, IRS form 4506-T or 4506T-EZ, and evidence of income.

interest-rate cap. The Freddie Mac 30-year fixed rate at the time of the modification determines the maximum rate for the modified loan.

investor. In this book, "investor" refers to the actual owner of a mortgage, which is the right to receive repayment of the loan amount and interest on outstanding principal. In the past, the financial institution lending the money was also the investor, on behalf of its depositors. Recently, money has been raised in financial markets through mortgage-backed securities (securities backed by a pool of similar mortgages), and the issuer of the securities is now the investor. *See* loan servicer.

judicial foreclosure. An action in court to enforce a lender's secured interest in real estate. In effect, it is a lawsuit for breach of contract when a borrower defaults on the promissory note. A costly and time-consuming alternative, it is seldom used when the mortgage includes a separate enforcement provision, as in a deed of trust.

lender. In this book, "lender" refers generically to the originator, servicer, and/or investor of the mortgage. Specifically, it refers to the recipient of a borrower's monthly payments and request for modification.

lien. A claim against property, typically to ensure repayment of a debt, but also to ensure payment for certain services to improve the property (e.g., "mechanics lien" for construction, repairs, and materials) or to ensure payment of charges against the property (e.g., "tax lien" for unpaid property taxes).

loan servicer. Collects payments as the investor's agent, keeping its fees, and then passing through the remainder. In this book, also referred to as "lender."

loan-to-value ratio (LTV). Calculated by dividing the senior loan amount by the property value. The lower the result, the less risk to a lender and the more equity vested in the owner. Any result greater than 100 percent, however, is commonly referred to as "negative equity" or being "underwater."

modification agreement. The agreement between a lender and a borrower that permanently changes the promissory note. It becomes effective upon completion of the trial period.

modification evaluator. A tool to help borrowers determine whether they might be eligible for HAMP. Go to http://makinghomeaffordable.gov/evaluator.html.

monthly debt ratio. See gross expense-to-income ratio.

monthly disposable net income. Income left after payroll deductions, all credit obligations, including housing and living expenses, but excluding the mortgage payment to be modified. *See* disposable net income.

monthly gross expenses. Though HAMP identifies specific expense items (refer to page 74), generally includes mortgage payments, other housing expenses, and credit obligations.

monthly gross income. *See* gross income.

monthly mortgage payment. *See* mortgage payment.

monthly mortgage payment ratio. *See* mortgage payment ratio.

monthly obligations. Include personal debts, revolving (credit card) accounts, installment loans, and household or living expenses.

monthly P&I. The principal and interest payment that traditionally has been considered the "mortgage payment." However, for HAMP purposes, P&I is a component of the monthly mortgage payment, which also includes escrow account payments. *See* amortization. *Contrast* negative amortization and interest-only payments.

mortgage. A lien or claim against real property (real estate) to ensure repayment of a loan, almost always for the purpose of buying the property, refinancing a previous loan, or liquidating equity accumulated from a down payment or value appreciation. The borrower owns the real estate, but the lender has a claim or interest in the real estate, specifically the right to sell it and collect what is owed from the sale proceeds if the borrower does not repay the loan as agreed. The term "mortgage" usually refers to both the loan agreement (promissory note) and the security instrument (mortgage or deed of trust).

mortgage payment. Combines the principal and interest paid to the lender, plus monthly allotments for property taxes and insurance, homeowner association fees, and certain other assessments. It does not include the payment for any second mortgage or for mortgage insurance, which are included in debt and in monthly obligations. *See also* target monthly mortgage payment.

mortgage payment ratio. Calculates the portion of income needed to pay housing expenses by dividing the monthly mortgage payment by gross monthly income. It is commonly referred to as the "housing-to-income" or "front-end" ratio. *See* target monthly mortgage payment ratio.

negative amortization. When loan payments are less than interest owed and the unpaid interest is added to the loan balance, the balance increases. This is opposite or negative compared to amortization, which reduces the loan balance.

negative equity. See equity. Also known as "underwater."

net income. *See* disposable net income.

net present value (NPV). The current value of future costs and benefits (cash flow) to a lender from modifying a mortgage versus foreclosing on it.

non-approval. Denial by a lender of a request for modification due to borrower's ineligibility or negative NPV Test findings, sometimes for failure to arrive at a viable monthly mortgage payment using the standard modification waterfall.

non-approval notice. Written explanation to the borrower from the lender that lists the reasons for the denying a request for modification.

nonrecourse agreement. Lender agrees not to make claims against assets of a borrower other than the property to compensate for any deficiency.

NPV input values. Individual credit, property, loan, and similar unique variables used when evaluating a borrower in the NPV test.

NPV test. The process of determining the net present value of a loan and comparing the results. If modification is more beneficial to the lender than foreclosure, then the results are "positive" and the lender is required by HAMP to modify. Otherwise, the lender may modify or not but should consider foreclosure alternatives.

payment constant. A number that corresponds to an interest rate and amortization term. The fully amortizing payment for any loan amount, at that rate and term, can be found by multiplying the loan amount by the payment constant.

payment reduction estimator. A tool available to help an eligible borrower estimate the payment resulting from a modification. Go to http://making homeaffordable.gov/payment_reduction_estimator .html.

pooling and servicing agreement. Governs the relationship between a loan servicer and investor. It may restrict loan servicers in applying HAMP to modify loans, even if the servicer has entered a Servicer Participant Agreement.

pre-foreclosure sale. *See* short sale.

principal balance. The amount of a loan that remains unpaid. Same as unpaid principal balance.

principal forbearance. A portion of the loan on which monthly payments are not required and interest is not charged (non-interest-bearing). Intended to further reduce the modified monthly mortgage payment. The amount must be paid as a balloon payment when the loan is due. *Contrast* principal forgiveness.

principal forgiveness. An actual reduction of the outstanding loan amount. Not due in the future. Also, effectively reduces the monthly payment.

promissory note. The agreement or contract that defines the terms and conditions of a loan and its repayment. A promissory note for a real estate loan should always be secured by a mortgage or deed of trust, which serves to enforce the promise to repay.

proposed principal balance. A tactic suggested in this book to reduce the estimated (capitalized) principal balance on which modified payments are calculated. It would require principal forgiveness by the lender.

qualification. In this book, refers to the credit analysis or underwriting of a borrower's ability to make modified loan payments. Contrast with "eligibility," which involves a set of threshold criteria.

reasonably foreseeable default. *See* imminent risk of default.

re-default. After modifying a delinquent loan, the borrower misses the modified payments and again becomes delinquent.

reinstatement. Pay by a specific date all back interest and principal owed in exchange for "reinstating" the loan to its pre-default status. Will take the loan out of delinquency status but will not reverse previous delinquency reports to credit bureaus. Typically combined with forbearance and the expectation of a windfall (e.g., bonus, investment, insurance settlement, tax refund).

repayment plan. An agreement between lender and borrower that apportions delinquent amounts to subsequent payments until all back interest, late fees, and other included amounts are paid. Results in a temporary or permanent increase in payments. May also be used to repay a forbearance amount. *See* forbearance.

Request for Modification and Affidavit. Former name of Request for Mortgage Assistance.

Request for Mortgage Assistance (RMA). Principal form in the initial package to initiate consideration for Making Home Affordable mortgage relief.

requestor. The borrower or authorized third party who escalates a disputed case.

servicer. See loan servicer. *See also* lender; used interchangeably in this book.

Servicer Participant Agreement (SPA). The agreement entered by loan servicers and lenders that participate in HAMP. In return for complying with HAMP guidelines, they are entitled to receive incentive payments from the federal government. The original deadline for signing an SPA is December 31, 2009.

short payoff. Lender agrees to accept less than the full amount owed, and the difference (shortfall) is forgiven, usually resulting in a lower loss to lender than foreclosure.

short refinance. Refinancing to a more affordable mortgage by a qualified borrower that results in a short payoff, often due to decline in property value. Has the effect of a principal reduction, and is unusual. Complicated by any junior lien or judgment.

short sale. A conventional sale when the net proceeds are less than the loan balance, resulting in a short payoff. Lender agrees to accept less than the full amount owed, releases the lien (security interest) so title may pass unencumbered to the buyer, and might waive (forgive) the unpaid portion of the loan principal (deficiency or shortfall).

short sale notice (SSN). Lender's agreement relating to a borrower's request for short sale, which sets an acceptable price ("minimum net" sale proceeds) and promises at least 120 days to market the property while a foreclosure sale may not occur.

single action rule. In some states, a lender must choose to foreclose based on the security instrument (mortgage or deed of trust) or sue for breach of contract (promissory note) but not both. In almost every instance, residential lenders will foreclose, thereby eliminating a lawsuit and a deficiency judgment.

single-family property. Any residential real estate with one to four units. In Making Home Affordable language, it is not limited to a single-dwelling structure.

Standard Modification Waterfall. The sequence of steps required by HAMP to reduce the interest rate, extend the amortization term, and forbear principal as needed to arrive at a mortgage payment that is "affordable and sustainable" for the homeowner.

target monthly mortgage payment. The modified payment calculated by multiplying gross monthly income by the target monthly mortgage payment ratio, which may not be less than 31 percent. The payment totals the reduced principal and interest payment, plus the other listed expenses.

target monthly mortgage payment ratio. The objective is to reduce the payment until this ratio closely approaches but does not fall below 31 percent. To determine the target monthly mortgage payment, multiply gross monthly income by 31 percent and round up when applying the modified interest rate, amortization, and principal forbearance.

Tier 1. The original HAMP modification program for homeowners was designated as Tier 1 in a major expansion of the program in June 2012.

Tier 2. Expansion of the HAMP modification program to rental property owners and to many homeowners not otherwise eligible was designated Tier 2 in a major expansion of the program in June 2012.

trial period. Precedes the actual loan modification. Typically lasts three months and involves a Trial Period Plan and preparation of the final modification agreement.

Trial Period Plan. Defines the terms of a trial period, primarily modified payments, and due dates. Modification requires completion of the trial period according to the plan.

trust deed. *See* deed of trust.

trustee sale. The foreclosure sale under a deed of trust. Also known as a nonjudicial foreclosure because it requires no further legal or judicial action for its enforcement.

underwriting. The process of analyzing the ability to repay and creditworthiness of an applicant for a loan or other extension or modification of credit.

unpaid principal balance (UPB). The unpaid portion of a loan. Same as principal balance.

Notes

Chapter 1

1. Version 4.4, as amended by Treas. Supp. Dir. 14-01 (March 3, 2014), and later amended and updated ("Guidelines").

Chapter 2

1. Chapter 3, "Getting Started: Initial Package," page 23.
2. Higher-risk loans offered potentially higher yields. However, the inability of high-risk borrowers to pay the escalating interest rates, which investors expected to yield high returns, was the undoing of the mortgage-backed securities market and, by extension, the credit and residential real estate markets and such venerable firms as Bear Stearns and Lehman Brothers.

Chapter 3

1. Access the actual RMA form with Adobe Acrobat at https://www.hmpadmin.com/portal/programs/docs/hamp_borrower/rma_english.pdf. Click the "Highlight Fields" button at the upper right corner. You cannot save the form, so I suggest printing it and completing it by hand when convenient. Then enter your information into the online form and print it. Lenders accept either format.
2. *Form 4506-T (Rev. September 2013)*, IRS, http://www.irs.gov/pub/irs-pdf/f4506t.pdf (last visited July 20, 2014).
3. *Form 4506T-EZ (Rev. January 2012)*, IRS, http://www.irs.gov/pub/irs-pdf/f4506tez.pdf (last visited July 20, 2014).

Chapter 4

1. Refer to chapter 5, "Delinquency Is Not Required: Risk of Default," page 39.

Chapter 5

1. Guidelines at page 96 (emphasis added).
2. Calculations 1 and 2 were originally from government-sponsored enterprise (GSE) guidelines, which have been replaced by a computerized tool unavailable to borrowers and their advisors. Calculation 3 is the preliminary (eligibility) requirement to begin the HAMP Standard Modification Waterfall sequence outlined in chapter 7, "Reduce Your Payments: The Modification Waterfalls," page 53. Income and expense line items used to calculate the ratios can be found in appendix G, "Financial Statement," page 161. Use this section for general direction.
3. PITIA is the mortgage principal and interest payment, property tax and insurance, and homeowner association fees, if any, on a monthly basis.
4. Chapter 2, "Where to Start: Eligibility," page 9.

Chapter 6

1. Chapter 2, "Where to Start: Eligibility," page 9.
2. Chapter 5, "Delinquency Is Not Required: Risk of Default," page 39.
3. Refer to appendix O, "Mortgage Relief Definitions," page 197, and glossary, page 205, for brief explanations.
4. For more about Tier 1 and Tier 2, refer to chapter 2, "Where to Start: Eligibility," page 9.
5. Refer to chapter 11, "Non-Approval: Required Disclosures and Remedies," page 91, and chapter 12, "Escalation: Challenging Noncompliance," page 97.
6. Refer to chapter 7, "Reduce Your Payments: The Modification Waterfalls," Principal Reduction Alternative, page 68.
7. Refer to chapter 11, "Non-Approval: Required Disclosures and Remedies," page 91, regarding NPV and valuation disputes. When disputing valuation, draw upon comments and suggestions in that chapter.
8. Contrast short sales, where market value is very important. Refer to chapter 16, "Short Sales: Modification Alternative," page 129.

Chapter 7

1. Use appendix G, "Financial Statement," page 161, to determine your gross monthly income.
2. For Tier 1, refer to page 59, and for Tier 2, refer to page 65. For PRA, refer to page 68.
3. Refer to Introduction to Modifying Your Loan of this chapter beginning on page 54 for details. Use appendix G, "Financial Statement," page 161, to determine your gross monthly income.
4. Refer to Introduction to Modifying Your Loan of this chapter beginning on page 54 for details.
5. Refer to Introduction to Modifying Your Loan of this chapter beginning on page 54 for details.
6. Appendix Q, "Payment Constant," page 201.
7. From what date—initial package, NPV data input, trial period, or modification—the guidelines are unclear.
8. Refer to Introduction to Modifying Your Loan of this chapter beginning on page 54 for details.
9. Find the PMMS 30-year fixed rate at http://www.freddiemac.com/ (scroll to the lower left of page).
10. Refer to Introduction to Modifying Your Loan of this chapter beginning on page 54 for details.

11. The Guidelines call this the "mark-to-market LTV," which simply means that it uses the current market value, rather than the property value when the loan was made. Refer to the Property Value section below.
12. Refer to PRA Policy paragraph below.
13. Refer to Step 3 for Tier 1 at page 62 and Step 4 for Tier 2 at page 67.

Chapter 9

1. Refer to chapter 12, "Escalation: Challenging Noncompliance," page 97.

Chapter 10

1. What about a homeowner who modifies, then later moves and rents the property to a tenant rather than selling it? Guidelines are silent about principal residence changes after modification. Tier 2, however, wants a landlord to rent for at least five years after modification, so converting a rental into a residence is restricted.
2. Refer to the author's book *The ABA Consumer Guide to Short Sales* (2014).
3. Refinancing an underwater mortgage might be possible through the Home Affordable Refinance Program (HARP). Refer to chapter 17, "Other Home Affordable Programs," page 136.
4. The TPP counts toward the first year.
5. Refer to appendix O, "Mortgage Relief Definitions," page 197.

Chapter 11

1. Dodd-Frank Wall Street Reform and Consumer Protection Act, Pub. L. 111-203, § 1482(a)–(b) (July 21, 2010) (guidance to servicers on implementation requirements).
2. Refer to chapter 2, "Where to Start: Eligibility," page 9.
3. Refer to chapter 6, "Modify or Foreclose? Net Present Value," page 45.
4. For additional comments and suggestions, refer to chapter 6, "Modify or Foreclose? Net Present Value," Principal Factors Influencing NPV Test Results, page 48.
5. This is a very rare instance of the borrower paying an advance fee during HAMP evaluation, which otherwise is prohibited.

Chapter 12

1. The HOPE Hotline telephone number is 888-995-HOPE (4673).
2. For identifying characteristics of scams, refer to appendix N, "Scam Avoidance: Making Home Affordable Statement," page 193.

Chapter 13

1. Refer to appendix G, "Financial Statement," page 161.
2. Refer to appendix F, "Profit and Loss," page 159.

Chapter 14

1. Also check *Contact Your Mortgage Company*, MAKING HOME AFFORDABLE (last updated July 12, 2013), http://www.makinghomeaffordable.gov, for an alphabetized list of participating servicers.
2. Refer to the author's book *The ABA Consumer Guide to Short Sales.*
3. Refer to chapter 11, "Non-approval: Required Disclosures and Remedies," page 91, and to chapter 12, "Escalation: Challenging Noncompliance," page 97, for actual requirements and suggestions.

Chapter 15

1. I.R.S. Publication 4681, Canceled Debts, Foreclosures, Repossessions, and Abandonments (2013).
2. The Mortgage Forgiveness Debt Relief Act of 2007. For more information, got to http://www.irs.gov/Individuals/The-Mortgage-Forgiveness-Debt-Relief-Act-and-Debt-Cancellation.
3. I.R.S. Publication 4705, Mortgage Forgiveness. For more information, see also I.R.S. Publication 523, Selling Your Home.
4. I.R.S. Publication 4705, Mortgage Forgiveness.
5. *Id.*
6. I.R.S. Publication 4681, Canceled Debts, Foreclosures, Repossessions, and Abandonments (for individuals, 2008 returns).
7. *Id.*
8. *Id.*
9. *Id.*
10. *Id.*

Chapter 16

1. Refer to the author's book *The ABA Consumer Guide to Short Sales.*
2. *Id.*

Chapter 17

1. Go to *Home Affordable Refinance Program (HARP)*, Fannie Mae, http://knowyouroptions.com/refinance/home-affordable-refinance-program (last visited July 30, 2014).
2. Go to *Check Your Potential Eligibility for HARP*, Freddie Mac, http://www.freddiemac.com/avoidforeclosure/harp_eligibility.html (last visited July 30, 2014).
3. Refer to chapter 7, "Reduce Your Payments: The Modification Waterfalls," Principal Reduction Alternative, page 53.
4. Refer to pages 87–88.

Appendices

1. *See* Making Home Affordable, http://www.makinghomeaffordable.gov/learning-center/Pages/beware.aspx.
2. *Report Fraud*, http://www.stopfraud.gov/report.html#mortgage.

Index